Frank Jacob
East Asia and the First World War

Frank Jacob

East Asia and the First World War

—

DE GRUYTER
OLDENBOURG

ISBN 978-3-11-073708-0
e-ISBN (PDF) 978-3-11-074567-2
e-ISBN (EPUB) 978-3-11-074571-9
DOI https://doi.org/10.1515/9783110745672

Library of Congress Control Number: 2022940533

Bibliographic information published by the Deutsche Nationalbibliothek
The Deutsche Nationalbibliothek lists this publication in the Deutsche Nationalbibliografie;
detailed bibliographic data are available on the internet at http://dnb.dnb.de.

© 2022 the author(s), published by Walter de Gruyter GmbH, Berlin/Boston
The book is published open access at www.degruyter.com.

Cover image: Tanaka Ryozo, The Illustration of The Great European War
No.16. - A humorous Atlas of the World. (Printing 13.09.1914).
https://commons.wikimedia.org/wiki/File:World_around_1900.jpg.
Typesetting: Integra Software Services Pvt. Ltd
Printing and binding: CPI books GmbH, Leck

www.degruyter.com

Contents

1 Introduction

Nobody would doubt that the First World War had a transnational impact or that it tremendously affected both participating and non-participating countries.[1] The "seminal catastrophe,"[2] as historian and diplomat George F. Kennan (1904–2005) would describe it, was indeed a global one. While much attention has been paid to the European theater of war and its major battles still have the potential to attract a large number of interested readers,[3] during the centennial of the events, one could observe a growing interest in non-European contexts and topics that went beyond "classical military studies."[4] However, there were also publications that, despite intending to cover the First World War in its broadest possible sense, did not succeed in offering more space for non-European and, in particular, East Asian perspectives.[5] The war was a watershed for many national histories, and its impact was not only felt politically or economically but went much further than that, as it changed human thoughts and beliefs as such.[6]

The present book is not especially interested in major battles, as there were not many of those in East Asia in the first place,[7] but rather in the impact of the

---

1 Exemplary among other studies and regions of the world, see Claes Ahlund (Ed.), Scandinavia in the First World War. Studies in the War Experience of the Northern Neutrals, Lund 2013; Michael Jonas, Scandinavia and the Great Powers in the First World War, London 2019; Lina Sturfelt, Introduction. Scandinavia and the First World War, in: Scandia 80 (2014) 2, online at: https://project2.sol.lu.se/tidskriftenscandia/index-q=node-1096.html. Accessed May 30, 2022.
2 George F. Kennan, The Decline of Bismarck's European Order. Franco-Russian Relations, 1875–1890, Princeton, NJ 1979, p. 3.
3 Olaf Jessen, Verdun 1916. Urschlacht des Jahrhunderts, second edition, Munich 2017.
4 Stefan Rinke, Latin America and the First World War, New York, NY 2017; Jan Schmidt and Katja Schmidtpott (Eds.), The East Asian Dimension of the First World War. Global Entanglements and Japan, China and Korea, 1914–1919, Frankfurt am Main 2020; Marcel Bois and Frank Jacob (Eds.), Zeiten des Aufruhrs (1916–1921). Globale Proteste, Streiks und Revolutionen gegen den Ersten Weltkrieg und seine Auswirkungen, Berlin 2020; Ana Paula Pires, Jan Schmidt and María Inés Tato (Eds.), The Global First World War. African, East Asian, Latin American and Iberian Mediators, London/New York 2021.
5 Jay Winter (Ed.), The Cambridge History of the First World War, vol. 1: Global War, Cambridge 2014.
6 For a broader debate of the war's impact on the humanities see Frank Jacob, Jeffrey Shaw and Timothy Demy (Eds.), War and the Humanities. The Cultural Impact of the First World War, Paderborn 2019. For the debates in East Asia in relation to the peace talks in Versailles and a possible new "world order" also see Urs Matthias Zachmann (Ed.), Asia After Versailles: Asian Perspectives on the Paris Peace Conference and the Interwar Order, 1919–33, Edinburgh 2018.
7 Jürgen Melzer, Warfare 1914–1918 (Japan), in: 1914–1918-online. International Encyclopedia of the First World War, ed. by Ute Daniel, Peter Gatrell, Oliver Janz, Heather Jones, Jennifer

First World War in this geographic region. It is also intended for a general audience as well as for introductory undergraduate courses on East Asian history or the history of the First World War from a global perspective, as the single chapters on China, Japan, and Korea, which could be read or assigned individually or in totality, provide basic introductions to the respective national histories and contextualize them to highlight the role and impact the First World War had in East Asia. The chapters have been written so that they can be understood without reading the others, and they can therefore also be rearranged to fit in different types of courses as well. The main aim is to arouse further interest in East Asian history in general and the region's involvement and transformation during the First World War in particular. Due to this specific intention, there are, of course, shortcomings with regard to a variety of topics that could have been more heavily emphasized or described in greater detail. However, the author still hopes that students and colleagues will find the work helpful and consider it an encouragement to look deeper into the relationship between the First World War and the respective histories of China, Japan, and Korea, which were much more impacted by the "European war" than Western historians have been willing to acknowledge or to emphasize in their works,[8] in which Asia is often nothing more than a side note.

A truly global understanding of the 20th century's "seminal catastrophe" demands a broader approach to the topic, and it is hoped that the present book will be part of the endeavor to provide it. As so many lives and individual stories were influenced by the First World War in East Asia,[9] the history of the region during and after the war cannot be ignored if the decisive developments related to the further history of the 20th century, especially in an Asian context, are taken into consideration from long-term perspectives. While the focus of the book is East Asia, repercussions from the European and American contexts are also highlighted to show and further emphasize that the history of the world at the beginning of Hobsbawm's "age of extremes" cannot be understood in national isolation. The history of East Asia during the First World War must consequently also be read as a regional one that was embedded into a global course of events.[10]

Keene, Alan Kramer, and Bill Nasson, issued by Freie Universität Berlin, Berlin, October 19, 2017. Accessed May 30, 2022. https://encyclopedia.1914-1918-online.net/article/warfare_1914-1918_japan.

8 See Jan Schmidt, Nach dem Krieg ist vor dem Krieg. Medialisierte Erfahrungen des Ersten Weltkriegs und Nachkriegsdiskurse in Japan (1914–1919), Frankfurt am Main 2021, pp. 9–16. The recently published study shows that the impact of the First World War on Japan was much more important than previous historical studies assumed.

9 Xu Guoqi, Asia and the Great War. A Shared History, New York 2017.

10 Sebastian Conrad, What is Global History? Princeton, NJ 2016, pp. 10–11 emphasized this as one central aspect of the study of global history.

2 China's Eruption after the First World War: Japanese Imperialism, Western Jingoism, and the Awakening of Chinese Nationalism

2.1 Introduction

Considering that China is one of the global players and a true world power today, it is almost hard to imagine that it was dominated by Western and Japanese imperialism 100 years ago.[1] For these imperialist nation states and their representatives, China had always been a "point of focus"[2] of the so-called Far Eastern problem, especially since all of the great imperialist powers aimed to get a piece of Chinese territory and access to the vast market there. The Chinese Empire under the Qing Dynasty (1644–1911) was torn into colonial spheres of influence,[3] and attempts to limit the foreign influence or to force all foreigners out of the country, e.g. the Opium War (1839–1842)[4] and the Boxer Rebellion (1899–1901),[5] were answered with brute force. The revolution of 1911 that British historian Rana Mitter called "unanchored"[6] was supposed to lead China

---

1 This chapter is an extended version of Frank Jacob, China's Eruption after the First World War: Japanese Imperialism, Western Jingoism, and the Awakening of Chinese Nationalism, in: Marcel Bois/Frank Jacob (Eds.), Zeiten des Aufruhrs (1916–1921). Globale Proteste, Streiks und Revolutionen gegen den Ersten Weltkrieg und seine Auswirkungen, Berlin 2020, pp. 171–213.

2 Wesley R. Fishel, The Far East and United States Policy: A Re–Examination, in: The Western Political Quarterly 3 (1950) 1, pp. 1–13, here p. 1.

3 Niels P. Petersson, Imperialismus und Modernisierung. Siam, China und die europäischen Mächte 1895–1914, Munich 2000, pp. 35–90. On the impact of these experiences on China and the Chinese see Matthew P. Fitzgerald/Peter Monteath (Eds.), Colonialism, China and the Chinese, New York/London 2019.

4 For dicussions of this war see Peter Ward Fay, The Opium War, 1840–1842, paperback edition, Chapel Hill, NC, 1997 [1975]; Haijian Mao, The Qing Empire and the Opium War. The Collapse of the Heavenly Dynasty, Cambridge 2016; Stephen R. Platt, Imperial Twilight. The Opium War and the End of China's Last Golden Age, New York 2019.

5 Susanne Kuß/Bernd Martin (Eds.), Das Deutsche Reich und der Boxeraufstand, Munich 2002; Mechthild Leutner/Klaus Mühlhahn (Eds.), Kolonialkrieg in China. Die Niederschlagung der Boxerbewegung 1900–1901, Berlin 2007; Jean Jaques Wendorff, Der Boxeraufstand in China 1900/1901 als deutscher und französischer Erinnerungsort. Ein Vergleich anhand ausgewählter Quellengruppen, Frankfurt am Main 2016. For a detailed discussion of German violence related to the Boxer Rebellion also see Susanne Kuß, Deutsches Militär auf kolonialen Kriegsschauplätzen. Eskalation von Gewalt zu Beginn des 20. Jahrhunderts, Berlin 2005.

6 Rana Mitter, 1911. The Unanchored Chinese Revolution, in: The China Quarterly 208 (2011), pp. 1009–1020.

into modernity and independence, but the First World War (1914–1918) would prove that these dreams had not yet been fulfilled, although the war was tremendously important for Asia in general and East Asia in particular, as Chinese historian Xu Guoqi remarked: "Research on the war's impact there and Asians' contributions has been insufficient, especially from Asian perspectives."[7] One simply has to agree with Xu's evaluation, and he claims that "given the relevance and importance of the Great War to Asian countries, it was as defining an event there as elsewhere."[8] When one considers how the war and its Asian events determined China's future, one of course cannot deny its impact on Sino–Japanese relations.

To quote Xu once more, "Asians may not be aware of the Great War, but that war nonetheless shaped their modern fate in significant ways," and it is important to consider "national aspirations and development, foreign relations, and Asians' perceptions of themselves and the world"[9] when talking about the First World War from a more global perspective. Asia is an important region of the world today, which is why it is even more important to better understand its past, as it was embedded in the global events of the 20th century. Many hopes, dreams, and aspirations were attached to the conflict in China, as well as in Japan, and the political leaders of both nation states attempted to profit from the war in Europe. Therefore, it is worth taking a closer look at the events in East Asia between 1914 and 1918, because they would determine the history of both countries in the years to come, even up to today. Contemporaries, like the British philosopher and mathematician Bertrand Russell (1872–1970), had realized that "[t]he most urgent problem in China's relations with foreign powers is Japanese aggression."[10] This aggression marked the 20th century from a Chinese perspective, because the Sino–Japanese War (1894–1895), the Russo–Japanese War

---

7 Xu Guoqi, Asia and the Great War. A Shared History, New York 2017, p. 2. This evaluation is correct, considering that Xu provided the only chapter on Asia in the three volumes of the Cambridge History of the First World War, edited by Jay Winter, historian and professor at Yale University. Xu Guoqi, Asia, in: Jay Winter (Ed.), The Cambridge History of the First World War, Vol. 1, Cambridge 2014, pp. 479–510.

8 Xu, Asia and the Great War, p. 2.

9 Ibid., p. 3.

10 Bertrand Russell, The Problem of China, London 1922, p. 130. On Russell's experiences in China see: Mirela David, Bertrand Russell and Ellen Key in China. Idividualism, Free Love, and Eugenics in the May Fourth Era, in: Howard Chiang (Ed.), Sexuality in China. Histories of Power and Pleasure, Seattle, WA 2018, pp. 76–98; Eric Hayot, Bertrand Russell's Chinese Eyes, in: Modern Chinese Literature and Culture 18 (2006) 1, pp. 120–154; Suzanne P. Ogden, The Sage in the Inkpot. Bertrand Russell and China's Social Reconstruction in the 1920s, in: Modern Asian Studies 16 (1982) 4, pp. 529–600.

(1904–1905), and the First World War brought Japan's ambitions for expansion to light.[11] However, the latter one also stimulated China's internationalization as a political power, and its representatives were interested in participating in as well as influencing matters of global politics. The war, regardless of its destruction, had also promised the establishment of a new international order, one from which Chinese intellectuals and politicians alike were hoping to receive a new chance to redefine China's fate and position in the world.[12]

The Japanese expansionist ambitions on the Asian mainland, however, left no space for such idealist hopes. Like Japan, the Chinese republican government had entered the war trying to secure its own position within the East Asian region, but all in all, as Xu correctly highlights, "[t]he China–Japan connection in the Great War is one of tragedy, irony, and contradiction."[13] Both governments tried to gain from their participation in the war, but while Japan used its Anglo–Japanese Alliance with Britain to be part of the winning side in the war and to gain control over Shandong, i.e. Chinese territory that had been leased by the German Kaiserreich, China only joined the Allies later to recover the rights to its own possessions. Between these two decisions, Japan presented the Twenty–One Demands, which will be discussed in more detail later, to China in 1915, which, according to Russell, "gave the Chinese Question its modern form."[14] The British philosopher continues his evaluation as follows:

> These demands involved, as is obvious, a complete loss of Chinese independence, the closing of important areas to the commerce and industry of Europe and America, and a special attack upon the British position in the Yangtze. We [the British, F.J.], however, were so busy with the war that we had no time to think of keeping ourselves alive. Although the demands constituted a grave menace to our trade, although the Far East was in an uproar about them, although America took drastic diplomatic action against them, Mr. Lloyd George never heard of them until they were explained to him by the Chinese Delegation at Versailles.[15]

Japan had clearly undertaken the quest to gain from the absence of the European powers in East Asia, and China could only hope for foreign intervention to

---

11 On Japan's growing military and expansionist ambitions in Asia between 1868 and 1905 see Da Yang, Leng yan jia wu. Kan Riben jun shi di guo de gou jian he bao fa (1868–1905), Beijing 2015. On the local and global impact of the Russo–Japanese War see Frank Jacob, The Russo Japanese War and Its Impact on the Twentieth Century, paperback edition, London/New York 2019 [2018].
12 Xu, Asia and the Great War, p. 10.
13 Ibid., p. 38.
14 Russell, Problem of China, p. 131.
15 Ibid., pp. 132–133.

avoid being ripped off and losing a large part of its territorial and political rights, even its independence. China's position, according to the understanding of many Chinese intellectuals and politicians, could only be saved by a new world order that was based on Woodrow Wilson's (1856–1924) demands for such an order.

When the peace conference at Versailles failed to deliver Wilson's principles in the form of actual politics, China and its people felt betrayed, and protests, namely the May Fourth Movement, demanded fair treatment for the Chinese Republic and a return of its rights to Shandong from the Germans. The movement therefore had a clearly anti–imperialist character, something that made Mao Zedong (1893–1976) interpret it in 1939 as a stage in the long–term history of the Chinese Revolution, "a step beyond the Revolution of 1911":

> The May [Fourth] Movement twenty years ago marked a new stage in China's bourgeois-democratic revolution against imperialism and feudalism. The cultural reform movement which grew out of the May [Fourth] Movement was only one of the manifestations of this revolution. With the growth and development of new social forces in that period, a powerful camp made its appearance in the bourgeois–democratic revolution, a camp consisting of the working class, the student masses and the new national bourgeoisie.[16]

For Mao, the movement resembled the awakening of Chinese intellectuals, who "were more numerous and more politically conscious than in the days of the Revolution of 1911." Of course, retrospectively, and from Mao's communist viewpoint and according to his theoretical assumptions, "the intellectuals will accomplish nothing if they fail to integrate themselves with the workers and peasants."[17]

Regardless of such doctrinaire evaluations, 1919 marked a watershed year in modern Chinese history, marking one of two attempts – the other being in 1898 – for an "intellectual break with the values of Confucian civilization." The May Fourth Movement was consequently not only an expression of anti–imperialist nationalism, but at the same time was seen by traditional elites "as an attack upon

---

16 Mao Tse–tung, The May 4th Movement, in: Selected Works of Mao Tse–tung, Vol. 2, https:// www.marxists.org/reference/archive/mao/selected-works/volume-2/mswv2_13.htm (17. 9. 2019). A similar evaluation can be found in Mao Tse–tung, The Chinese Revolution and the Chinese Communist Party, in: Selected Works of Mao Tse–tung, Vol. 2, https://www.marxists.org/refer ence/archive/mao/selected-works/volume-2/mswv2_23.htm#p4 (17. 9. 2019), where Mao states: "The Opium War, the Movement of the Taiping Heavenly Kingdom, the Sino–French War, the Sino–Japanese War, the Reform Movement of 1898, the Yi Ho Tuan Movement, the Revolution of 1911, the May 4th Movement, the May 30th Movement, the Northern Expedition, the Agrarian Revolutionary War and the present War of Resistance Against Japan – all testify to the Chinese people's indomitable spirit in fighting imperialism and its lackeys."
17 Mao, May 4th Movement.

the traditional moral and social orders as well."[18] Modernizing universities under an enlightened leadership – Beijing University (Beida) was led by Cai Yuanpei (1868–1940), a philosopher educated in China and Germany (Leipzig University)[19] – provided the ground for the "great intellectual upsurge of 1919," because students were presented with new educational opportunities when men like Yuanpei "welcomed ideas from all over the world and collected a faculty of brilliant young men of diverse backgrounds."[20] These academic changes created a self–confident student body, whose representatives were interested in China's modernization and wanted to gain recognition for their nation within the international order as well. They shared this latter aspect with a large number of Chinese people, who had realized that Japan's ambitions, well and clearly expressed in the Twenty–One Demands, threatened not only the integrity of China but even its whole existence as an independent nation state. Eventually, when more than 3,000 students protested on 4 May 1919 at the Gate of Heavenly Peace (Tiananmen), whose protests were violently met by the government, it was "[t]he whole patriotic public [that] was aroused,"[21] and the consequence was further student protests in around 200 places, as well as strikes in factories in Shanghai and other cities. The American political scientist and Sinologist Benjamin I. Schwartz (1916–1999) therefore described the events correctly when he characterized them as "[a] student movement [that] was born in which women participated, broad public support was enlisted, and the sanction of saving China was invoked to achieve an unprecedented degree of student organization and activism. This was a new political expression of nationalism, all the more significant because it was unpremeditated."[22]

Nevertheless, the events of 4 May 1919 and its consequences should not solely be understood from a political perspective, but must be analyzed with all

---

18 Charlotte Furth, Intellectual Change. From the Reform Movement to the May Fourth Movement, 1895–1920, in: Denis Twitchett/John K. Fairbank (Eds.), The Cambridge History of China, Vol. 12: Republican China 1912–1949, Part 1, Cambridge 1983, p. 322.

19 Ibid., p. 323. For a more detailed analysis of Cai's role in early 20th century China see Cai Jianguo, Cai Yuanpei. Gelehrter und Mittler zwischen Ost und West, Münster 1998; William J. Duiker, Ts'ai Yuan–p'ei. Educator of Modern China, University Park, PA 1977. On Cai's educational concepts see Peili Wang, Wilhelm von Humboldt und Cai Yuanpei. Eine vergleichende Analyse zweier klassischer Bildungskonzepte in der deutschen Aufklärung und in der ersten chinesischen Republik, Münster/New York 1996.

20 Benjamin I. Schwartz, Themes in Intellectual History. May Fourth and After, in: Denis Twitchett/John K. Fairbank (Eds.), The Cambridge History of China, Vol. 12: Republican China 1912–1949, Part 1, Cambridge 1983, p. 406.

21 Schwartz, Themes, p. 407.

22 Ibid.

its cultural complexities, since a new generation was beginning to demand a new China that was not only politically independent, but also culturally and intellectually different from its past.[23] The present chapter will therefore show why 1919 must be considered a watershed year in Chinese history and what role the First World War played in it. At first, China's situation at the beginning of the war will be described and then the country's role and development during the global conflict will be discussed. Eventually, China's position at the Peace Conference in Versailles will be analyzed before a closer look is taken at the May Fourth Movement. The chapter will thereby show how the global conflict shaped the Chinese position in the early 20th century and which forces were awakened by Japanese imperialism, Western jingoism, and Chinese conservatism to be finally combined in a national protest movement. The First World War is consequently considered to have acted as a cataclysm that provoked this national upheaval in China as part of an international wave of protest movements in the aftermath of the war that was considered to end all conflicts and to introduce a new international order, based on the liberal ideas of Wilson and his like–minded colleagues.

2.2 China in 1914

Economically, China as a whole seemed to change only between 1912 and the end of the civil war in 1949.[24] The average individual's income neither increased nor decreased, and the rapid growth since the late 19th century seems to have been stopped by internal turmoil and the wars the Chinese have been involved in since their revolution in 1911. American historian Albert Feuerwerker highlighted that "[t]he relative factor supplies of land, labour and capital remained basically unaltered" and "[t]he occupational distribution of the population was hardly changed."[25] China, and this might have been one of the most important problems of the May Fourth Movement in 1919 as well, was mainly agricultural, with people in this sector making their living on family farms that numbered from 60 to 70 million across the country. 50% of these farms were owned by peasants, while 25% were partly rented farms, and the

---

23 Fabio Lanza, Behind the Gate. Inventing Students in Beijing, New York 2010, p. 101.
24 The description of China's economy follows, if not indicated otherwise, Albert Feuerwerker, Economic Trends, 1912–49, in: Denis Twitchett/John K. Fairbank (Eds.), The Cambridge History of China, Vol. 12: Republican China 1912–1949, Part 1, Cambridge 1983, pp. 28–127.
25 Ibid., 28.

remaining 25% were in the hands of tenant farmers. Most Chinese were consequently living in smaller villages, making their living as peasants. They were consequently not only hard to reach in the centralizing attempts by the government, but also for those who chanted the song of Chinese nationalism in 1919.

While the larger cities with ties to foreign powers became hubs of economic and intellectual exchange, the rural areas of the country remained peripheral. The consequence was "larger regional marketing complexes" with important centers that linked "inter–provincial and inter–regional commerce."[26] In cities like Nanking, Hankow, Chungking, etc., along with the capital Beijing and internationally important trade centers like Hong Kong and Shanghai, an economic increase was visible and changed the urban environments, but almost none of it was felt in the far–away provinces, where local identity determined the daily life of the Chinese farmers. Due to the economic processes that could be observed in these larger cities, the urban population of China was growing during the late 19th century, even increasing the speed of urbanization after 1900. Nevertheless, in 1938, only around 27 million people – out of a population of 500 million – were living in cities with more than 50,000 inhabitants. China could therefore hardly be called an urban society, which is why Mao's claim from 1939, that a revolutionary party would need to include the workers *and* peasants to be successful, is correct, especially when one wants to explain one of the problems of the May Fourth Movement, which will be taken into closer consideration later.

The contacts with Western and Japanese traders had an impact on China, for sure, but primarily on those who operated in the named economic centers, where national companies got connected to the global market. Most of the 430 million Chinese people (1912) did not gain from the economic developments in these, sometimes far away, urban centers. Twenty years after the First World War, almost 80% of people were still working in the agrarian sector, although the end of the Qing Dynasty in 1911 had stimulated the founding of manufacturing companies and mining enterprises that were privately owned by Chinese rather than foreign investors. These more than 500 enterprises, however, could only accumulate a capital of around Ch.$ 20 million, i.e. only a fraction of the invested foreign capital in China at the time.[27] Before and also during the war,

---

26 Ibid., 32.
27 For a detailed discussion of the development of capitalism in China see Wu Chengming, A Brief Account of the Development of Capitalism in China, in: Tim Wright (Ed.), The Chinese Economy in the Early Twentieth Century. Recent Chinese Studies, London 1992, pp. 29–43. For an analysis of China's relation to the global market William N. Goetzmann/Andrey D. Ukhov/Ning Zhu, China and the World Financial Markets 1870–1939. Modern Lessons from Historical Globalization, in: The Economic History Review 60 (2007) 2, pp. 267–312 is recommended.

however, Chinese–owned industry expanded, and more than 2,000 new factories had been established by 1920.[28] The Chinese economy, like that of the
Japanese (as will be shown in another chapter), profited from the absence of
European competition during the First World War. That China would be unable to use this positive trend, however, is related to political instabilities
rather than economic incapacities. Most of the said companies, to name just
one problem, were based in Shanghai or other urban centers, so the gained capital was not equally invested in the growth of a national economic sector. In addition, the immense growth of the Chinese industry of more than 13% that was
reached between 1912 and 1920 also led to a post–war recession, especially in
1921–1922, when foreign, i.e. first and foremost European, competitors returned
to the Asian markets.

The traditional manufacturing of handicrafts at the same time declined further "as a result of competition from both imported foreign goods and the output of Chinese– and foreign–owned modern industry in China."[29] By 1919, the
output in two out of three of China's main industries – coal, cotton yarn, and
cotton cloth – was still dominated by foreign firms (Table 2.1).

Table 2.1: Percentage of total output for China's main
industries in 1919.[30]

	Chinese	Foreign
Coal Industry	24.4%	75.6%
Cotton Yarn	57%	43%
Cotton Cloth	41%	59%

Although China could claim the majority of the production with regard to cotton yarn, more than 60% of the spindles were working in Shanghai, keeping
the industrial progress within an urban environment. In addition, "[t]he con-
centration of modern industry in coastal cities, the large foreign–owned component, the predominance of consumers' goods, and the small size and technical
backwardness of most factories – all of these are correlates of the very small
share of modern industry in China's national product before 1949."[31]

---

28 Feuerwerker, Economic Trends, pp. 41–42.
29 Ibid., p. 51. China's cotton industry and trade is discussed in Kang Chao, The Development
of Cotton Textile Production in China, Cambridge, MA 1977, ch. 4–6.
30 Numbers according to Feuerwerker, Economic Trends, p. 60.
31 Ibid., p. 62.

In the republican period, the country was also suffering from its very poor transportation system that could hardly link the modernizing industrial centers in the coastal regions with the agrarian hinterland of peripheral provinces. High transportation costs made Chinese–produced coal coke and pig iron more expensive than competing products from Japanese or Western sources of production. China might have had the advantage of comparatively extremely low wages, but "[t]he wages of coolie labour were incredibly low, but the economic efficiency of the human carriers who dominated transport at the local level was even lower."[32] Between 1912 and 1927, there were only around 3,500 kilometers of railways built through China, which is not surprising when one considers that railways were early on financed through foreign capital and were often used as instruments for informal imperialism.[33] Considering that the initial wave of railway building in China between the end of the Sino–Japanese War in 1895 and the Chinese Revolution of 1911 caused the construction of more than 9,000 kilometers of track, the outcome for the first one and a half post–revolutionary decades is rather low. This lack of infrastructure had tremendous consequences on the attempts to industrialize China, since the "inland [. . .] continued to depend much more on traditional means of transport, by water and land, for local and regional carriage than it did on motor vehicles or trains."[34] During the First World War, junk tonnage would even increase before this river–related transportation method was replaced by modern steamships in the early 1920s and railway track construction intensified.[35]

Another economic problem for China was its lack of financial centralization. The republican government was unable to collect revenues on a broader scale, which is why many possible modernization–oriented measures were hard to finance and why "government policies, while not without far–reaching

---

32 Ibid., p. 91.

33 The best examples are probably the South Manchurian Railway or the Eastern Chinese Railway, financed by Japan and Russia respectively. Files of the Peking Legation: South Manchurian Railway, The National Archives London, Foreign Office and Foreign and Commonwealth Office Records, FO 676/140. See also S.C.M. Paine, The Chinese Eastern Railway from the First Sino–Japanese War until the Russo–Japanese War, in: Bruce A. Elleman/Stephen Kotkin (Eds.), Manchurian Railways and the Opening of China. An International History, New York/London 2009, pp. 13–36 and Y. Tak Matsusaka, Japan's South Manchuria Railway Company in Northeast China, 1906–34, in: ibid., pp. 37–58; Mi Rucheng, Di guo zhu yi yu Zhongguo tie lu, 1847–1949, Beijing 2007; Okabe Makio (Ed.), Minami Manshū tetsudō gaisha no kenkyū, Tokyo 2008.

34 Feuerwerker, Economic Trends, p. 98.

35 Wang Yuru, Economic Development in China between the Two World Wars (1920–1936), in: Tim Wright (Ed.), The Chinese Economy in the Early Twentieth Century. Recent Chinese Studies, London 1992, pp. 58–77, here pp. 66–67.

consequences for the economy, were never realistically capable of pushing the Chinese economy forward on the path of modern economic growth."[36] After the revolution in 1911, the government struggled with the transformation of the old fiscal system, however, without being able to better control the financial resources of the country, i.e. taxes. New regulations could hardly be enforced, especially since China was becoming more and more politically fractured. The provinces remained responsible for most of the taxes, however most of the money remained in the provincial capitals, where warlords began to act according to their own political and economic agenda without paying much attention to the demands of the central government. As a consequence, foreign loans needed to fill the financial gaps and, starting in 1913, the Chinese government had to take on obligations of around US$ 270 million during the next two decades. The so-called Nishihara loans in particular, granted by Japan, also increased the Chinese dependency on Japan.[37] China was, however, not only weakened by economic problems, but also by the political factionalism that prevented a united national front against the menace of Japanese imperialism and Western jingoism during and after the war. Therefore, the reasons for the political weakness of China should also be addressed here, before the impact of the First World War is dealt with in more detail.

After the death of Yuan Shikai (1859–1916), the first president of the Chinese Republic, China would be divided between powerful warlords, eventually showing the division of the country, and was prepared by those who controlled the prefectures and would use taxes to secure their own position instead of supporting the central government. While the central government officially represented the state's power after Yuan's death in 1916, especially since no dynasty or dominant ruler existed, in reality, different families and warlords were pursuing their own goals in the provinces, waiting for their bid for power.[38] This factionalism, however, already existed before the First World War. The early republican governments were led by a generation born around 1870, who were

---

36 Feuerwerker, Economic Trends, p. 99.
37 Murao Hideo, The Ideas and Philosophy of Nishihara Kamezō. In the Context of His Role in the Nishihara Loans, in: Nagasaki kenritsu daigaku ronshū 30 (1997) 3, pp. 433–473; Michael Schiltz, "Separating the Roots of the Chrysanthemum". Nishihara Kamezō and the Abortive China Loans, 1917–18, (2007), MPRA Paper No. 7100 https://mpra.ub.uni-muenchen.de/7100/1/MPRA_paper_7100.pdf (3. 10. 2019); Suzuki Takeo (Ed.), Nishihara shakkan shiryō kenkyū, Tokyo 1972.
38 Andrew J. Nathan, A Constitutional Republic. The Peking Government, 1916–28, in: Denis Twitchett and John K. Fairbank (Eds.), The Cambridge History of China, vol. 12: Republican China 1912–1949, Part 1, Cambridge 1983, pp. 256–283, here p. 256.

interested in securing their own position as traditional elites on the one hand, but who were also, due to their experience as students abroad at Western or Japanese universities, interested in modern forms of government and economy on the other. Sun Yat-sen (1866–1925) was also recruiting his revolutionary followers among Chinese students in Japan and at home, waiting to launch a new revolutionary attempt against the old order.[39] The revolution, however, did not create a united China, although the government in Beijing operated on the basis of the provisional constitution of 1912 from Yuan's death in 1916 until 1928. The ruling president, "elected by parliament for a five-year term, had the symbolic functions and potentially the prestige of a head of state," yet it was "his personality and factional backing [that] determined whether he could translate these into real power."[40] The cabinet, in the meantime, was usually unable to agree upon a political course because its members were supporting different factions, each of them longing for their own political goals. Only a strong president was able to at least partly rule, usually based on the control of crucial ministries, like the Ministry of Finance or Ministry of the Interior. Since essential decisions, e.g. budgets or war declarations, needed the support of parliament, it was hard to rule in the aftermath of the revolution in 1911. In 1914, China was consequently not only suffering from economic problems but also from political instability. When the Chinese government eventually declared war against Germany in 1917, it did so because it hoped to gain from such a step. Next to a better stance against Japanese imperialism, it was hoped that the prestige of being one of the victors at the peace conferences after the war would help to better position China within a new world order. Its financial dependency on Japan and foreign capital in general, as described above, however, further weakened the position of the central

---

39 Sun Yat-sen's relationship to Japanese right-wing pan-Asianist organizations and military representatives, who were interested in a pro-Japanese order in a possible post-revolutionary China is described in detail by Marius B. Jansen, The Japanese and Sun Yat-sen, Stanford 1970 [1954]. Some of the right-wing contacts of the Chinese revolutionary are also discussed in detail in Frank Jacob, Japanism, Pan-Asianism, Terrorism. A Short History of the Amur Society (Black Dragons) 1901–1945, Palo Alto, CA 2014 and Frank Jacob, Die Thule-Gesellschaft und die Kokuryūkai. Geheimgesellschaften im global-historischen Vergleich, Würzburg 2013. There were, however, also pro-Chinese supporters of the revolutionary movement in Japan. For one source of such a supporter see Miyazaki Tōten, My Thirty-Three Year's Dream. The Autobiography of Miyazaki Tōten, transl. and ed. by Marius B. Jansen and Etō Shinkichi, Princeton 2014. On the different varieties of pan-Asianism in Japan, see: Sven Saaler/J. Victor Koschmann (Eds.), Pan-Asianism in Modern Japanese History. Colonialism, Regionalism and Borders, London 2007.
40 Nathan, Constitutional Republic, p. 264.

government, whose constitutional role during and in the aftermath of the First World War was purely a facade.

In reality, power lay in the hands of the different factions and "personal followings, cutting across the boundaries of official institutions," wherein each faction was "centred on a particular leader and composed of his individually recruited, personally loyal followers."[41] There were several factions that had gained influence since the revolution and would struggle for influence during the war years. Some of them were military cliques, like the Zhili Clique[42] or the Fengtian Clique,[43] while others were formed by politicians or journalists, like the so-called Research Clique.[44] Regardless of such categorizations, it has to be emphasized that the larger and more successful cliques were heterogeneous with regard to their supporters and followers in parliament. The first elected parliament (1913–1914) was dissolved twice in its first three years of existence when Zhang Kun (1854–1923) proclaimed himself Prime Minister of the Imperial Cabinet in early July 1917 while trying to reinstall Emperor Puyi (1906–1967), who had abdicated.[45] Eventually, it was the Anfu Club, the political wing of the Anhui Clique, represented by Duan Qirui (1865–1936),[46] who served as Prime Minister between 1916 and 1918, that won a majority in parliament after Zhang's failed imperial restoration attempt. Of 470 seats, 342 were controlled by the Anfu Club. Due to its dominance, parliamentarian politics, at least for a while, functioned much better; this becomes obvious when considering that 1918 saw a new prime minister and cabinet in Beijing, both of whom went through the supposed process of confirmation by the Chinese parliament.[47] Nevertheless,

---

41 Ibid., p. 271.

42 The Zhili clique was led by General Feng Guozhang (1859–1919) and General Cao Kun (1862–1938), who also served as President of the Chinese Republic between 1923 and 1924.

43 The Fengtian clique was led by Zhang Zuolin (1875–1928), who started his career as a bandit, became warlord of Manchuria, and was eventually assassinated by officers of the Japanese Kwangtung Army. On his role in Northeast China between the revolution and his death see David Bonavia, China's Warlords, New York 1995, ch. 2; Gavan McCormack, Chang Tso-lin in Northeast China, 1911–1928. China, Japan, and the Manchurian Idea, Stanford, CA 1977.

44 For a more detailed survey of factionalism in China, especially in the years after the First World War, Andrew J. Nathan, Peking Politics, 1918–1923. Factionalism and the Failure of Constitutionalism, Berkeley/Los Angeles 1976; Hsi-sheng Ch'i, Warlord Politics in China 1916–1928, Stanford, CA 1976 and Hatano Yoshihiro, Chūgoku kindai gunbatsu no kenkyū, Tokyo 1973 are recommended. For a short survey see Edward A. McCord, Warlordism in Early Republican China, in: David A. Graff/Robin Highman (Eds.), A Military History of China, Lexington KY, 2012, pp. 175–192.

45 Madeleine Chi, China Diplomacy 1914–1918, Cambridge, MA 1970, p. 127.

46 Duan Qirui was also provisional President of the Chinese Republic between 1924 and 1926.

47 Nathan, Constitutional Republic, p. 278.

this short period of dominance would later lead to new fractions within China's political landscape again. The protests in 1919 were consequently not only stimulated by foreign events, but also by the anger about the lack of a clear national political agenda within the parliament, where factional struggles rather than national necessities dominated political decisions. There were numerous moments during the First World War when intellectuals and students alike might have hoped for a more China–oriented political agenda by the ruling power, but eventually these hopes were disappointed, since power and influence were the main driving forces of political action within the parliament. This political weakness was also obvious to foreign observers, and Japanese military officers in particular believed that the First World War provided a good opportunity to expand the influence of Japan on the Asian mainland.[48] Japan had kept forces on the continent after the Russo–Japanese War, namely in Manchuria, where it maintained "some garrison troops [. . .] on the pretext of protecting their railways and they exerted significant military influence over Manchuria, despite China's official sovereignty in this region."[49] The First World War naturally provided Japan with an opportunity, one that not only its military leaders but also the politicians in Tokyo were willing to use to extend its influence in China. The war consequently tied both countries' ambitions to each other: while China wanted to regain its sovereignty, Japan wanted to further expand on the cost of its East Asian neighbor. Both had high expectations, triggered by the conflict, which paralyzed the West. Needless to say, the war was a watershed moment in the history of Sino–Japanese relations, as it was in both national histories. The following section will show how the war as such determined developments in East Asia.

2.3 China and the First World War

After Japan had issued an ultimatum and then declared war against Germany on 23 August 1914, China was something of an observer of the war in East Asia since Yuan Shikai and his supporters had decided to stay neutral, and had to watch as Japan occupied Shandong on 7 November 1914, taking over the imperial rule in the region from Germany.[50] As American historian Stephen G. Craft correctly

---

48 On the expansive policy of the Japanese military see Kitaoka Shin'ichi, Nihon rikugun to tairiku seisaku, 1906–1918, Tokyo 1978.

49 Asada Masafumi, The China–Russia–Japan Military Balance in Manchuria, 1906–1918, in: Modern Asian Studies 44, no. 6 (2010), pp. 1283–1311, here p. 1285.

50 Ian Nish, Japan and the Outbreak of War in 1914, in: The Collected Writings of Ian Nish, Vol. 1, Tokyo 2001, pp. 173–187.

evaluated, China could not do much about it: "Without a powerful army, and with the European powers preoccupied with the Western Front, China had no choice but to use diplomatic means to regain control."[51] Yuan had multiple reasons to keep China out of the war and therefore used his military power and the backing of his decision by the Western powers to suppress the voices that demanded Chinese action in 1914. One problem he had to face was the increase in the number of bandits and criminal organizations in Republican China, who, among other things, regularly kidnapped foreigners.[52] Yuan had also realized that while all the European powers were involved in the war, American support alone might not have been enough to keep Japan's imperial ambitions with regard to China in check. He consequently did not want to "waste" his power in a solely European war, leaving Chinese interests undefended. Otherwise, Yuan realized, Japan could have used the political and probably military vacuum to further extend its sphere of influence.[53] He consequently declared Chinese neutrality on 6 August 1914, demanding that the United States and Japan guarantee it. Japan, however, did not address this demand, but rather, in accordance with Great Britain, declared war against Germany. While Britain needed Japanese support, especially with regard to its battleships for control of and protection of transports in the Mediterranean Sea, the British Minister to China, John Jordan, promised Chinese diplomat V. K. Wellington Koo (1888–1985) on 19 August 1914 that the Chinese rights to Shandong, and its capital Qingdao, would be returned to China in the aftermath of the war.[54] Yuan, and with him the Chinese people, therefore "maintained an expedient, watchful neutrality, which would last until August 1917, and was prepared to give it up the moment the opportunity rose."[55]

It only took Japan two weeks to land 20,000 soldiers on the Liaodong Peninsula on 3 September 1914 in order to gain control of Qingdao and the Shandong Railway as fast as possible. The 3,000 German soldiers and 3,000 reservists who defended the Chinese possession of the German Kaiserreich did not stand a chance. Japan eventually gained control of the whole province of Shandong,

---

51 Stephen G. Craft, Angling for an Invitation to Paris: China's Entry into the First World War, in: The International History Review 16 (1994) 1, pp. 1–24, here p. 1.
52 On banditry in Republican China see Phil Billingsley, Bandits in Republican China, Stanford 1988; Cai Shaoqing (Ed.), Minguo shiqi de tufei, Beijing 1993. Due to the rise of the warlords in China since 1916, the number of bands of robbers would even further increase.
53 Dieter Kuhn, Die Republik China von 1912 bis 1937. Entwurf für eine politische Ereignisgeschichte, 3. überarbeitete und erweiterte Auflage, Heidelberg 2007, p. 146.
54 Xu, Asia and the Great War, p. 39.
55 Ibid., p. 40.

which was de facto transformed into a Japanese protectorate on the Asian mainland.[56] This process received relatively little attention from the European powers, who were just realizing that a fast end to the war had been a wish based on wild assumptions rather than on facts. Japan had only done what it had been longing to do since the end of the Russo–Japanese War, namely to secure its influence in Manchuria and to extend it if at all possible. During the Chinese Revolution, the government in Tokyo only feared for its possessions in China, which is why Foreign Minister Uchida Kōsai (1865–1936) and Minister to Peking Ijūin Hikokichi (1864–1924) argued in favor of support for the Qing Dynasty so as not to endanger Japan's rights in Manchuria. An unknown revolutionary government seemed less reliable than the autocrats they had been dealing with since the 1860s.[57] Agreements were signed and Japan would sell arms to the government, but at the same time, it proposed a joint military intervention in China to Britain. Yuan Shikai, using British intermediaries, would, however, eventually reach an agreement with the revolutionaries, who were holding the provinces Great Britain was mainly interested in, and a military intervention became unnecessary. In the meantime, Japanese "patriots" (*shishi*) had been sent to China by the Black Ocean Society (Gen'yōsha) and the Amur Society (Kokuryūkai), supporting the Chinese revolutionaries in the hope of gaining influence over the post–revolutionary government. Kita Ikki (1883–1937) was one of those sent on such a mission, but the revolutionary leaders realized relatively fast that these Japanese agents had a more expansionist interest and interpretation of pan–Asianism.[58] During the so–called Second Revolution against Yuan's rule by Sun Yat–sen and others like General Li Liejun (also referred to as Li Lieh–chun), Japan also granted asylum to the defeated revolutionaries, since it was unclear if their service, according to Japan's long–term goals in the region, could be

---

56 Kuhn, Republik China, p. 146.

57 Shinkichi Etō, China's International Relations, 1911–1931, In: John K. Fairbank/Albert Feuerwerker (Eds.), The Cambridge History of China, Vol. 13: Republican China 1912–1949, Part 2, Cambridge 1983, pp. 74–115, here p. 92.

58 Kita Ikki had already worked with Chinese revolutionaries in Japan before 1911, e.g. on the publication of the *Naigai jiji gekkan* (*Monthly Correspondence on Home and Abroad*). See: Ōshima Tōto, Tōyama-ō no doko ga erai ka, in Fujimoto Hisanori (Ed.), Tōyama seishin, Tokyo 1940, pp. 82–110, here p. 86; Hatsuse Ryūhei, Dentōteki uyoku. Uchida Ryōhei no kenkyū, Fukuoka 1980, p. 214. For Kita Ikki's vita see Kimura Tokio, Kita Ikki to Ni-niroku jiken no inbō Tokyo 2007, pp. 318–322; Marion Laurinat, Kita Ikki (1883–1937) und der Februarputsch 1936. Eine historische Untersuchung japanischer Quellen des Militärgerichtsverfahrens, Berlin 2006, pp. 46–48; Matsumoto Ken'ichi, Kita Ikki ron, Toyko 1996, pp. 348–359; Tanaka Sōgorō, Kita Ikki. Nihonteki fashisuto no shōchō, second edition, Tokyo 1971, pp. 427–453.

used at a later time.[59] There were also incidents related to the Second Revolution in China that riled the Japanese miliary: "the detention of a Japanese army captain, the arrest of an army second lieutenant, and acts of violence by Yuan's troops as they entered Nanking which resulted in the deaths of three Japanese."[60] The relations between the two East Asian countries were consequently already bad when the First World War opened another window for Japan to deal with the main antagonist to its claim for leadership in the region.

China had declared its neutrality and demanded "that belligerents were not to occupy or conduct warfare on Chinese soil or in Chinese territorial waters,"[61] but these claims were simply ignored by the Japanese government as it launched the above–described attack against the German possessions in Shandong. The government in Tokyo had willingly voted for the Japanese Empire to play an active role during the war, and once the territory of interest had been occupied by its troops, it would be no easy task to get it back from Japan. The military operations already showed that the Japanese military did not care for Chinese neutrality at all when the leading officers "decided to attack German fortifications from the rear, [because] to do so it would have to pass through Chinese territory and violate"[62] it. Pressured by Tokyo, the government in Beijing eventually had to take Shandong off its map of neutral territory, since Japan had presented a fait accompli in Shandong. It was clear from the beginning of the military operations by the Japanese army that Tokyo had no interest in taking just Qingdao from the Germans because, early on, railway lines and geostrategic places in the province were captured by Japan's soldiers. Once Germany had surrendered, the Japanese military just left its troops where they were to secure rule over the whole province, while China could only observe, according to its declared neutrality. The European powers, in the meantime, did not pay attention to this at all, and if they did, it was because they had their own ambitions for China that determined their non–intervention. Britain, allied with the Japanese, did not favor the larger intervention of Japan in China, but its strong presence in the northeastern provinces might have had a positive and stabilizing impact on China's central and southern provinces, where the main British interests were centered. With the pressing developments of the war in Europe, the British military planners and politicians felt a more intensive need for Japanese assistance, which is why they might simply have looked the other way. China could only rely on American help and sympathy.

---

59 Etō, China's International Relations, p. 94.
60 Ibid.
61 Ibid., p. 95.
62 Ibid.

In Japan, the situation stimulated the demands of right-wing pressure groups like the Amur Society, whose leader Uchida Ryōhei (1874–1937) declared in October 1914 that Japan had the chance to solve its Asian problems due to the absence of the European powers. He criticized the reluctant position of the Japanese government and urged the politicians in Tokyo to act in favor of a more aggressive foreign policy towards China.[63] Uchida formulated ten demands – very similar to the official Twenty–One Demands of 1915 – that requested special rights for Japan in China, including a right for military intervention. And he was correct insofar as the European powers really could not have intervened, since they "had no time or resources for Asian concerns."[64] The Chinese wish to regain control over its own territory in Shandong was eventually countered by the Twenty–One Demands, which were drafted by Prime Minister Ōkuma Shigenobu (1838–1922) and Foreign Minister Katō Takaaki (1869–1926) and handed over to Yuan Shikai by the Japanese on 18 January 1915.[65] The Japanese cabinet had agreed on 14 demands, grouped into four sections, as well as on a fifth section of "wishes" on 11 November 1918. An acceptance of the Twenty–One Demands would have degraded China to the status of being a servant state to Japan. The Japanese not only demanded the German rights to Shandong, but also the acceptance of special interests in the Manchurian provinces of Liaoning and Jilin as well eastern Inner Mongolia, the elongation of leasing rights in Lushun and Dalian, including for the local railways, a joint venture between the two countries for the Hanyeping iron and steel works, and a prohibition for further concessions or lease treaties for coastal or domestic harbor towns with other states.[66] Two demands directly threatened China's sovereignty, because the Japanese demanded their own consultants for Chinese politics, economy, and finances. Furthermore, Tokyo demanded a combined police force and a joint defense industry.[67]

While Yuan was requested by the Japanese representative in Beijing, Hioki Eki (1861–1921), to keep the demands secret, they were leaked by Wellington Koo[68] who, due to his good contacts with the US Minister in China, Paul Reinsch

63 Kokuryūkai, 8 Tai–Shi mondaikaiketsu iken, 9 October 1914, Gaimushō gaikōrshiryōkan (Archive of the Foreign Ministry of Japan), B–1–1–2–156; Uchida Ryōhei, 15 Tai–Shi mondaikaiketsu iken, 29 October 1914, Gaimushō gaikōrshiryōkan, B–1–1–2–151.
64 Etō, China's International Relations, p. 96.
65 For a detailed description of the initial demands see ibid., pp. 98–99; Xu, Asia and the Great War, p. 40.
66 Kuhn, Republik China, p. 147.
67 Ibid.
68 For Koo's vita see Stephen G. Craft, V.K. Wellington Koo and the Emergence of Modern China, Lexington, KY 2003.

(1869–1923), hoped for support from the Americans. Yuan, in contrast, dealt directly with the Japanese politicians in more than 40 negotiation meetings, and after 84 days, a revised version of the initial demands was finally presented. Regardless of the negotiations, when the international press, like *The Times* of London, reported the Japanese demands, the wider public opinion in the West, as far as it was concerned with the events and developments in the Far East, expressed sympathy for the Chinese.

In the end, Tokyo had to abandon the fifth group of its demands, since these would have transformed China into a Japanese protectorate, but still, the acceptance of the first four groups would have been a humiliation for the Chinese, who had initially hoped to regain their own territory but instead had to accept further political degradation by the Japanese.[69] The fact that Yuan eventually agreed upon a final, much-diffused version of the demands, however, further separated him from revolutionaries like Sun Yat-sen who, in contrast to Yuan, did not consider the final agreement a Chinese success, but treason.[70] With its aggressive policy, Japan now left no doubts about its aims in East Asia and lost some of its prestige, especially since the political procedure was almost amateur-like. Etō Shinkichi's overall evaluation should therefore be quoted here in some detail:

> What was distinctive about the demands was the insensitivity and clumsiness of Japanese diplomacy. The world, and especially America, saw a crafty Japan taking advantage of its weaker neighbour at a time when the Western powers were preoccupied elsewhere. Japanese diplomats, by requesting secrecy, enabled Chinese statesmen to build up alarm and distrust by leaking the contents of supposedly non-existent demands. The final ultimatum served on Yuan Shih-k'ai in May 1915 completed the picture of Japanese insensitivity. It gained Japan little the Chinese had not already agreed to, and provided the symbolism for what became, each 25 May, a Day of National Humiliation.[71]

The acceptance of the demands by China could consequently only be considered to be a "Pyrrhic victory,"[72] and it was not only the American public that began to look at Japan more critically. During the negotiations, China also was shaken by a first wave of anti-Japanese resentment when more than 40,000 demonstrators assembled in Shanghai in March 1915 to protest against the Twenty-One Demands, because intellectuals like Liang Qichao (1873–1929) had criticized the content of the demands and warned the government as well as the people that

---

69 Etō, China's International Relations, pp. 97–99.

70 Kuhn, Republik China, p. 148.

71 Etō, China's International Relations, p. 99.

72 Ibid., p. 100.

Japan was trying to turn China into a second Korea.[73] Anti-Japanese protests took place in most of the larger Chinese cities – like Shanghai, Beijing, Shenyang or Hankow – where students went on strike, held protest meetings, organized rallies and delivered pamphlets and leaflets to the wider public, and where merchants organized a boycott against Japanese products. The government, in the meantime, decided to suppress these protests, as they were considered to be acting against the rule of Yuan Shikai, and violence was used to force the protesters to dissolve.[74] Mao Zedong not only realized in 1915 that "Japan is a powerful enemy," but he also concluded that China as a nation "could not survive without fighting in the next twenty years."[75] The people who remembered the national humiliation by Japan 20 years before, when China had been defeated in the First Sino–Japanese War, were now being challenged again by Japanese imperialism. The students, who had considered Japan to be a successful example of Asian modernization, were disappointed and now realized that the Japanese government had no real interest in solidarity with its neighbors, but rather wanted to replace the Western imperialist powers as the leader of East Asia. This knowledge stimulated a wave of nationalism in China, which, however, was not exclusively related to the foreign menace.

China's leaders, due to the Japanese bid for expansion, also realized that they needed to try to counter the imperialist behavior of their neighbor and tried to link their own aims with the Allies, who were still struggling to decide the war in Europe. Britain had had an interest in China's participation in the war, but the Japanese government had declared its reservations, especially since a stronger Chinese voice within the international community was against the natural interests of Japan. Due to the Japanese reservations, Britain eventually decided against negotiating with China about its participation in the war.[76] The war, however, transformed the British Empire into a rather unfelt presence in China, where its activities decreased, and eventually Britain was reduced to a minor power in East Asia when Japan took over its political and economic might in the region.[77]

---

73 Xu, Asia and the Great War, p. 40.

74 Kuhn, Republik China, p. 148.

75 Mao to Xiao Zisheng, 25 July 1916, in: Stuart R. Schram (Ed.), Mao's Road to Power. Revolutionary Writings, 1912–1949, Armonk, NY 1992, Vol. 1, p. 103, cited in Xu, Asia and the Great War, p. 41.

76 Etō, China's International Relations, p. 100.

77 Clarence B. Davis, Limits of Effacement. Britain and the Problem of American Cooperation and Competitionin China, 1915–1917, in: Pacific Historical Review 48 (1979) 1, pp. 47–63, here p. 47. For two studies about the Anglo–Japanese relations during and after the First World War see Peter Lowe, Great Britain and Japan, 1911–1915. A Study of British Far Eastern Policy,

Regardless of these developments, the British government kept its pro–Japanese stance and did not criticize its East Asian ally either for the Twenty–One Demands or for its aggressive policy in Shandong. Actually, only a few officials in the Far Eastern Department were worried about the developments in China, but their voices could hardly be heard during the loud and heated debates about the Western Front. That the Japanese had shown that they considered the British as their rivals in East Asia since the Chinese Revolution in 1911 seemed to be unimportant during the war, due to which the British Empire needed to tighten all its muscles and activate all its allies, no matter how avaricious they may have been.[78] Even America's attempts, namely by Paul Reinsch as well as Edward T. Williams (1854–1944),[79] who led the US State Department's Far Eastern Division, and President Woodrow Wilson himself, could not persuade the British to be more aware of their East Asian ally. However, once the details of Japan's demands had been leaked, Britain also put diplomatic pressure on the government in Tokyo, although the Chinese Minister in London, Alfred Sao–ke Sze (1877–1958),[80] was informed by Foreign Minister Edward Grey (1862–1933) that the British government recommended the acceptance of the final version of the Japanese demands.

Regardless of his position, Yuan Shikai did not seem too concerned by his lack of allies against Japan, especially since he, as mentioned before, considered the final version of the demands of the Japanese government a success of his long negotiations. In fact, Yuan was rather more interested in internal matters, since he was trying to overcome China's post–revolutionary republican order. He was trying to reestablish the monarchy in China and longed for himself to be the first post–revolutionary emperor of the country.[81] His plans, however, met resistance, even from former supporters. Liang Qichao, who had supported Yuan in the past, began to publicly criticize his bid for a reinstallation of the monarchy and was supported by some of the military leaders who had supported Yuan in the past but were, however, unwilling to serve him in the role of a Chinese Emperor. On 11 December 1915, Yuan's preparations were

New York 1969 and Ian Nish, Alliance in Decline. A Study in Anglo–Japanese Relations, 1908–1923, London 1972.

78 Davis, Limits of Effacement, p. 50.

79 Williams' letters related to "Chinese problems" can be found in Box 1 of the Edward Thomas Williams Papers at the Bancroft Library of the University of California, Berkeley. For his later involvement in the peace talks in Paris, see his diary, Carton 3, Vol. 7.

80 Ian Nish, Japan and China, 1914–1916, in: F. Harry Hinsley (Ed.), British Foreign Policy Under Sir Edward Grey, Cambridge 1977, pp. 452–465.

81 Kuhn, Republik China, p. 149.

finished and a process began that would lead to further fractions within Chinese politics. The Deputy Council for Legislation (*daixing lifayuan*) requested Yuan to take on the throne and the title of Emperor, but the general declined the offer. When asked for a second time on 13 December 1915, Yuan agreed and declared that he would reign the country as its new emperor under the maxim "great constitution" (*hongxian*), beginning on 1 January 1916. Two weeks after these events, Cai E (1882–1916), a disciple of Liang and the former military governor of Yunnan Province, established the National Protection Army (*huguojun*) and declared Yunnan's independence.[82] Other military leaders followed Cai's lead and also revolted against the self–proclaimed emperor.

The revolt in Yunnan prevented Yuan Shikai from following his original plan, and he postponed his inthronization until 9 February 1916, but the antagonism against his person in the south of China clearly showed that he would be unable to keep the power for himself. His decline had begun. Yuan was internally and externally isolated, unable to gain any valuable support for his claim, which is why he eventually had to abandon his ideas and the throne itself. On 22 March 1916, Yuan officially renounced his claim.[83] Regardless of the end of the ambitious imperial plans of the formerly mightiest military leader in China, the break up of the provinces and the growing power of individual generals was irreversible. In early April 1916, Guangdong declared its independence from Beijing, and other provinces would follow. Duan Qirui, who as Prime Minister had been summoned to the capital to try to solve this crisis, was also unable to repair the damage that had been done to the country by the ambitions of Yuan. The latter had laid the foundations for the era of the warlords, who would determine the fate of the Chinese republics in the years to come until Chiang Kai–shek (1887–1975) began his rule in 1928, though this was not fully uncontested by the continuing existence of autonomous warlords. Duan did, however, keep control in northern China, where he ruled the remains of the Beiyang government, while the south, the southwest, and the northeast were held by powerful military leaders. The Japanese had stimulated these developments in northern China as well when they supported a Manchu–Mongol movement that longed for independence from the republic. Japan's foreign ministry had supported this movement, but when Yuan eventually died on 6 June 1916, it withdrew its support since China had been weakened already and no additional separatist movement was needed to weaken the central government further. After Yuan's death, the Japanese changed

---

82 Xie Benshu, Cai E yu minchu zhengju, in: Shehui kexue zhanxian 6 (1996), pp. 220–226, cited in ibid., p. 150.
83 Ibid., pp. 150–151.

their tactics with regard to their foreign policy, and when Ōkuma Shigenobu was replaced as Prime Minister by Terauchi Masatake (1852–1919) in October 1916, the latter, together with the new foreign minister, Motono Ichirō (1862–1918), attempted to gain influence over the new Chinese cabinet by sending a personal envoy to Beijing, namely the businessman Nishihara Kamezo (1873–1954), who would initiate the so–called Nishihara Loans, a form of indirect imperialism that would achieve what the Twenty–One Demands could not.[84]

The death of Yuan, however, also created another opportunity for China to gain some more weight in the international theater, because the opponents against the active involvement of the Chinese Republic in the First World War could no longer resist the urge felt by so many of his fellow politicians. Since 1915 a scheme had been worked out, according to which China would provide labor for the war in Europe. According to the motto "laborers in place of soldiers" (*yigong daibing*),[85] Beijing was willing to support the war effort of the allied powers with human capital. After Yuan Shikai's death, the way was clear for laborers to go to Europe, and "his successors feuded with each other but managed to provide ca. 150,000 laborers,[86] who worked on the Western Front during the war."[87] China thereby sent a number of working men to Europe, surpassing the number of involved civilians of any other country. When the British Legation in Beijing requested support and demanded that British missionaries could recruit men in north China for the Chinese Labor Corps, it was clear that the Chinese government would eventually participate in the war and could hope for better treatment once the enemy in Europe had been defeated. A lot of laborers, however, would be sent to France as well. It is ironic that a French ship with Chinese workers was sunk on its way to Europe in February 1917, not only causing 542 deaths among the workers, but also leading to a further request by the Allies to the Japanese government, demanding support from its navy for protection against German submarines. Japan, on the other hand, used this request to demand the former German possessions in China and the Pacific above the equator, something that was secretly granted by Britain, France, Russia, and Italy.[88] While China was still recruiting and sending its workers to

---

84 Etō, China's International Relations, p. 101.

85 On this strategy see Xu, Asia and the Great War, pp. 45–48.

86 Xu claims a number of 140,000 laborers, Wang speaks of 175,000. Peter Chen–main Wang, Caring beyond National Borders. The YMCA and Chinese Laborers in World War I Europe, in: Church History 78 (2009) 2, pp. 327–349, here p. 327.

87 Xu, Asia and the Great War, p. 45.

88 Etō, China's International Relations, p. 101.

foreign countries, its hopes to thereby regain its sovereignty as a state could already never be fulfilled.

As such, recruitment was not an easy task for the foreign missionaries. Most of the laborers were illiterate and had never even heard of the countries they were supposed to be working for or sent to. The British missionaries, who were able to use the Chinese language and were accustomed to China's culture, were obviously helping with the progress, but the involvement of the Chinese government during the process to ensure its successful operation seemed to be inevitable.[89] In Europe, the workers were eventually housed in camps that were provided and run by the British, French, and American militaries (Table 2.2).

Table 2.2: Chinese Labor Camps on the Western Front.[90]

	French organization	British organization	American organization
Number of camps	87	23	10
Size of camps	25–2,000 men	7 camps of more than 3000 men Other camps with 100–1,000 men	Ca. 1,500 men in each camp

Contractually, the Chinese workers had a right to food, clothing, and a salary, but the contractual agreement was obviously not kept in every camp, which is why conflicts between the men and their military supervisors occurred early on. While the laborers from China were allowed to move around their new environment freely and even to travel to other cities, if the required documents had been obtained before, the foreign workers were also confronted with racism and jingoism from the Western soldiers.[91] Eventually, however, China not only benefitted economically from sending workers to Europe but also through exports, e.g. rifles that were secretly sent to the British through Hong Kong. In

---

89 Wang, Caring beyond National Borders, p. 330.

90 Data according to ibid., p. 332. For a more detailed analysis of the role of the Chinese Labor Corps on the Western Front, see: Xu Guoqi, Strangers on the Western Front. Chinese Workers in the Great War, Cambridge, MA 2011 and Alex Calvo/Bao Qiaoni, Forgotten Voices from the Great War. The Chinese Labour Corps, in: The Asia–Pacific Journal 13 (2015) 1, http://apjjf.org/-Bao-Qiaoni-Alex-Calvo/4411/article.pdf (30. 9. 2019).

91 Michael Summerskill, China on the Western Front. Britain's Chinese Work Force in the First World War, London 1982 provides a more detailed account for those Chinese laborers, who worked under British surveillance.

contrast to Japan, whose government and businesses gained immense surpluses during the war, no long–lasting or major impact could be seen in China. The government in Beijing, especially due to its political problems, needed money, and Japan seemed to be the only option to hand.

Nishihara had arranged a first loan to the Chinese government in January 1917, due to which Duan's government was receiving five million Yen in gold.[92] These loans were funneled through Zhang Zuolin, who ruled in the northeast of the country. Due to the incoming money, Duan was able to keep his allies around him, namely Zhang and the conservatives of the Chinese Republic, represented in the national assembly. The revolutionaries, gathered around Sun Yat-sen, in the meantime opposed the Chinese participation in the war, fearing that it would further strengthen the position of the current government. The Japanese eventually decided to put their lot in with Duan's rule and centered their loan policy on his person, abolishing any support for the revolutionaries in the south, who had been traditionally supported through existent pan–Asianist connections. This, in the end, created a political schism, because Duan's opponents, i.e. more than 130 members of the national assembly, met in Guangzhou (Canton) in August 1917, where they elected Sun as the new leader of a southern military government.[93] Between 1917 and 1918 the northern government therefore received further eight Nishihara loans – a total of 145 million Yen – that were supposed to strengthen Duan's position against his enemies, but which also stimulated nationalist and anti–Japanese feelings among the population, who felt betrayed and sold out to a foreign power. It was, however, not solely the corruption of the government but also, and especially, the dissolution of China, which was becoming more and more divided among warlords, that would eventually stimulate the protests of 1919. Accordingly, the early warlord period from 1916,[94] as one of the long–term reasons for the national upheaval after the First World War, should be discussed in a bit more detail, after which the occasion for the protests in 1919, i.e. the Chinese attempts at Versailles to be treated as an equal by the other great powers, will be thoroughly analyzed.

The warlord period determined China's further political development and, in a way, prevented it from taking a united stand against the Japanese imperialist

---

92 Etō, China's International Relations, p. 101.

93 Ibid., p. 102.

94 The description will, if not explicitly stated otherwise, follow James E. Sheridan, The Warlord Era. Politics and Militarism under the Peking Government, 1916–28, in: Denis Twitchett/John K. Fairbank (Eds.), The Cambridge History of China, Vol. 12: Republican China 1912–1949, Part 1, Cambridge 1983, pp. 284–321.

menace, especially during the second half and the aftermath of the First World War. A warlord is usually considered as someone "who commanded a personal army, controlled or sought to control territory, and acted more or less independently,"[95] but the group of these men, who determined China's political fate, was very heterogeneous. Some might have started their career in the military, others as bandits, and their values and motives were definitely as different as the characters themselves. There were hundreds of warlords in China and only some of them, especially the ones who ruled larger territories, have been intensely studied so far. Controlling their own armies, they were first and foremost trying to expand their own influence, looking for allies if necessary, but then suppressing them if possible. Chinese politics between 1916 and 1928 consequently offers a rich field for Machiavellian studies, as power was the only motive for these "princes," who obviously did not identify with the Chinese nation and the vision of a strong nation state in the region.

For the warlords, there existed no national community, imagined or real,[96] but they considered other ties as valuable, namely family ties, which is why many of them tried to install their own family members in key military or political positions. In addition, marriages continued to be used as a political instrument, while personal bonds between officers and their military subordinates would also help to strengthen the position of the warlords. If they wanted to remain in control, the warlords needed to control territory, because revenue secured loyalty within their private armies. Without territory, the army would dissolve and the warlord would consequently lose his position at the top of the province he controlled. Naturally, a helix of violence and attempted expansion by the warlords to increase their own power by increasing their army and the territory they controlled was the consequence of these simple interrelations between possession and rule. For the common people, this helix, however, created actual problems, especially when they were living in a contested area. There, different warlords might have claimed possession of the territory and demanded tax payments at the same time. The loyalty of his subordinates was the most important but also, at the same time, the most expensive asset of a warlord. In addition, a steady supply of weapons, ammunition, and other military goods was necessary, next to the payments for food and other necessary supplies. Since it

---

95 Ibid., p. 284. On the warlord definition and related questions see also Harold Z. Schiffrin, Military and Politics in China. Is the Warlord Model Pertinent?, in: Asia Quarterly 3 (1975), p. 195 and Arthur Waldron, The Warlord. Twentieth-Century Chinese Understandings of Violence, Militarism, and Imperialism, in: The American Historical Review 96 (1991) 4, pp. 1073–1100.

96 Benedict Anderson, Imagined Communities. Reflections on the Origins and Spread of Nationalism, revised edition, New York 1998 [1991].

was not certain that the occupied territories would still belong to them in the near future, most warlords tended to try everything to financially drain the occupied regions as far as possible. In addition to taxes, successful businessmen in particular would draw the attention of a warlord, as they promised to provide exactly what the military leaders were looking for: easy money. Loyalty to the different cliques was also almost always negotiable, depending on the cui bono of the moment. Some warlords had rather loose ties with other cliques or other generals, while some had developed closer relations, usually fortified by a common enemy. The Anhui, Zhili and Fengtian cliques dominated the early warlord period. The warlords, like Zhang Zuolin, could have had very interesting biographies, and like the condottieri of earlier times, they rose to power through opportunity, pure will, and an acceptance of the violent deaths of those who opposed their own ambition for power. Once in power, some of the warlords were successful in expanding their local rule into the riparian territories. Once they had occupied larger territories and could claim rule their uncontestedly, they became a nationally important factor and were able to counter the interests of the government in Beijing in the region. The warlord period was consequently a very violent episode in Chinese history, because it was determined by hundreds of smaller and larger conflicts between single warlords or different cliques. They might have fought for influence in a whole province, but there were also smaller battles for geostrategically important spots or due to specific economic interests. While "China was nominally a republic, with a parliament, a premier, a president, political parties and elections,"[97] nothing could be done in most parts of the country without the consent of a warlord.

Politically the warlords' positions were also very diverse. Yan Xishan (1883–1960), who controlled Shanxi Province, was a modernizer, while Zhang Xun (1854–1923) was interested in the re–establishment of a Chinese Dynasty. There were of course other political forces in the years between 1916 and 1928, like the republican government in Beijing, the intellectuals and their agenda for modern education, new political forces based on the impact of Marxism–Leninism, especially since the Russian Revolution in 1917, and the students and workers who protested against a growing Japanese influence on China's politics, but they were all unable to overcome the rule of the warlords and were consequently in some way dependent on their decisions. The warlords were eventually responsible for a fragile China, where the political structure remained republican but where, in twelve years, one can count four presidents and, depending on the counting

---

97 Elisabeth Forster, 1919 – The Year That Changed China. A New History of the New Culture Movement, Berlin/Boston 2018.

method, 25 to 45 cabinets, as well as seven different constitutions.[98] In these years, 26 people served as prime minister, with terms ranging from two days to 17 months. More than 90 ministers were part of the different governments, in which the south dominated overall by a ratio of 2:1. The nationalists and the communists alike would later refer to the warlords as a junta, a term that emphasized the egocentric aspect of their politics, which was irresponsible and in no way interested in the needs and sorrows of the ordinary people.[99] The rise of the warlords went hand in hand with increasing criminality, as bandits and other criminal organizations often cooperated with the new military rulers or were even incorporated into their armies. Many common people, i.e. civilians, were also victims of the violent conflicts between the 1,300 warlords, who waged around 140 small-scale wars within or between different provinces. The civilian death count has been estimated at more than 600,000 people. None of these wars was waged to reunite China under one political leadership, but rather for the profit and territorial expansion of the warlords.[100]

The steady wars between China's military rulers increased the demand for soldiers, arms and ammunition, as well as war-related supplies, while more and more provinces were drawn into these violent conflicts (Table 2.3).

Table 2.3: War-related increases in soldiers between 1916 and 1928.[101]

Year	Soldiers in China	Provinces involved in conflicts between the warlords
1911	570,000	
1916	700,000	
1918	850,000	1
1919	940,000	
1920		3
1922	1,050,000	
1924		5
1925/26	1,470,000	12
1928	1,830,000	12

The permanent need to arm larger forces stimulated an arms trade with the foreign powers, who exported weapons to China. In addition, the warlords tried to establish their own arms production facilities in larger cities like Shanghai or

---

98 Kuhn, Republik China, p. 164.
99 Ibid.
100 Ibid., pp. 164–165.
101 Data according to ibid., p. 166 and Ch'i, Warlord Politics, p. 137.

Wuhan, from where their troops would be supplied with firepower. Due to these industrial structures, Chinese logistics were also improved, although an overall economic increase was prevented by the violent destruction wrought by the wars between the single bidders for power. It was first and foremost Britain and Japan that exported infantry rifles and other weapons to China and therefore gained from the warlords twice over. Not only were they paid for the arms, but they also used them to keep the country politically unstable, a factor that was quite useful for the imperialist interests of the two exporting powers. As well as rifles, the warlords also imported artillery and were able to count close to 1,500 field guns in 1918. Compared to the Western powers, the provision of field guns or machine guns was still rather sparse, however, because there was only one of them for every 1,000 soldiers.[102]

Regardless of the lack of unity and the further division of large parts of the country among several mighty warlords, the Chinese government, led by President Li Yuanhong (1864–1928), who had taken over that position after Yuan Shikai's death, and Prime Minister Duan Qirui, discussed China's possible participation in the First World War to secure its interests in the aftermath of the global conflict.[103] After heated internal discussions and negotiations with the United States, who had given China some hope of regaining its territory after the war, i.e. Shandong Province, the Chinese government declared war against Germany on 14 August 1917. This happened after a debate that had lasted five months, but the internal struggles in China did not end with the declaration. Members of the revolutionary party, i.e. the Guomindang (Nationalist Party of China), including its leader Sun Yat–sen, opposed China's participation in the war, since they also realized that Duan intended to use it to strengthen his own position further. The country was more divided than others, and, due to the secret agreements between Japan and the other allies, had no chance of regaining its territorial rights anyway.

Regardless of China's willingness to participate in the war effort of the Allied Powers, it was hardly necessary to send troops to Europe, since the Chinese soldiers were not well equipped enough and the Western powers were rather uninterested in a military contribution, but they appreciated, as mentioned above, the support of laborers from China, who could be used for the logistics related to the war effort on the Western Front. In mid–1918, therefore, between 140,000 and 200,000 workers represented China's contribution to the Allied victory. Among them were also close to 30,000 students and other intellectuals,

---

102 Kuhn, Republik China, pp. 166–167.
103 Craft, Angling for an Invitation, p. 1.

who came into contact with socialist and communist ideas, which they would spread at home after their return in the 1920s.[104] In the meantime, in China, the national turmoil intensified more and more. Parliament, which had been dissolved in June 1917, was not summoned again. Instead, Duan Qirui continued to extend his own power. Many members of parliament, as already mentioned above, eventually fled to the south, where they supported Sun Yat-sen, who established, backed by the Chinese Navy, a military government in Guangzhou (Canton) in September 1917. Sun and his supporters claimed to protect the constitution of 1912, but the existence of two governments would make it difficult for China to demand something from the other Allied Powers in the aftermath of the war. A disunited nation state could hardly demand anything from the West. Sun could not remain in his leading position for very long and had to abandon it in early May 1918, but the north-south division of China had been intensified by his actions and a united front against Japanese and Western imperialism was impossible.[105]

The political schism had also intensified the dependency of Duan Qirui on Tokyo's financial support and opened the door for an economic form of Japanese imperialism. He needed money for the military operations of the Anhui clique and therefore was responsive to the offer of the Nishihara loans, which, on the other hand, further increased Japan's control over the political fate of China. 40 million Yen would be used to modernize the military and the banking system of the country, as well as the development of a phone and telegraph network, 30 million Yen were supposed to be invested in mining and forestry, and likewise 50 million Yen for the railway networks in Manchuria and Shandong, which would have supplied the Japanese with another tool with which to strengthen their grip in these regions. Japan, in exchange, received guarantees that were related to Chinese natural resources as well as special trading rights in the country. The loans made Duan's position particularly strong and he was politically uncontested in fall 1918, but he had sold out China's integrity to gain such a powerful rule.[106] Japan had supported Duan's rise to power since 1916, when the government in Tokyo had "launched a policy of full support to [his] government [. . .]

---

104 Some of the students also remained in France, some Chinese arrived after leaving China after the May Fourth Protests. Zhou Enlai (1898–1976) was one of those, active in France in the 1920s, before later becoming influential within the communist movement in China. Chae-jin Lee, Zhou Enlai. The Early Years, Stanford 1994, pp. 75–117; Han Suyin, Eldest Son. Zhou Enlai and the Making of Modern China, 1898–1976, New York 1995, pp. 50–62.

105 On Sun's southern government see Marie-Claire Bergère, Sun Yat-Sen, trans. Janet Lloyd, Stanford 1998, pp. 270–273.

106 Kuhn, Republik China, pp. 174–175.

to establish close ties of political and economic cooperation, and financial obligation between China and Japan."[107] The Japanese government had realized that an informal empire would secure its interests much better than open and aggressive demands, which had failed in 1915. The money invested in military training and modernization, of course, did not serve the war effort of China as a member of the Entente Powers in the First World War, but was rather used to suppress internal enemies of Duan's government. The Japanese consequently perfectly understood how to exploit the internal turmoil in China and to use money where diplomatic pressure had failed in the past. At the same time, the government in Tokyo tried to gain exclusive influence in northeast China by supporting Zhang Zuolin:

> While the imperial government is not unwilling to give friendly consideration to financial aid according to circumstances, it is important to do so by means of economic loans, especially by adopting the form of investment in joint enterprises, in order to avoid the suspicion of the powers and the jealousy of the central government. If [Zhang] too will strive increasingly to promote the reality of Sino-Japanese cooperation, exerting himself, for example, in relation to the lease of land, the management of mines and forests, and other such promising enterprises, and if he will apply every effort to implementing the principles of so-called coexistence and coprosperity and devise methods of joint control both in already existing and in newly-to-be-set-up Sino-Japanese joint venture companies, then the finances of the Three Eastern Provinces can be made to flourish of their own accord and in an inconspicuous way.[108]

It was China's political instability, the rivalry of the warlords, and the lack of a truly national agenda that made it easy for Japan to economically infiltrate the country, to use its leaders as puppets for its own agenda, and to not waste any doubts on its position within China related to the peace conferences after the First World War. Japan was uncontested, since the one and only Chinese government as such did not exist and, since Tokyo had already secretly prepared its territorial gains for the aftermath of the war, it could simply wait to harvest the fruits of its long-term strategy in East Asia.

The philosopher and founding member of the Communist Party of China, Chen Duxiu (1879–1942), would argue in an article on the foundations for the realization of democracy ("Shixing minzhu de jichu", 1 December 1919) that the reasons for the failure of the republic were diverse:

---

107 Sheridan, Warlord Era, p. 304.
108 Gaimushō, Nihon gaikō nenpyō narabi ni shuyō monjo, Vol. 1, p. 525, cited in ibid., p. 305.

1) The Republic of China is still young.
2) The revolutionaries underestimated the problems related to the foundation of a republic.
3) The warlords control the military in China.
4) The parties do not understand the true nature of democracy.

Chen also criticized the fact that the people were not involved in Chinese politics, as the country was ruled by bureaucrats, not by true representatives of the people.[109] The peace negotiations at Versailles and the failure of the delegation to secure Chinese interests, however, would eventually lead to a first national outcry in China and would stimulate the genesis of a first national movement and the discussion about the nation state's political fate in the aftermath of the First World War.

2.4 China at Versailles

Recent publications have dealt with the Treaty of Versailles and its political shortcomings, and the German historian Jörn Leonhard correctly called it a "global epochal threshold" ("*Globale Epochenschwelle*").[110] For China, the trip of its delegation to France would end with another national trauma that would mark the direct cause for the May Fourth Movement. While the members of the Chinese delegation had to counter only one imperialist antagonist, namely Japan, because the Czarist Empire had fallen victim to the Russian Revolution, and the Bolshevists were not represented in Paris but would deal with China in bilateral treaties later,[111] it was from the beginning no easy task for the government in Beijing to reach its aims. Ge–Zay Wood, who had published an analysis of the Sino–Japanese conflict in 1919 for the Chinese Patriotic Committee in New York, highlighted that "[t]he arrival of peace in Europe has lifted the velvet curtain on the Far East which has been hidden behind the scene of world

---

109 The text can be found in Hans J. van de Ven, From Friend to Comrade. The Founding of the Chinese Communist Party, 1920–1927, Berkeley 1991, pp. 19–20, and is also cited in Kuhn, Republik China, pp. 151–152.

110 Jörn Leonhard, Der überforderte Frieden. Versailles und die Welt 1918–1923, Munich 2018, p. 1254. Also see Eckart Conze, Die große Illusion. Versailles 1919 und die Neuordnung der Welt, Munich 2018.

111 Allen S. Whiting, The Soviet Offer to China of 1919, in: The Far Eastern Quarterly 10 (1951) 4, pp. 355–364.

politics for the last four years of war."[112] The Chinese author made it clear that the peace conference would not only determine the future fate of Europe, but would have a tremendous impact on East Asia as well:

> The war in Europe has come to an end. It is high time to consider, not only peace in Europe, but peace in the whole world. The war is a world war, and the problem of peace is certainly and necessarily a world problem. Now can this problem be solved with any satisfaction without rightly settling the Far Eastern question? Can the world have peace while China is every day threatened with War [sic!]?[113]

For Wang, it was also clear that "the Far Eastern is essentially a [S]ino–Japanese question"[114] and that China's treatment during the peace conference would decide the fate of the whole region.

A lot of Chinese hoped that the peace negotiations in France would provide opportunities to regain the territorial rights to Shandong Province and to overturn some of the Twenty–One Demands that had had to be accepted by the government of Yuan Shikai in 1915. There was unity about these goals and a political compromise between the northern and southern governments of China was achieved, due to which they would send a shared delegation led by Lu Zhengxiang (1871–1940) for the north and Wang Zhengting (1882–1961) for the south. The conference in Paris was the first international one that China attended, and Wellington Koo used the opportunity there to give a speech that emphasized the Chinese interest in a new world order that would supposedly follow the ideals US President Woodrow Wilson had spread during the First World War. Regardless of the hopes in China that were also shared by some of its delegates, the East Asian nation state did not receive equal treatment and the Chinese government was not considered to represent one of the victorious Allied Powers, but was considered an inferior participant in the peace talks. This position towards China was influenced by jingoist stereotypes, which were shared by many British diplomats, to name just one example, like Edward T.C. Werner, who wrote about his experiences in the consular service and as a Sinologist in 1920. In his work *China and the Chinese*, he provided a negative image of the Chinese people:

> Emotionally the Chinese are mild, frugal, sober, gregarious, industrious, of remarkable endurance, but at the same time cowardly, revengeful, very cruel, unsympathetic, mendacious, thievish, and libidinous. They are taciturn, but spasmodically vehement. [. . .] Intellectually the Chinese are non–progressive; though in modern times some have shown a desire for Western learning, most have always been and still are slaves to uniformity and

---

112 Ge–Zay Wood, China Versus Japan, New York 1919, p. 3.
113 Ibid., p. 7.
114 Ibid., p. 9.

mechanism in culture. They are unimaginative, imitative, lacking free individuality and creative power, slow in organizing, lacking reflection and foresight, vague in expression, unable to take a comprehensive grasp of a subject; they attach little importance to accuracy. They are also exceedingly suspicious and superstitious.[115]

The Chinese delegation soon realized that many Western diplomats had similar views about China and that they would not receive equal treatment. Eventually, they failed, like Japan failed in its attempt to be considered equal by the Western allies. However, Japan was important enough to secure its territorial interests in Paris, while "Chinese diplomats rallied their meager resources but were ignored in their efforts to recover what had been taken from China."[116]

For the British delegation, it was clear from the beginning that Japan would not accept less than the German rights to Shandong, which, as mentioned before, had been secured in secret agreements with the Western allies already. The Japanese press, as observed by the British Foreign Office, had also made clear the main points of interest:

1. Questions in Europe were not the concern of Japan.
2. Qingdao must not be returned to Germans but the question of its future disposal must be settled directly between China and Japan.
3. If Great Britain retains the South Sea Islands south of the equator, Japan would certainly want to retain those to the north.
4. Japan would have something to say as regards the settlement in Eastern Siberia.
5. The question of discrimination against the Japanese in America, Canada, and Australia would appear likely to be brought up at the Conference as arising out of the proposal for a League of Nations.[117]

To avoid discussions about racism and Japanese immigration to the British dominions, London might also have been in favor of letting Japan take its stand against China. The Chinese rights for self-determination and territorial integrity were consequently sacrificed for the interests of the British Empire as a whole. Since the Japanese "came to Paris with three demands: first, a formal recognition of the principle of racial equality; second, title to the German islands of the North Pacific; and third, acquisition of Germany's economic and other rights in the Chinese province of Shandong,"[118] it was clear that not all of them could be denied.

---

115 Edward T.C. Werner, China of the Chinese, London 1920, pp. 7–8.
116 Xu, Asia and the Great War, p. 153.
117 British Embassy, Tokyo to Balfour, November 12, 1918, FO 608/211, cited in ibid., p.155.
118 Ibid., p. 157.

The American position towards the Chinese was not as bad as the British one, but only because the US diplomats distrusted the Japanese, as they were competing with them over economic interests in the Pacific region in general, and in China in particular. Robert Lansing (1864–1928), a member of the US delegation, even compared Japan with Germany, with the former claiming a position for itself in East Asia as Germany had claimed in Europe. The Japanese expansionist demands as such consequently represented a threat to the new liberal and peaceful order that Wilson had not only recommended but requested to secure peace after the war.[119] The Japanese delegation, however, pressed for the rights to Shandong, and even threatened on 24 and 30 April 1919 not to sign the peace treaty at all. Furthermore, they would not only withdraw from the conference, but also from the League of Nations and thereby sabotage Wilson's project of a new international and peaceful order from its beginning. As Xu remarked, the US President's "dilemma was this: if he gave Shandong to Japan, China might not vote for the League; if he gave Shandong to China, Japan would not vote for the League."[120] In the end, China's national division and lack of international recognition as a worthy and powerful ally in East Asia were responsible for the final swing towards Japan. Since Italy had already left the peace talks due to its claims for Fiume, Wilson could not afford another power leaving, because "the defection of Japan might well break up the conference and destroy the League of Nations."[121] Considering the later problems the League of Nations had to face in the United States, as well as with Japan in its more aggressive and expansionist period, one could critically ask if its establishment was worth the sacrifice of Chinese interests in Versailles.[122] Regardless of the future developments, China had to live with the new facts, despite the hopes for a better and more equal world to live in having been so high in the East Asian country.

When the war in Europe ended, the people in China were happy to read news about the allied victory in the war against the Central Powers. An official national holiday was declared by the government, and three days off work did their part in cheering up the common people. When it became known that Wilson would be in Paris to negotiate over the new world order, people across the

---

119 For Lansing's memoirs of the peace talks see Robert Lansing, Die Versailler Friedensverhandlungen. Persönliche Erinnerungen, Berlin 1921.

120 Xu, Asia and the Great War, p. 159.

121 Ibid., p. 160.

122 On Japan and the League of Nations see Thomas W. Burkman, Japan and the League of Nations. Empire and World Order, 1914–1938, Honolulu, HI 2007. For the Chinese relations to the League see Alison Adcock Kaufman, In Pursuit of Equality and Respect. China's Diplomacy and the League of Nations, in: Modern China 40 (2014) 6, pp. 605–638.

country cheered, because they were hoping for the US President's success at the green table. The mood in the capital was good, and especially the students were full of hope:

> Chinese students in Beijing gathered at the American Legation, where they chanted 'Long live President Wilson!' Some of them had memorized and could easily recite his speech on the Fourteen Points. Chen Duxiu, Dean of the School of Letters at Peking University, a leading figure in the New Cultural Movement, and later a co–founder of the Chinese Communist Party, was then so convinced of Wilson's sincerity and noble objectives that he called Wilson 'the best good man in the world.'[123]

The intellectuals, like Cai Yuanpei, connected Wilson's ideas and the end of the war with a watershed moment in history, since the future seemed brighter and the League of Nations promised peace, based on the self–determination of nations and an international sister– and brotherhood of human beings. In Beijing, more than 50,000 people marched through the streets during the national holiday as participants in the victory parade.[124] In Paris, however, the expectations many Chinese had for the peace talks were bitterly disappointed and would consequently turn the joy about the end of the war into anger, especially since imperialism had shown its face again, just at the moment the destruction of so many lives due to imperialist aims had ended. Nothing had changed, and the diplomats the Chinese had sent to France could only try to resist the imperialism and anti–Chinese jingoism of the Western powers and Japan.

60 delegates were led by Lu Zhengxiang and Wang Zhengting, representing their respective Chinese governments, and many of the diplomats involved had been active in China's diplomatic service in several Western countries, some even for decades, having started their careers under the Qing Dynasty. Considering the intellectual power the Chinese government had mobilized for the peace talks in France, it is obvious that it was attempting to achieve bigger things than just being treated as an inferior participant. In contrast to Japan, whose government was granted five seats at the negotiation table and therefore was ranked as a great power, China was granted only two seats and therefore degraded to the status of an unimportant participant. The high expectations related to former promises and to Wilson's declarations during the war had been replaced by blunt great power policy again. The Chinese could do nothing to overcome the jingoist treatment it had had to deal with since the Opium Wars of the previous century. Regardless of this treatment, however, the Chinese delegation and its

---

123 Xu, Asia and the Great War, p. 161.
124 Ibid., pp. 162–163.

diplomats did everything possible to achieve the goals the government in Beijing had announced to regain its political and territorial sovereignty:

1) The restoration of rights related to foreign concessions in China and related lease treaties, i.e. the Shandong issue,
2) the sovereignty of China as a nation state by abolishing the so-called Boxer protocol of 1901, i.e. first and foremost the end of foreign troops and jurisdiction in China, and
3) the reintroduction of tariff autonomy.[125]

The expression of these aims was answered with a rejection from the other powers, who were not interested in discussing things unrelated to the First World War, although China could insist on a discussion of the Shandong issue.

Wellington Koo, who presented the Chinese demands on 28 January 1919, provided a detailed explanation of this issue, arguing on behalf of the self-determination of nations – the people of Shandong were Chinese – and emphasizing that the existent agreements with Japan, which had been signed during the war, had only been accepted due to Japanese pressure. The peace conference could hardly accept such treaties, so Koo's argument went, and since Germany had been at war with China as well, it could have hardly transferred Chinese rights to a third power, i.e. Japan. The Chinese made these points because they truly believed in the idea of the League of Nations and that there was a genuine interest at the peace conference to establish equality and a secure peace. They must have been surprised, to say the least, when it emerged that the Western powers had already signed secret treaties with Japan, in which the question of Shandong had already been dealt with. Another treaty between Duan Qirui and Japan showed that the Japanese government had also already received rights with regard to the territory that ran along the railway tracks in the province.[126]

China was one of the victims of the peace negotiations in France. Wilson's claim for the self-determination of nations obviously only counted when geostrategically relevant for the Western powers, and nobody seemed to be willing to challenge Japanese expansionism. China was consequently robbed by its neighbor while the world discussed a future without war. Considering these issues, the peace talks were rather more interested in securing the interests of the Entente than in truly preparing the ground for a solid post-war order based on peace and equality.[127] The delegation from China could hardly do anything, although

---

125 Ibid., p. 165.
126 Kuhn, Republik China, pp. 175–176.
127 Stephen G. Craft, John Bassett Moore, Robert Lansing, and the Shandong Question, in: Pacific Historical Review 66 (1997) 2, pp. 231–249, here p. 233.

they had prepared themselves by recruiting international help in advance as well. An authority on international law, John Bassett Moore (1860–1947), had been recruited as a legal advisor for the Chinese delegation to serve and assist it during the Paris Peace Conference. He had signed a three–year contract, receiving US$ 4,000 per year for his services. The agreement was secret, because China, while knowing that it would need such a specialist to help their cause, did not want to arouse too much interest in its preparations. Moore, however, was aware that it would not be international lawyers who would be discussing the future of the world in general, and China's fate in particular. He let his daughter know "that they [Wilson, as well as other political leaders of the Western powers] do not want 'international lawyers,' as they are likely to be prejudiced in favor of the past, with all its evil associations and practices."[128] Regardless of his considerations, he tried to help the Chinese delegation with a legal claim to get their rights to Shandong back, but Wilson was not willing to argue about any Sino–Japanese treaties. In the end, China had only two choices: sign the Versailles Peace Treaty with reservations or not sign it at all. The Big Four of the conference – Britain, France, Italy, and the United States –, however, declared that a signature with reservations was not going to be accepted and that China would only have the right to complain after signing the treaty.[129]

The Japanese at the same time offered a compromise, namely the declaration of 30 April 1919, according to which China would receive its rights to Shandong back at a future moment in time; however, it did not define when exactly that was supposed to be. Although the economic privileges for Japan would remain, this declaration was considered a friendly offer from Japan's delegation by the diplomats representing the Western powers. Next to Wilson, British Prime Minister David Lloyd George (1863–1945) and French Prime Minister Georges Clemenceau (1841–1929) eventually took a pro–Japanese stance. Ultimately, Germany, according to paragraph 156 of the Treaty of Versailles, had to transfer its rights in Shandong to Japan. The Chinese delegation, on the other hand, did not sign the treaty in the end.[130] Of course, this was a bitter moment for China, and on 2 May 1919, its "delegation asserts that the reported action of the Council of Three in transferring the German rights to Japan is not in keeping with the principles of peace laid down by the Allied and associated powers."[131] What happened needed no explanation, as the motives for the decisions of the major Allied powers were well

---

128 Cited in ibid.
129 Ibid., pp. 238–240.
130 Kuhn, Republik China, pp. 177–178.
131 China Calls Decision of Big 3 'Unfair', in: New York Tribune, 4 May 1919, p. 4.

known. The explanation in the *New York Tribune* was as frank as possible when it stated: "It appears clear, then, that the council has been bestowing on Japan the rights, not of Germany, but of China; not of an enemy, but of an ally. The more powerful ally has reaped a benefit at the expense, not of the common enemy, but of the weaker ally."[132] And from a Chinese perspective, as *The Sun* (New York) declared, nothing but injustice had been done: "in the opinion of the Chinese delegation the decision had been made without regard for justice or the protection of the territorial integrity of China."[133] The violation of Chinese rights was the direct reason for the protests, but, as has been shown before, the long–term reasons also played a role. Now, with another humiliation at hand, a nationalist protest would arise in China that criticized the Treaty of Versailles, but at the same time demanded reforms to the political structures so as to eventually achieve Chinese unity that would secure the nation state's sovereignty and territorial integrity.

2.5 The May Fourth Movement

The May Fourth Movement (*wusi yundong*) in China was a heterogeneous protest movement that was in a way a direct result of the Treaty of Versailles and the political mistreatment of the Chinese nation state by Japan and the West; however, it was also the result of long–term developments in China, e.g. the factionalism that divided the country or the increase of violence in the era of the warlords. The movement combined different protests into one national upheaval that shook the country in the direct aftermath of the First World War. It might have begun as a student movement on 4 May 1919, but it became a national protest movement rather fast. While the focus is usually on the year 1919, one can also consider the events in May as a culmination of an intellectual renewal movement that spanned over the years between 1917 and 1921. It was a clash between tradition and modernity, young and old, so to speak, and the struggles would supposedly decide China's fate and future. The intellectuals at Beijing University were interested in a Chinese modernity that would break with the conservative traditions and confronted the students at this institution with new thoughts and alternatives. The demand for a break with the past was even more imminent due to the results of the Paris Peace Conference, as the negotiations showed that while new ideas were prominently promoted during the war, nothing had changed. China was still treated like a colonial sphere, equality was

---

132 Ibid.
133 China Also Balks, in: The Sun, 7 May 1919, p. 1.

a wish rather than a reality, and corruption still determined Chinese politics, as Duan Qirui was considered as responsible for China's misery as the Allied Powers, whose demands against imperialism and for the self–determination of nations were nothing more than a tool, only to be used when it fitted the great power policies of the West. Capitalism and therefore imperialism still dominated world politics, and the frustration about the fact that nothing had changed was an immense factor with regard to the outbreak of protests in Beijing in May 1919.

It has been argued that it makes sense to trace the May Fourth Movement back to 1915, when the journal *Xin qingnian* (*New Youth*) had been founded in Beijing, and to extend its impact and role until the mid–1920s.[134] In a political sense, the May Fourth Movement marked the awakening of the Chinese nation as well as the starting point of a broader anti–Japanese and therefore anti–imperialist movement in China, which not only demanded a fight against the warlord system, but would also lead to the establishment of the Communist Party of China (CPC) in 1921.[135] The working class joined forces with the students for the first time, although China's industrial working class was not large enough to claim representation for the mass of people. Others who protested demanded the emancipation of women and equality of the sexes. It was consequently a broad revolutionary and nationalist movement, combining heterogeneous forces that were brought together by their wish for a better China. To claim that the Treaty of Versailles was the only reason for the existence of the May Fourth Movement would consequently not be sufficient.[136] Of course, the decision about Shandong was perceived as "unjust" and had "violated the principles of international law,"[137] and Chinese students in the US claimed that "for Japan to retain these concessions and claim them by the right of conquest is to justify the retention of the plundered goods of a burglar."[138] Nobody who had believed in Wilson's motto of self–determination could believe that Japan was supposed to keep the rights it had received during the war years, and the editors of *The Chinese Students' Monthly*, a journal for Chinese students in the US, declared that the

> treaty of 1915 [i.e. the acceptance of the attenuated Twenty–One Demands, F.J.] was made under circumstances which would render it null and void. It was made with a threat of war.

---

134 Kuhn, Republik China, pp. 188.
135 On the early years of the CPC see Hans J. Van de Ven, From Friend to Comrade. The Founding of the Chinese Communist Party, 1920–1927, Berkeley, CA 1991.
136 Kuhn, Republik China, p. 189.
137 China's Grievances over Shantung, in: The Chinese Students' Monthly 15 (1919) 1, pp. 3–6, here p. 3.
138 Ibid., p. 4.

> It was signed under the duress of an ultimatum. The consent contained therein was wrested from China at the point of the bayonet, and as such, it could not justify Japan's retention of the German concessions. [. . .] No more can Japan justify her possession of the German concessions in Shantung by the Treaty of 1915 than can a burglar justify his claim to the possession of the robbed goods by a written consent signed at the point of the revolver.[139]

Nobody in China could stand by in 1919, just observing these events, which so resembled Chinese weakness, due to its leaders' incapacities as well as the nation state's lack of modernization. Therefore, multiple forces that had criticized the current state of political affairs, the rise of the warlords, and the lack of a Chinese national identity – namely, the modernization or Westernization movement of the 1860s (*yangwu yundong*),[140] the reform movement of 1898 (*wuxu bianfa*),[141] and the revolutionaries of 1911 (*xinhai geming*) – eventually joined forces and became part of the larger national movement, i.e. the May Fourth Movement.

Many of the intellectuals who supported the movement had been studying abroad, and when they returned to China, they had naturally become agents of modernization.[142] For them especially, who might have been true believers in the chances of a better world after 1918, the events in France were more than humiliating. They naturally became important leaders of the new protest movement.[143] In the years during the First World War, many new journals had been founded and offered a broader variety of discussions, especially to students, whose most important concern was the future of education. A conflict about the right path to a better future was naturally occurring when traditionalists, who wanted to stick with social values and tradition, as they were related to

---

139 Ibid.

140 Ding Xianjun, Yangwu yundong shihua, Beijing 2000. In English see John King Fairbank/ Merle Goldman, China. A New History, second edition, Cambridge, MA 2006, pp. 217–234.

141 Mao Haijian, Wuxu bianfa shi shikao, Beijing 2005. For a broader discussion of the reform movement in English see Paul A. Cohen/John E. Schreckner (Eds.), Reform in Nineteenth–Century China, Cambridge, MA 1976.

142 For a contemporary discussion of Chinese students abroad see Y. S. Tsao, A Challenge to Western Learning. The Chinese Student Trained Abroad – What He Has Accomplished – His Problems, in: News Bulletin (Institute of Pacific Relations), December 1927, pp. 13–16. For a broader discussion of Chinese students abroad, especially in Germany and the US, Thomas Harnisch, Chinesische Studenten in Deutschland. Geschichte und Wirkung ihrer Studienaufenthalte in den Jahren 1860 bis 1945, Hamburg 1999; Edward Rhoads, Stepping Forth into the World. The Chinese Educational Mission to the United States 1872–1881, Hong Kong 2011 and Weili Ye, Searching Modernity in China's Name. Chinese Students in the United States, 1900–1927, Stanford 2001 are recommended.

143 Nancy F. Sizer, John Dewey's Ideas in China 1919 to 1921, in: Comparative Education Review 10 (1966) 3, pp. 390–403, here p. 390.

Confucianism, and modernists, who depicted a more Western modernization for China, clashed over who was rightfully determining the country's eventual course. What a majority of intellectuals shared in 1919 was a belief in a democratic form of government as well as evolutionary progress that was based on modern education.[144] While Chinese students had traditionally had to memorize the classics and not critically think and argue, Cai Yuanpei considered education "a means of cultivating virtuous or moral character in the young. This moral training was to be supplanted by an industrial and military education and rounded out by an aesthetic one."[145] Students initially admired Japan, whose modernization process since the beginning of the Meiji Restoration in 1868 had been considered successful. The May Fourth Movement, however, was directed against both Chinese traditional education and Japan as an idolized modern Asian nation state. The protesters were seeking other solutions for what a modern education and an independent and sovereign Chinese nation state should be based on. The students who returned from abroad, not only from Japan but the US and Germany as well, brought new ideas with them and wanted to use their newly gained knowledge to transform the existent society at home.

The people who initially formed the May Fourth Movement, like in many protest and probably revolutionary movements, represented a young generation, mostly born in the 1890s, who longed for change because they did not consider the current state of China to be a place where their ambitions and dreams could be reached or fulfilled. Intellectuals like Hu Shi (1891–1962), Gu Jiegang (1893–1980), Fu Sinian (1896–1950), and Mao Zedong dreamed of a new Chinese society, especially since they had witnessed the Russian Revolution of 1917, which seemed to promise a chance for a new age and a more equal and classless society. In 1919, not too much information about the internal state of Soviet Russia and the corruption of the revolution by Lenin was known abroad, and intellectuals and revolutionaries worldwide hoped for a near world revolution in the name of equality.[146] It was argued that the Chinese Revolution of 1911 had failed because people were not willing to modernize, but rather were trapped between tradition and modernity, paralyzed and unable to bring

---

144 Ibid.

145 Cyrus H. Peake, Nationalism and Education in Modern China, New York 1932, p. 76 cited in ibid., p. 391.

146 Criticism was often seen as an attempt to undermine the achievements of the Russian Revolution, and even later critics had initially believed that it would change the world instead of establishing another regime. Frank Jacob, From Aspiration to Frustration. Emma Goldman's Perception of the Russian Revolution, in: American Communist History 17 (2018) 2, pp. 185–199.

the revolution to a fruitful end. Modernization could hardly change the Chinese mentality, and therefore the revolutionary attempt was incomplete. While a Chinese Republic had been created on paper, the Chinese people were still living in the past. Charles K. Edmund (1876–1949),the President of the Canton Christian College in 1918 and 1919, described the problems modern educators faced in China as follows: "Religion, government, and reverence for antiquity have been the dominant influences in shaping the course of Chinese education."[147] He also emphasized that the country was simply too large, and since the revolution in 1911, there was an insufficient number of higher education institutions to offer a broader education to the Chinese people.[148]

For the reformers and revolutionaries like Sun Yat–sen, who demanded a "national rescue" in 1911, Western education was only considered a tool, and the slogan "Chinese learning for fundamental principles, Western learning for practical applications" (*zhongxue wei ti, xixue wei yong*) was promoted; however, in contrast to Japan's government–promoted "Japanese spirit, Western technology" (*wakon yōsai*) strategy, it failed to achieve permanent results.[149] The attempts to enlighten China, i.e. to overcome the Confucian tradition of ritualized submission, were not easy to achieve, since the three principles (*sangang*) that ordered the relationships between ruler and subordinate, father and son, and husband and wife were essential to the lives of the Chinese, as were the five basic relations (*wulun*) between ruler and minister, father and son, older and younger brother, husband and wife, and between friends.[150] To prepare the path towards a new China meant breaking these existent relations and the rules they were based on. Of course, education played an important role because new values needed to be taught. As a consequence, academics, educators, and intellectuals in general "were experiencing major upheavals and innovations in the 1910s, trying to define their institutional structure, intellectual ideals and intellectuals' role in society."[151]

---

147 Charles K. Edmunds, Modern Education in China, Department of the Interior, Bureau of Education, Bulletin 1919, No. 44, Washington 1919, p. 5.
148 Ibid., pp. 24–25.
149 Geng Yunzhi, An Introductory Study on China's Cultural Transformation in Recent Times, Berlin 2014, pp. 79–116. On wakon yōsai see Peter Lutum, Das Denken von Minakata Kumagusu und Yanagita Kunio. Zwei Pioniere der japanischen Volkskunde im Spiegel der Leitmotive wakon–yōsai und wayō–setchū, Münster 2005 and Hirakawa Sukehiro, Wakon yōsai no keifu. Uchi to soto kara no Meiji Nihon, Tokyo 1992.
150 Kuhn, Republik China, pp. 191–192.
151 Forster, 1919, p. 20.

In 1905, Empress Dowager Cixi (1835–1908) was responsible for a first reform when she abolished exams for civil servants. In the past, civil servants had to be familiar with Confucian works. Now, students were learning in schools and universities that were teaching according to Western or often Japanese examples. Their learning experiences were consequently totally different, and although the classics were still part of their education, the students had to read them "as part of history or the history of literature, rather than as timeless truths."[152] Due to these changes it also became easier for intellectuals to criticize politics, because they were acting based on reason than following traditional paradigms of submission. The consequence was some kind of Chinese Enlightenment, and the corruption as well as failures of the warlords' politics were more openly discussed. Such discussions were in addition more public, as the press created a new sphere of publicity in the early 1900s when more and more newspapers, periodicals and journals reached an increasing number of readers, thereby stimulating nationalist discourse at the same time.[153] Schools and universities were also responsible for this increase in periodicals because many of them published their own newspapers or journals, like the *Beijing University Daily*. Eventually, there was an overlap between academia and the press, between intellectual discourse and politics. The weakness of the government during the warlord period also gave more room to critical voices, and many intellectuals began open and critical discussions about the future of China. In these circles, especially at Beijing University, however, traditionalists (Old Faction) and modernizers (New Faction) also clashed over their opinions on the form of education as well as the future of the nation.[154]

On the face of it, they might have discussed the use of language, i.e. traditional vs. actually spoken Chinese, but this was not all. Nevertheless, the front line between the two factions was not always clear, as it was often presented later, because there were many blurred positions that tended to be found on both sides from time to time.[155] While the intellectuals as Beijing University struggled over the correct use of language, they indirectly fought over the future of China as such. Conservative ideas and positions, on the one hand, demanded a stronger focus on genuinely Chinese values, while progressive intellectuals pressed for the modernization of China by a stronger focus on values and thoughts that

---

152 Ibid., p. 21.
153 The Shanghai News sold 20,000 issues in 1917, and 30,000 in 1920, while the number of periodicals as such reached more than 800 in the late 1910s and 2,000 in the early 1920s. Ibid., p. 23.
154 For a more detailed analysis of the struggle between the two academic factions at Beijing University see ibid., pp. 30–32.
155 Ibid., p. 39.

had been imported to the country from abroad. That such discussions origi-
nated at the university of the Chinese capital is not surprising. Beijing University was the only remnant of the Hundred Days' reform in 1898.[156] Before Cai
Yuanpei took over the presidency in December 1916, his predecessors like Yan
Fu (1854–1921) had already begun to implement initial reforms with regard to
the education of the university's students.[157] Other intellectuals like Chen
Duxiu, Hu Shi and Li Dazhao (1889–1927) followed Cai's call to serve at Beijing
University, where they would provide the core group of educators that stimulated a more open and critical education, poetically named the "wind of learning at Beijing University" (*Beida xuefeng*).[158] The new educational program,
"education with a worldview" (*shijieguan jiaoyu*), also positively influenced
the position of the students, who became more involved, more active, and
eventually more demanding. Confucianism was criticized as something that
prevented China's modernization, and an active struggle with the nation's own
past began. Some clamored "Down with Confucian teachings" (*dadao ruxue*),
others "Down with tradition" (dadao chuantong).[159] Li Dazhao, who worked in
the university library before being promoted to the rank of professor, studied
and taught Marxism there, and referred to the Russian Revolution as a historical
success that could be an example for China. Like Lenin in Russia, he considered
a revolution possible, as long as the majority of peasants were led by an intellectual avant–garde. For that, the agrarian population of China needed to be liberated from its suppression by the corrupt warlords as well as the government of
men like Duan Qirui.[160]

In spring 1918 Li founded a study group for socialism (*shehui zhuyi yanjiu-
hui*) at the university, and a special issue of the journal *New Youth* (*Xin qingnian*)
provided a detailed discussion of Marxism in May of the same year. Li published an article in this issue, in which he provided a survey of his own views
on Marxism, "My Views on Marxism" ("Wo de Makesi zhuyiguan"), and therefore became one of the early influential Marxist leaders in China. When Mao
Zedong had finished his studies in Hunan, he supposedly also joined the student group that mostly consisted of Marxists as well.[161] However, it was not

---

156 Rebecca E. Karl/Peter Gue Zarrow (Eds.), Rethinking the 1898 Reform Period. Political
and Cultural Change in Late Qing China, Cambridge, MA 2002.
157 Kuhn, Republik China, pp. 192–193.
158 Ibid., p. 194.
159 Ibid., p. 197.
160 On Li see Maurice Meisner, Li Ta–Chao and the Origins of Chinese Marxism, Cambridge,
MA 1967.
161 Kuhn, Republik China, pp. 199.

only Marxist ideas that were discussed. New input was received in many fields, such as economics, literature, art, etc. All in all, the years of the First World War had been very vibrant at Beijing University. The results of the Paris Peace Conference would eventually set the critical potential of the students free, and they not only went onto the streets to protest against Western and Japanese imperialism, but they also protested against an antiquated China that should exist no longer: too traditional, disunited, corrupt, and, most importantly, weak. The May Fourth Movement was supposed to break the chains that constrained the Chinese nation, no matter if they had been forged in foreign environments or at home.

The events of 4 May 1919 clearly showed that the students were not willing to accept another humiliation from Western or Japanese imperialism, that they wanted to change their country, and that they wanted to live in a sovereign and independent nation that was ruled according to reason and by the masses of the people, not by a corrupt government that would sell out Chinese territory to the Japanese just to remain in power. The reaction of the young intellectuals showed that the republican policy since the revolution in 1911 had failed to create a modern nation state that the young generations could identify themselves with and in which they felt they had a perspective. The universities had become revolutionary hubs where a generation was educated that would no longer accept the existent structures. When the news arrived from Paris on 2 May 1919, it was clear that the barrel was going to overflow. Demonstrations and protests that had been planned for 7 May 1919, the day China had received an ultimatum to sign the final version of the initial Twenty–One Demands in 1915, were brought forward to 4 May.[162] Fu Sinian,[163] who had been radicalized at Beijing University, was one of the initiators of the movement and, as a native of Shandong Province, felt particularly humiliated by the decision that Japan should receive the German rights there. On 3 May 1919, he was nominated at a meeting of the planning committee of all universities and colleges of the city to act as their chairman, and it was decided that the protests should begin the next day, Sunday, at the Gate of Heavenly Peace (Tiananmen).

Around 3,000 male and female students had gathered on Tiananmen Square by 1:30 pm, more than 50% of all students in Beijing at that time, representing the 13 universities and colleges as well as the Female Teacher College (Beijing

---

[162] Ibid., p. 206. On the heterogenous organization of the protests and the involved groups and ideas see Arif Dirlik, Ideology and Organization in the May Fourth Movement. Some Problems in the Intellectual Historiography of the May Fourth Period, in: Republican China 12 (1987) 1, pp. 3–19.

[163] On Fu's life and work see Wang Fan–sen, Fu Ssu–nien. A Life in Chinese History and Politics, Cambridge/New York 2006.

nüzi shifan). They marched to the Legation Quarter wearing flags and banners bearing anti–Japanese slogans and demands for the return of Shandong to China. They protested against Japanese imperialism as well as against their own political leadership, which was deemed corrupt and unable to lead China to a prospective future. Flyers were handed out, demanding that the Allied Powers rethink their decision and give Shandong back to China. The manifesto of the May Fourth Movement had been provided by the author Luo Jialun (1896–1969), who, together with Fu Sinian, edited the journal *New Flood* (*Xinchao*). The protesters wanted to march to the embassies of the United States, Great Britain, France, and Italy, but the police did not allow them to enter the Legation Quarter. Consequently, the students changed their route and instead continued their protest march to the house of former Vice–Minister of Foreign Affairs Cao Rulin (1877–1966), who was a member of the Anhui Clique and had negotiated with the Japanese over the Twenty–One Demands. He was one of the politicians that were friendly to Japan, and due to his involvement in the talks with the Japanese government during the war years, he was a natural target for the protesters.[164]

It was originally not the intention of the organizers of the demonstration to use violence, but when they reached the house of Cao, some of the students went in and, since the pro–Japanese politician was no longer there, they destroyed the interior and looted some rooms. The students found Zhang Zongxiang (1879–1962), a politician responsible for Japanese matters, in hiding, and he was eventually beaten up by the protesters until he lost consciousness. When the police arrived, most of the students had fled, but Fu Sinian, Luo Jialun, and some 30 others were arrested. They, however, had to be released again, because the government was under extreme pressure and public opinion demanded freedom for the protest's leaders. In fact, a nationalist wave went through the country, and sympathy for those who had protested on 4 May 1919 could clearly be felt. The demonstrations spread across the country, and more protests, no longer only by students, were witnessed in other cities.[165] Businessmen called for a boycott of Japanese goods, and workers and artisans went on strike. In the harbors, the ships from Japan remained loaded, and in Hangzhou, rickshaw drivers would no longer offer their services to the Japanese. Until July 1919, the import of cotton and cement from Japan collapsed, and the amount of other imported goods was also decreasing.[166] The students in Beijing had already begun to strike on 19 May,

---

164 Kuhn, Republik China, pp. 207–208.
165 For Shanghai, to name just one example, see Joseph T. Chen, The May Fourth Movement in Shanghai. The Making of a Social Movement in Modern China, Leiden 1971.
166 Kuhn, Republik China, p. 209.

and many from other cities solidarized themselves with their fellows in the capital when they began to strike in Shanghai, Wuhan and other cities. Luo Jialun described the national wave of protests on 23 May when he argued that the spirit of the students ended the lethargy of society.[167] It was this spirit, as Luo highlighted, that was necessary for the birth of a new, nationally united China. Three days later, 12,000 students and pupils protested in Shanghai, hoisting the flag of the Chinese Republic to express their national identity. In Wuhan, the pro–Japanese military governor suppressed the protests and ordered his soldiers to beat up or even shoot the students if they did not comply with his orders. Chinese President Xu Shichang (1855–1939) declared that the students should go to the universities and learn, instead of protesting in the streets. Regardless of such attempts to contain the protest movement, it had reached a national level.[168] The strikes had motivated workers, artisans, and soldiers to follow the students' example, but in Beijing the government answered the national outcry with mass arrests in early June 1919. When more than 1,000 students were held prisoner in the rooms of Beijing University, 60–70,000 people protested in Shanghai on 5 June 1919. On the same day, thousands of female protesters gathered at Xu Shichang's residence to show solidarity with the imprisoned students.[169]

The protest could not be localized and suppressed by the government, and it eventually reacted to some of the demands when pro–Japanese ministers, including Cao Rulin, were dismissed from their duties. In Paris, the Chinese delegation did not sign the Treaty of Versailles on 28 June 1919, and thereby at least protested symbolically against the imperialist nature of the document's contents. In 1916, Chen Duxiu had already demanded a form of democracy that really represented the will of the people, who should rule and hold the political power within an independent nation state.[170] On 1 December 1919, he published an "Idealist Manifesto of the New Youth" ("Xin qingnian xuanyan") in which he argued that the demand for possessions, be it by plutocrats or warlords, must be countered and that democracy demanded equal rights for all people. The parties, who only represented the wishes and needs of a few, of the privileged classes so to speak, should not be something the common people would be members of. The manifesto also demanded the emancipation of women,

---

167 Vera Schwarcz, The Chinese Enlightenment. Intellectuals and the Legacy of the May Fourth Movement of 1919, Berkeley 1986, p. 22.

168 Kuhn, Republik China, pp. 210–211.

169 Ibid., 211.

170 Edward X. Gu, Populistic Themes in May Fourth Radical Thinking. A Reappraisal of the Intellectual Origins of Chinese Marxism (1917–1922), in: East Asian History 10 (1995), pp. 99–126, here p. 109.

among other changes that would establish a better society in the future.[171] It was, in a way, the disappointment of the hopes and dreams of the young generation in China that had stimulated the outbreak of the protests on 4 May 1919. For Li Dazhao, with the end of the First World War, a new epoch had begun in 1919:

> [T]his new epoch has brought with it new life, new civilisation, a new world. [. . .] From today onwards we realise the gross error [of imperialism and social Darwinism] for we now know that material evolution does not rely upon competition, but rather mutual aid. The weakness of mankind is that they wish for survival, wish to enjoy happiness and wellbeing, for which purpose the relationship between us should be fraternal love, we should not slaughter each other by force of arms.[172]

The reality, however, had proved the Chinese hopes wrong. Western and Japanese imperialism did not end with the First World War, nor did China receive a more democratic government. Hence the students were also no longer willing to accept that as their eternal fate and demanded change. Others in China listened to their demands and joined the protests, because they had realized that change demanded action.

Elisabeth Forster is consequently absolutely correct when she calls 1919 "a year of radical cultural transformation in China,"[173] and many of the students who protested as part of the May Fourth Movement would have an immense impact on China's further historical course. In the summer of 1919, the term "New Culture Movement" was coined to describe the heterogeneity of the protest movement as such, "with a matrix of reference points [. . .] used to sell a variety of the cultural reform agendas that were then competing" and used "as a buzzword [it supposedly] determined which of the agendas would be successful in the competition they were all engaged in, and in this way it shaped China's cultural path."[174] All participants, especially the intellectuals involved, projected their own agenda on the movement, which consequently was a heterogenous rally (*Sammlungsbewegung*) whose participants all channeled their own ideas through it, or, to quote Forster again, "May Fourth intellectuals were people of

---

171 Chen Duxiu, Duxiu wencun, Xianggang 1965, Vol. 1, pp. 366–368, cited in Kuhn, Republik China, pp. 212–213.

172 Li Dazhao, Xin jiyuan, in: Li Dazhao quanji, Shijiazhuang 1999, Vol. 3, p. 128, cited in: Xu Jilin, Historical Memories of May Fourth. Patriotism, but of What Kind?, in: China Heritage Quarterly 17 (2009), http://www.chinaheritagequarterly.org/features.php?searchterm=017_mayfourthmemories.inc&issue=017 (30. 9. 2019).

173 Forster, 1919, p. 1.

174 Ibid., p. 13.

flesh and blood, not abstract agents of a vision."[175] The protesters, however, did not long solely for a Western modernity, as Rana Mitter has Eurocentrically argued, but demanded their own modernity, which would, of course, have been partly influenced by Western thoughts, but was definitely not solely Western in its nature.[176] A breakup of the Chinese traditions would not have meant the abolition of China's identity as such. All in all, the movement achieved larger publicity because the actions of activists from different origins – academia, public media, and politics – joined with each other to express their criticism together.[177] Since people from different regions participated, due to being able to coordinate their actions through modernized means of transportation and print capitalism, the rise of nationalism as described by Karl W. Deutsch (1912–1992), Ernest Gellner (1925–1995), and Benedict Anderson (1936–2015) was a natural consequence, especially since it could also turn against a foreign and antagonistic Other, i.e. Japan.[178]

2.6 Conclusion

Regardless of China's political instability and its division by the imperialist claims from the Western powers and Japan, political scientist Brantly Womack is correct to highlight that "it has never scattered."[179] The bipolarity of Japan and China in East Asia, however, was very openly and aggressively emphasized by the actions of the Japanese government, whose representatives used the First World War as a good opportunity to extend its sphere of influence, or, to quote American historian Ernest R. May (1928–2009), it "liberated Japanese ambitions."[180] At the same time, it stimulated Chinese nationalism, as many intellectuals, students, workers, businessmen, women, soldiers, etc. felt humiliated by both Japan's Twenty–One Demands and the Treaty of Versailles alike. They gathered to protest against these events, but eventually formed part of a heterogeneous

---

175 Ibid., p. 15.
176 Rana Mitter, A Bitter Revolution. China's Struggle with the Modern World, Oxford 2004.
177 Forster, 1919, p. 16.
178 Anderson, Imagined Communities; Karl W. Deutsch, Nationalism and Social Communication. An Inquiry into the Foundations of Nationality, Cambridge, MA 1953; Ernest Gellner, Nations and Nationalism, Ithaca, NY 1983.
179 Brantly Womack, China between Region and World, in: The China Journal 61 (2009), pp. 1–20, here p. 6.
180 Ernest R. May, American Policy and Japan's Entrance into World War I, in: The Mississippi Valley Historical Review 40 (1953) 2, pp. 279–290, here p. 279.

protest movement, whose members demanded a better future for a united and strong Chinese nation state that would resist any further humiliation from Japan or the West.

Regardless of the potential of the May Fourth Movement to overcome Chinese fragmentation, as this was caused by the corruption of its politicians, the rise of the warlords, and the imperialist expansion of Japan, the protests lacked consistency beyond 1919 and were not able to achieve or enforce any political changes.[181] Mao Zedong's evaluation, as quoted before, highlighted two problems. China, to become a true and unified nation, needed to include the majority of its people, i.e. the agrarian population, and, as history would prove, it would have to fight Japan. The ordinary people did not have any idea about some of the abstract demands of the intellectuals – e.g. political sovereignty or the dignity of women – and therefore could neither identify themselves with the protest movement nor with China as a nation in general. The May Fourth Movement was a first national upheaval, directed against Japanese and Western imperialism, and would be an important step for the development of the Chinese communist movement. While it was unsuccessful in 1919, its impact would be tremendous. It would be the communists who would gain from the initial combination of anti–imperialism and nationalism in China, but they would eventually succeed in one aspect that the May Fourth Movement could not. It was the communists who reached out to the provinces, to the common Chinese people, the uneducated masses, and who could use the war against Japan to form a true political mass movement, whose leaders and their successors determined the fate of China and continue to do so even today. That Chinese nationalism turned from an anti–imperialist to an imperialist one is probably the fate of that of any nation state, no matter if it claims to be communist or not. Today, the bipolarity in East Asia and the struggle between China and Japan still determines the fate of the region, but the relationship is still poisoned by its past, especially the Twenty–One Demands and the loss of Shandong in 1919. Due to the centennial, tensions rose again when the humiliation of China by the Japanese was remembered, even though the Chinese eventually achieved national unity, at least on paper. The events in Hong Kong in 2019 show that there is now a new generation of students who demand change and a different future to the one proclaimed by the government in Beijing. It remains to be seen if they have the right ideas and the means to reinvigorate a national protest movement in the near future or if they will be crushed by a violent regime, as their predecessors were on Tiananmen Square in 1989.

---

181 Kuhn, Republik China, p. 226.

3 Japan and the Great War: Imperialist Ambitions Abroad, Social Change and Protest at Home

3.1 Introduction

Regardless of the recent centennial the Great War,[1] the focus of many studies published in the last four years, has remained Eurocentric as "[b]oth popular and academic accounts of the First World War often omit East Asia, and any reference to Japan,"[2] despite the war having "permanently laid to rest a Europe-centered power system."[3] The war changed East Asia tremendously and had a great impact on the national level in this region because it caused a "regional restructuring" there, namely the transition from a China-centered to a Japan-centered political and economic system.[4] For Japan the Great War was therefore naturally very important and caused change in multiple ways, although works on Japan and that period mainly focus on the political history of the country, and the centennial did not change this perspective too much.[5] On the one hand, this change is emphasized by Western scholars like the Dutch historian Dick Stegewerns, who critically discussed the war's character as a turning point in Japanese history, but for Japanese historians the landmark was and often still is the Russo–Japanese War of 1904/05, while the First World War was often, especially by Western historians, considered

---

1 This chapter is a revised and extended version of Frank Jacob, Japan and the Great War: Imperialist Ambitions Abroad, Social Change and Protest at Home, in: Marcel Bois/Frank Jacob (Eds), Zeiten des Aufruhrs (1916–1921). Globale Proteste, Streiks und Revolutionen gegen den Ersten Weltkrieg und seine Auswirkungen, Berlin 2020, 352–391.
2 Oliviero Frattolillo/Antony Best, Introduction: Japan and the Great War, in: Oliviero Frattolillo/Antony Best (Eds.), Japan and the Great War, New York 2015, pp. 1–10, here p. 1.
3 Thomas W. Burkman, Japan and the League of Nations. Empire and World Order, 1914–1938, Honolulu 2007, p. 2.
4 Tosh Minohara/Tze–ki Hon/Evan Dawley, Introduction, in: Tosh Minohara/Tze–ki Hon/Evan Dawley (Eds.), The Decade of the Great War. Japan and the Wider World in the 1910s, Leiden 2014, pp. 1–17, here p. 2.
5 Frederick R. Dickinson, War and National Reinvention. Japan and the Great War, 1914–1919, Cambridge, MA 1999; idem., World War I and the Triumph of a New Japan, 1919–1930, Cambridge, MA 2013; Tosh Minohara/Tze–ki Hon/Evan Dawley (Eds.), The Decade of the Great War. Japan and the Wider World in the 1910s, Leiden 2014. Two works by German scholars changed this and provided important new insights for the study of the topic. Jan Schmidt, Nach dem Krieg ist vor dem Krieg. Medialisierte Erfahrungen des Ersten Weltkriegs und Nachkriegsdiskurse in Japan (1914--1919), Frankfurt 2020; Jan Schmidt/Katja Schmidtpott (Eds.), The East Asian Dimension of the First World War. Global Entanglements and Japan, China and Korea, 1914–1919, Frankfurt 2020.

as a bilateral conflict between Japan and Germany[6] of second rank from a national perspective.[7] The Japanese political scientist Maruyama Masao (1914–1996), in addition, did not characterize 1919 as the climax of Taishō democracy, but rather called it the starting point for Japanese fascism.[8] In a way this characterization was correct, as Japan contradicted the new political world order of the interwar period, as it was supposed to be established in Versailles, with its colonial policies in the years leading to the full–scale expansion of the Japanese Empire during the early Shōwa period (1926–1945).

For other Japanese researchers, like the political scientist Hosoya Chihiro (1920–2011), the First World War rather marked the beginning of a new order of Japanese–American rivalry that was eventually cemented by the Washington Conference (1921/22).[9] Nevertheless, it was the European conflict between 1914 and 1918 that allowed Japan to replace China in the East Asian political order and allowed the Japanese economy to grow due to the absence of European competitors. With regard to its own status in the region of East Asia, for Japan, the war and its consequences can hardly be called less than decisive.[10] The war against Germany in Shandong, a Chinese province, was not "a brief, narrow, bilateral conflict that was limited to East Asia in the autumn of 1914," but "part of the profound global clash between two opposing alliance systems that lasted for four long years."[11] One also has to emphasize that the impact of the First World War on Japan as a nation state, and in consequence on East Asia as a region, was not limited to the political level, but, to quote the work of historians

---

6 Minohara/Hon/Dawley, Introduction, p. 1.
7 Dick Stegewerns, The End of World War One as a Turning Point in Modern Japanese History, in: Bert Edström (Ed.), Turning Points in Japanese History, London/New York 2002, pp. 138–162, here p. pp. 142–151. The number of Japanese works published on the First World War was in the years leading to and even during the centennial period rather little. Publications include: Yamanoue Shōtarō, Dai–ichiji Sekai Taisen. Wasurerareta sensō, Tokyo 2010; Yamamuro Shin'ichi et al., Gendai no kiten Dai–ichiji Sekai Taisen, 4 vols., Tokyo 2014; Kimura Seiji, Dai–ichiji Sekai Taisen, Tokyo 2014; Itaya Toshihiko, Nihonjin no tame no Dai–ichiji Sekai Taisenshi. Sekai wa naze sensō ni totsunyū shita noka, Tokyo 2017. In contrast, a three volume history of the Russo–Japanese War was published in 2016. Handō Kazutoshi, Nichiro SensōshI, 3 vols., Tokyo 2016. For a very detailed survey of the Japanese historiography related to the First World War see Schmidt, Nach dem Krieg ist vor dem Krieg, pp. 33–74. Schmidt's extremely important study also highlights that the war had actually caused important debates within Japan and therefore must not be only seen as a Western event that aroused little attention in the Japanese context. It is therefore hoped that Schmidt's book will soon be translated into English as well.
8 Cited in Stegewerns, End, p. 146.
9 Hosoya Chihiro, Ryō taisenkan no Nihon no gaikō, 1914–1945, Tokyo 1988, p. 75.
10 Minohara/Hon/Dawley, Introduction, p. 3.
11 Frattolillo/Best, Introduction, p. 1.

Oliviero Frattolillo and Antony Best again, "both Japan's experience within the war and its observations of the impact of the conflict were major catalysts for change and . . . its effects went beyond the further expansion of Japanese political and military influence in continental East Asia."[12]

Japan had not only succeeded in "display[ing] its national glory"[13] but, as a signatory power of the Treaty of Versailles, helped to create what Japanese Foreign Minister Uchida Yasuya (1865–1936) had called the "Magna Carta of a new world"[14] in Tokyo's *Asahi Shimbun* on 23 January 1920. If the Russo–Japanese War had introduced Japan to the international stage as a world power, the First World War strengthened this role and underlined Japanese demands in a more globalized world after 1918. For the Japanese nation state, as the American historian Frederick R. Dickinson correctly remarked, "the interwar years were an extraordinary era of change kindled by a singular global event."[15] In addition, in the later part of the Taishō period (1912–1926), namely the years between 1918 and 1926, a more democratic expression of the wishes of the Japanese people seemed to be possible, even against old elites like the military or navy.[16]

The present chapter will provide a survey of the impact and the consequences of the First World War in Japan. It will therefore cover the political perspectives of Japan's war participation and the economic impact of the war. Afterward, the social changes, as they were achieved due to the war, will be described in more detail. Eventually, the protests in 1918 and in the aftermath of the war shall be taken into closer consideration to show how Japan was shocked by an increase in social unrest and democratic forms of criticism against capitalism and an economic crisis created by a globalized conflict and its consequences.

3.2 Political Perspectives

The Meiji period (1868–1912) was one of transition, because the Meiji Restoration had transformed the country as a whole since 1868[17] and created a modern nation

---

12 Ibid., p. 2.
13 Frederick R. Dickinson, The First World War, Japan, and a Global Century, in: Oliviero Frattolillo and Antony Best (Eds.), Japan and the Great War, New York 2015, pp. 162–182, here p. 162.
14 Cited in ibid.
15 Dickinson, World War I and the Triumph, p. 6.
16 Harukata Takenaka, Failed Democratization in Prewar Japan. Breakdown of a Hybrid Regime, Stanford, CA 2014, p. 87.
17 On the Meiji Restoration see: Inoue Kiyoshi, Meiji ishin, Tokyo 2003; Osatake Takeki, Meiji ishin, Tokyo 1978; Tōyama Shigeki, Meiji ishin, Tokyo 2018.

state that was industrialized and whose economy was no longer based on rice cultivation.[18] The struggle of the Japanese people with Westernization and the defense against Western imperialism was consequently expressed in ideas that wanted to combine a Japanese soul with Western technology (*wakon yōsai*)[19] on the one hand, while preparing the country for self-defense with riches and a strong army (*fukoku kyōhei*) on the other.[20] The Meiji state had fought two wars to consolidate its position within East Asia and to counter Chinese and Russian ambitions in Korea. During these wars, the Imperial Japanese Army and Navy were not only able to wage a fast and successful war against the much bigger Chinese Empire but were also, as the first Asian nation state, able to defeat a European army on the battlefield. However, the Peace Treaty of Portsmouth did not secure Japanese interests in the region, especially since the United States considered the island empire in the Far East as its antagonist of the future.[21] Nevertheless, the Meiji period saw the establishment of a politically and militarily consolidated Japanese state whose policy makers were interested in the Asian mainland, especially since the costs of the war against Russia needed to be paid and Japan's economy needed access to the raw materials and resources of the continent.

When the First World War began in 1914, the Japanese policy makers and military planners alike realized that this war would be more than just a European conflict.[22] They eventually considered the war to be a chance to solve some of the problems that had been troubling the country since the Meiji Restoration, because, as Frattolillo and Best so expertly described it,

> Japan had a dual identity. On the face of it, it appeared on the world scene as an up-and-coming country, militarily and economically. Indeed, it was the only Great Power in Asia and, moreover, was allied with the only world power, Britain. Beneath the surface, though, it was troubled in a number of ways. At the broadest social level, many of the issues that it faced were a natural result of the modernization process that it had begun after 1868.[23]

---

18 David H. James, The Rise and Fall of the Japanese Empire, London/New York 2010 [1951], p. 157.

19 Hirakawa Sukehiro, Wakon yōsai no keifu. Uchi to soto kara no Meiji Nihon, Tokyo 1992; Peter Lutum, Das Denken von Minakata Kumagusu und Yanagita Kunio. Zwei Pioniere der japanischen Volkskunde im Spiegel der Leitmotive wakon–yōsai und wayō–setchū, Münster 2005.

20 Ban'no Junji, Meiji kenpō taisei no kakuritsu. Fukoku kyōhei to minryoku kyūyō, Tokyo 1992; Nakano Takeshi, Fukoku to kyōhei. Chisei keizaigaku josetsu, Tokyo 2016.

21 For a detailed discussion of the US role during the Russo–Japanese negotiations at Portsmouth and the American interest in a pro–Russian peace treatey, see Frank Jacob, The Russo–Japanese War and Its Shaping of the Twentieth Century, London 2018, pp. 90–113.

22 Dickinson, The First World War, p. 164.

23 Frattolillo/Best, Introduction, p. 2.

Representatives of the Japanese Imperial Navy in particular had realized that the war in Europe offered a chance to regain both influence on the political scene and support for a restrengthening of the naval power of Japan. In January 1914 the Siemens Scandal (*Shīmensu jiken*) had weakened the position of the navy, whose representatives were accused of corruption.[24] In addition, the national expenditure for the Japanese navy had been steadily cut since 1911 (Table 3.1).

Table 3.1: Navy Expenditure 1911–1914.[25]

Year	Expenditure in ¥
1911	100,463,000
1912	95,486,000
1913	96,446,000
1914	83,700,000

The navy's leaders had initially hoped for an expansion of its budget in early 1914, but due to the scandal these hopes were destroyed. In an attack in the Lower House Budget Committee meeting, Shimada Saburō (1852–1953) of the Dōshikai[26] accused the navy's leaders of having lost their "moral integrity" and, even worse, of having "soiled Japan's reputation abroad."[27] In the following days the pressure on the government increased, although a motion of no confidence was rejected by 205 votes to 164 in the Diet.[28] Eventually, however, Prime Minister Admiral Yamamoto Gonnohyōe (1852–1933) resigned, and he was then degraded, together with Navy Minister Saitō Makoto (1858–1936), by a naval court, which also punished leading officers in Japan's navy with fines and jail time. The months before the First World War were therefore a troublesome time for the navy, whose representatives realized that the war in Europe might help them to get back on track quickly. However, when the war began in August 1914, it was not yet clear what Japan would do. Of course, the elderly

---

24 On the scandal see: J. Charles Schencking, Making Waves. Politics, Propaganda, and the Emergence of the Imperial Japanese Navy, 1868–1922, Stanford, CA 2005, pp. 187–191. On Siemens' role in Japan Toru Takenaka, Siemens in Japan. Von der Landesöffnung bis zum Ersten Weltkrieg, Stuttgart 1996 is recommended.
25 Numbers were taken from Schencking, Making Waves, p. 186.
26 The party, originally called Rikken–Dōshikai (Association of Allies of the Constitution) founded by Prime Minister Katsura Tarō (1848–1913) in 1913 only existed until 1916.
27 Schencking, Making Waves, p. 191.
28 Ibid., p. 193.

statesmen (*genrō*) around Yamagata Aritomo (1838–1922) were responsible for the fate of the country, but they were not really interested in being drawn into a larger European conflict. Allied with Britain through the Anglo–Japanese Alliance since 1902, it was likely that they would support the Allied Powers, but the German–ruled Chinese province of Shandong also triggered the Japanese interest in the region as a reason to get involved, as it represented an opportunity to extend Japan's influence in East Asia while supporting a European war effort.[29]

Historian J. Charles Schencking clearly describes the ambivalence of the First World War, with regard to its European and East Asian perspectives, when he states that "the cataclysmic event that forever altered European history was a war, if not the war, of opportunity for Japan."[30] The military commitment to the war effort in Europe was limited to naval support for the security of British convoys, while East Asia, especially China, got quite unprotected and therefore presented a good opportunity for Japan to gain what it had not been able to during its own wars there in the Meiji period. For the navy, the war was also a game changer. To quote Schencking again: "Acting opportunistically in the opening months of the war, initially without the consent of the cabinet, the navy used the war to further its institutional, strategic, and budgetary aims, and did so with astonishing success."[31] The increase of naval necessities could be explained by the demands of its British allies as well as the growing navy of the US, which must have been considered as a competitor for the Pacific Rim in the days after the war was over. Financially, the increased spendings were made possible by the overall economic boom that will be discussed in more detail later. However, due to a surplus of almost ¥ 1.5 billion between 1915 and 1918 and ¥ 1.3 billion in 1919, the navy could demand, and was granted, more money for new ships and increased personnel costs.[32]

Japan's Foreign Minister Katō Takaaki (1860–1926), in contrast, contacted British Foreign Secretary Sir Edward Grey (1862–1933) to find out what Japan was supposed to do according to Britain's war plans.[33] The situation for the British government was, however, really ambivalent when it came to the question of Japanese support: "On the one hand, certain members of the British government, namely in the Admiralty Office, strongly desired Japanese naval assistance. On the other hand, British diplomats in China and Hong Kong believed that Japanese

---

29 A. Morgan Young, Japan under Taisho Tenno 1912–1926, London/New York 2010, p. 70.
30 Schencking, Making Waves, p. 201.
31 Ibid.
32 Ibid., p. 202.
33 Ibid., p. 203.

participation would diminish Britain's 'future political influence in China and our prestige in Asia generally' and 'would involve deplorable complications now and hereafter.'[34] Identifying the war as an opportunity to extend Japan's influence in China while supporting the British war effort in Europe, Katō, as well as Prime Minister Ōkuma Shigenobu (1838–1922), agreed to get involved. The support of the Entente and the war against Germany also provided Japan, and especially its navy, with the opportunity to acquire an empire in the Pacific, where the German colonial islands were waiting for the ambitious Japanese to take them into their possession.[35]

On 15 August 1914 the Japanese government sent an ultimatum to Germany, demanding the Germans' surrender in Shandong, the transfer of their rights in this province to Japan, and the dismantling of warships in Chinese waters. The note did not receive any reply, which is why Japan formally declared war on 23 August.[36] Due to the lack of a German war plan for the East Asian theater of war and the Japanese superiority therein, the campaign against the central power in China was a rather short one, as were the operations against German warships in the Pacific. According to the Japanese perspective, they were only at war and fighting against the German Empire due to their obligations related to the Anglo–Japanese Alliance. The former ambassador to America and lecturer at Columbia University, Iyenaga Toyokichi (1862–1936), explained this fact to a US audience in Buffalo, New York on 7 February 1915: "Japan entered the war [at] last. [. . .] I will assure you, she will not be the last to quit the bloody scene, but will leave it at the same time and in company with her ally."[37] By stating this, the former Japanese ambassador highlighted the role of the British request for Japanese participation in the global conflict, because "[t]o capture this stronghold of Germany in the Far East, and to destroy the warships that preyed upon British merchantmen, was then the duty that was imposed upon Japan when she was called by her ally to her assistance."[38] Regardless of the attempt to create an image of the Japanese decision makers that resembled the idea of a reluctant Japan when it had to enter the war,[39] the military

---

34 Ibid., p. 204.
35 Ibid., p. 206.
36 Young, Japan under Taisho Tenno, pp. 71–73.
37 Frederik R. Coudert et al., Why Europe Is At War? The Question Considered from the Points of View of France, England, Germany, Japan and the United States, New York/London 1915, p. 115.
38 Ibid., p. 121.
39 Iyenaga makes this point quite clear, when he writes: "Japan whole-heartedly went to her ally's aid in fulfilment of the obligations imposed upon her by her Anglo–Japanese Treaty. Had Japan desisted from taking such action she would have been forever branded as a cowardly, selfish nation, and none would in future have trusted or befriended her." Ibid., p. 134.

operations in China[40] soon revealed the real interest of the government in Tokyo. Iyenaga had already claimed the Japanese right for expansion in Shandong to be just in early 1915, because to him it was more than obvious that "if the Allies finally win, Japan will have proper claims to make for the blood and treasure expended for the capture of Kiao–chau [sic!] and in running the great risk of having for her foe a power so formidable as Germany. Even should Japan decide to retain Kiao–chau, it would not be a violation of China's integrity, for Kiao–chau was not a part of China; its complete sovereignty, at least for ninety–nine years, rested in Germany."[41] With regard to the European theater of war, it was declared that the Japanese soldiers were no "hirelings" and would never fight for money, as for example many Hessian soldiers had done in the past. It was rather hoped "that the Allies will be able to crush by their own hands the German militarism."[42] The ambivalence of the Japanese perception of the First World War was consequently already visible early on. On the one hand, the war, supposedly only waged for the sake of the Anglo–Japanese Alliance, would secure Japanese rights in Asia, especially since Japan had to fight a strong enemy there, i.e. Germany. On the other hand, it was natural that the Japanese nation state should be granted the German rights in the region, once the enemy's troops in Shandong had been defeated.

Consequently, the Japanese operations in Shandong focused on a fast siege of the German fortress of Kiao–chow. In contrast to the experience of Port Arthur during the Russo–Japanese War a decade before, a combined naval–land assault secured the Japanese victory quickly and without the large number of casualties caused by the siege of Port Arthur in 1904/05.[43] This time, the Japanese were much better prepared and did not face an enemy that neither had a larger amount of soldiers in the region nor was similarly willing to resist as the Russians had been a decade before. It seemed unlikely that the Japanese would face any problems in Shandong. The Bay of Kiao–chow was blocked by the Second Squadron of the Japanese Navy under the command of Vice–Admiral Katō Sadakichi (1861–1927) by late August 1914, and the landing of troops began on 2 September. Again, Japan sent troops to fight a war against a foreign power on Chinese soil, ignoring China's neutrality. The Japanese commanders, experienced and with vivid memories of the Russo–Japanese War, prepared the attack

---

40 Ibid., pp. 121–122.
41 Ibid., p. 138.
42 Ibid., pp. 138–139.
43 Joseph I. C. Clarke, Japan at First Hand. New York 1918, pp. 384–385.

on the German fortifications in Shandong with caution as well as care, and therefore landed large siege guns and naval guns.[44] The majority of casualties of the Japanese Army or Navy were rather related to accidents, like the sinking of the Takachiko, an old cruiser that hit a mine in mid–October 1914 and whose crew of 280 sailors drowned in the sea.[45] The German garrison was bombarded by Japanese shells for a week before its commander decided to surrender. 8,000 people, of whom 3,000 had been soldiers, became prisoners of war of the Japanese, whose army had lost 200 men – in addition to almost 900 wounded – in the last assault. On 7 November 1914 the German capitulation was received, and the relatively short campaign ended for the Japanese Empire with a victory and the takeover of the colonial rights in Shandong Province.[46]

Although the Japanese victory was celebrated at home, Germany was not really considered an enemy, especially since Japan's military had been trained and educated by German officers in the past, and because Russia was rather considered the natural enemy of the Japanese Empire in East Asia. In Europe, the war, however, went on, and some politicians and military leaders there hoped that Japan would also participate in the fight against Germany on European soil, but the Japanese government did not want to take such responsibilities. In addition, suspicions in London and Washington argued against the further incorporation of Japan with regard to the Allied war effort. Japan had already shown in Shandong that it was willing to take over the rights and possessions of the German Empire, and it was feared that its further involvement in the war could lead to tremendous demands related to the postwar era.[47] With regard to Japan's influence on the Asian mainland, the course of Tokyo seemed clear: "It had been determined in Japan that there had never been an opportunity like the present, and that there was never likely to be one so favourable again, for bringing China under Japanese control."[48] The First World War had created a window of opportunity for Japanese imperialism on the Asian continent, or as Frattolillo and Best described it, "the power vacuum created by the retreat of the European Powers from the region allowed Japan not only to seize Germany's Qingdao lease and resolve the Guandong issue, but also to begin to exercise a degree of influence over the Chinese government."[49] By the time the war ended, Japan had increased its influence in East Asia quite

---

44 Young, Japan under Taisho Tenno, p. 73.
45 Ibid., p. 74.
46 Ibid.
47 Ibid., pp. 75–76.
48 Ibid., p. 76.
49 Frattolillo/Best, Introduction, p. 4.

dramatically, while the Japanese Navy ruled in German Micronesia and parts of the Pacific Rim in 1919 as well.[50] The victory over the German troops in Shandong in 1914 was essential for this development, as it not only allowed them to take over the islands in the Pacific controlled by the German Empire, but also to intensify the pressure on Beijing, where Japanese politicians attempted to replicate their imperial policy in Korea before 1910. China was supposed to be transformed into a Japanese protectorate, something that was solely possible because the Western imperial powers were involved in the First World War, trying to destroy each other on the European battlefields.

A "turning point in Japanese diplomatic history"[51] was reached in 1915 when Japan issued the Twenty–One Demands, according to which the colonial transformation of China was to be completed within the coming years, with Japan as the sole and exclusive colonial power. It was solely due to American diplomatic intervention[52] and the pressure of a nationalist wave at home that the government in Beijing was able to achieve changes to the demands, especially the last group of them that was dropped in the end, as this would have really damaged China's national integrity and "brought much criticism because it attempted to violate Chinese sovereignty and clashed with existing British privileges."[53] While the Japanese government had requested to keep Group V[54] of the demands secret, the leaking of their content provided the Chinese leadership with international support and a chance to resist Japan's aggressive imperial policy. The Japanese

---

50 Dickinson, The First World War, p. 166.
51 Sōchi Naraoka, A New Look at Japan's Twenty–One Demands. Reconsidering Katō Takaaki's Motives in 1915, in: Tosh Minohara/Tze–ki Hon/Evan Dawley (Eds.), The Decade of the Great War. Japan and the Wider World in the 1910s, Leiden 2014, pp. 189–210, here p. 189.
52 The US intervention, however, was not an expression of a pro–Chinese policy, but of an imperialist anti–Japanese agenda. An article in the journal "The Revolutionary Age" from 1919 therefore criticized the US position: "The motive behind these protests about Shantung are purely imperialistic. China, before the war, was the scene of a fierce struggle, between competing Imperialisms for control; and the struggle must become more acute now. The only considerbale competitor in the Far East of American Imperialism is the Imperialism of Japan; and there is a natural protest, accordingly, against soldifying Japenese control in China." The Shantung Controversy, in: The Revolutionary Age 2, no. 4, July 26, 1919, p. 2.
53 Naraoka, A New Look, 189.
54 These demands would have turned China into a Japanese puppet state, as Naraoka's short summary confirms: "The fifth group was the most notorious and controversial. It included the following articles. China was to engage some influential Japanese people as political, financial and military advisers (article 1); Sino–Japanese control of the police was to be implemented where necessary (article 3); and China was to grant Japan the right to construct railways in the Yangtze (article 5)." Ibid., p. 191. A detailed description of all demands is provided by Young, Japan under Taisho Tenno, pp. 76–77.

image abroad was damaged by this imperialist attempt, especially since "some in the West felt that Japan, despite the I[mperial] J[apanese] N[avy] having contributed to the defence of the Indian Ocean and the Mediterranean, had done relatively little to support the Allied cause and that its outlook in international affairs was selfish and increasingly anachronistic in a world that was being redefined by Wilsonian internationalism."[55]

Regardless of such animosity against Japan's expansionist actions, the government in Tokyo continued its overall policy of attempting to use every opportunity to extend the borders of the Japanese Empire. The Russian Revolution and the international participation in the Russian Civil War against the Bolsheviks provided them with another opportunity to do exactly that. Due to the revolutions in February and October 1917, the Czarist Empire not only dropped out of the war, but it also ceased to exist and was replaced by a Bolshevik party regime under Lenin's (1870–1924) leadership, who had corrupted the revolution as a whole.[56] Due to the attempt of the Czech Legion[57] that had been fighting in the Czar's army to reach their home by crossing Asia, as they wanted to sail from Vladivostok to America and then back to Europe, an international intervention on their behalf and against the Bolsheviks was initiated by the British and French governments, who were aiming at a containment of the communist menace as well.[58] The United States and Japan were informed about the case and an intervention was requested, and both agreed to send a small force of 7,000 soldiers to Russia. The Japanese Army eventually sent 9,000 men from its Twelfth Division on Kyūshū in August 1918, and on 23 August, a combined force of British, Czech, French, and Japanese troops led by Ivan Kalmikoff, a Cossack, began the war

---

55 Frattolillo/Best, Introduction, p. 4.
56 Frank Jacob, 1917 – Die korrumpierte Revolution, Darmstadt 2020. For the impact of the Russian Revolution on anti–left sentiments and politics in Japan, see: Tatiana Linkhoeva, The Russian Revolution and the Emergence of Japanese Anticommunism, in: Revolutionary Russia 31 (2018) 2, pp. 261–278; Tatiana Linkhoeva, Revolution Goes East, Imperial Japan and Soviet Communism, Ithaca, NY 2020. For a more general discussion of the Russian Revolution and its impact on Japan, see: Hosoya Chihiro, Roshia kakumei to Nihon, Tokyo 1972.
57 On the Czech Legions see: Gerburg Thunig–Nittner, Die Tschechoslowakische Legion in Russland. Ihre Geschichte und Bedeutung bei der Entstehung der 1. Tschechoslowakischen Republik, Wiesbaden 1970 and Joan McGuire Mohr, The Czech and Slovak Legion in Siberia from 1917 to 1922, Jefferson, NC 2012.
58 Sumiko Otsubo, Fighting on Two Fronts. Japan's Involvement in the Siberian Intervention and the Spanish Influenza Pandemic of 1918, in: Tosh Minohara/Tze–ki Hon/Evan Dawley (Eds.), The Decade of the Great War. Japan and the Wider World in the 1910s, Leiden 2014, pp. 461–480, here p. 468.

against the Bolshevik Red Army at Kraevski.[59] Additional troops were sent from Japan and Manchuria to the Siberian Transbaikal province, where a strong contingent of the Red Army, supposedly 30,000 men, was waiting for the foreign invaders. An advance of the latter to the city of Chita in September was successful and Japan could strengthen its control over the Chinese Eastern and Amur railway lines in the province, although smaller struggles with Russian partisans continued there in the following weeks. By November 1918 Japan had sent more than 70,000 soldiers to Eastern Siberia, and the three provinces in that region were under the firm control of the international troops that stayed there uncontested during the winter.[60]

Regardless of its rather promising start, the Siberian Intervention became rather a disaster for Japan. On the one hand, the Spanish flu was imported to Japan as a consequence of the intervention, because Japanese soldiers got infected with it due to their operations in Siberia,[61] and on the other, the Bolshevik victory in the Russian Civil War could not ultimately be prevented by the international intervention and the troops sent from Britain and its empire, France, Italy, China, and Japan. The military operations were costly and, with regard to the gains, rather a waste of Japanese financial and military capacities, but the government in Tokyo had hoped to achieve its expansionist vision in Siberia, which had been expressed since the early Meiji period.[62] What turned out to be nothing more than a costly "adventure" in Siberia, however, was also an essential part of the overall wartime strategy of Foreign Minister Uchida Yasuya, who intended to strengthen

---

59 Ibid., pp. 468–469.

60 Ibid., pp. 469–470. For a more detailed analysis of Japan's Siberian Intervention see: Izao Tomio, Shoki shiberia shuppei no kenkyū. Atarashiki kyūseigun kōsō no tōjō to tenkai, Fukuoka 2003; Hosoya Chihiro, Shiberia shuppei no shiteki kenkyū, Tokyo 2005; Paul E. Dunscomb, Japan's Siberian Intervention, 1918–1922, Lanham, MD 2011.

61 Hayami Akira, Nihon o osotta supein infuruenza. Jinrui to uirusu no dai ichiji sekai sensō, Tokyo 2006, pp. 284–293. According to Iijima Wataru, the Spanish flu had hit China between 1918 and 1920, from where the disease supposedly reached China. Wataru Iijima, Spanish Influenza in China, 1918–20. A Preliminary Probe, in: Howard Phillips/David Killingray (Eds.), The Spanish Influenza Pandemic of 1918–19. New Perspectives, London 2003, pp. 101–109, here p. 109, cited in Otsubo, Fighting on Two Fronts, p. 466. On Epidemics in Modern Asia, including the Spanish flu, also see Robert Peckham, Epidemics in Modern Asia, Cambridge 2016.

62 Especially right wing secret societies, like the Gen'yōsha or the Kokuryūkai had demanded a Japanese expansion until the Amur River, which was considered the natural border of a Japanese interest zone on the continent. For a detailed analysis of these societies, their positions, and impact, see: Frank Jacob, Japanism, Pan-asianism and Terrorism. A Short History of the Amur Society (the Black Dragons) 1901–1945, Bethesda, CA 2014.

Japanese interests in Northern Manchuria and China alike. The Twenty–One Demands and the dispatch of Japan's troops to Siberia were meant to achieve these
goals and therefore present Tokyo's overall strategy during the war, namely to use
it to further extend and strengthen the Japanese Empire on the Asian continent,
where Korea (since 1910) and the railway rights in Southern Manchuria only provided the necessary bridgeheads for the further expansion of Japan's imperialist
ambitions.[63]

The eventual end of the Siberian Intervention was the result of a strong parliament, whose members, with the support of Army Minister, and later Prime
Minister (1926–1929), Tanaka Giichi (1864–1929), were able to avoid the interference of the Japanese Imperial Army. The General Staff was only informed once
the Emperor had already approved parliament's decision.[64] This act further emphasized the rather powerful position of the elected leaders of Japan, in contrast
to the previous Meiji period and the later Shōwa years, when the military would
decide the political course of the country. Regardless of the fact that Japan had
failed to reach its ultimate aims in China and Siberia, the war had left its impact
on the island country, and for many people a new age seemed to have begun in
1918/19.

When news of the armistice between the Entente and the Central Powers
reached Japan, a national school holiday was declared and more than 60,000
businessmen and shopowners gathered for a lantern parade.[65] In 1922, they
also sponsored the Tokyo Peace Exposition in Ueno Park and the Japanese
League of Nations Association kept the commemoration of the armistice alive
through the 1920s. In Japan, many people believed in the proclaimed new age
of internationalism, reflected in Wilson's idea for the League of Nations. That
these dreams at the end of the conflict in Europe went beyond the later realities
was already expressed during the negotiations of the peace treaty in Versailles,
where Japan was present as a victor nation as well.[66] In November 1918, Foreign Minister Uchida had drafted a memorandum, outlining something like a
general agenda for Japan's delegates who were supposed to participate in the
peace treaty negotiations.[67] The Foreign Minister of Japan was well aware that

---

63 Rustin B. Gates, Out with the New and in with the Old. Uchida Yasuya and the Great War
as a Turning Point in Japanese Foreign Affairs, in: Tosh Minohara/Tze–ki Hon/Evan Dawley
(Eds.), The Decade of the Great War. Japan and the Wider World in the 1910s, Leiden 2014,
pp. 64–82, here p. 65.
64 Takenaka, Failed Democratization, p. 88.
65 Dickinson, The First World War, p. 174.
66 Ibid., p. 166.
67 Kobayashi Tatsuo (Hrsg.), Suiusō Nikki, Tokyo 1965, pp. 285–286.

the League of Nations was rather an idealistic project, determined by racism and jingoism from the beginning, and therefore unable to solve the main questions related to the postwar era, in which the main imperialist powers would try to regain as much control, and even intensify their influence, in the colonial world to become as powerful as they had been before the war. Uchida's overall strategy suggested being a complying voice in the choir of the great powers and not creating any form of antagonism. While the League of Nations might not have been attractive for Japan, the latter could not afford to stay outside.[68] The Foreign Minister knew that the Japanese attempts to expand its control and influence on the Asian continent needed to be accepted in Versailles, or as the American historian Rustin B. Gates explained it, "[w]ith the end of World War I, Uchida had to go along with the trends of the times to pursue his past policy of cooperation. This policy would be tested in Paris over the question of Japanese control of Shandong."[69] While the years between 1912 and 1926 were often referred to as a more democratic period in Japan, where internationalist ideas, represented by the League of Nations, were stronger than nationalist ones, this is contradicted by the continuity of Japanese imperialism, here expressed in Uchida's considerations about the expansion of the empire in China and Manchuria. Japan's interest in its neighboring regions was not related to Wilsonian ideals, but "a consistent line in Japanese policies towards Asia" becomes very obvious and "has little to do with a new spirit of democratic international cooperation."[70]

The main interest of the Japanese delegation in Paris was consequently not to establish a new peaceful international order, but to secure gains from the war, especially the German rights in Shandong, which naturally had to lead to a conflict with China.[71] Manchuria and Mongolia were also considered rather exclusive zones of interest for Japan, which is why they were not supposed to be discussed as part of the Chinese question.[72] The talks in Paris were consequently quite ambivalent: "[W]orld leaders forged the institutional framework for a new system that they believed would relieve humanity of the threat of

---

68 Gates, Out with the New, p. 72.

69 Ibid.

70 Kurt W. Radtke, Nationalism and Internationalism in Japan's Economic Liberalism. The Case of Ishibashi Tanzan, in: Dick Stegewerns (Ed.), Nationalism and Internationalism in Imperial Japan. Autonomy, Asian Brotherhood, or World Citizenship? London/New York 2003, pp. 169–195, here p. 180.

71 See the chapter by Jacob on China in the present volume for a more detailed discussion of this conflict at the Versailles Peace Conference.

72 Radtke, Nationalism, p. 182.

war. For Japan the rapid changes in international affairs produced uncertainty concerning future relationships with its Asian neighbors and the victorious powers."[73] While Wilson had hoped to recreate an international political system, the Japanese in particular had gained from disrupted relations during the war years, as the East Asian region could now be politically and economically dominated by the Japanese. Their interest in the latter field increased due to the transformation of its production, as their main export goods were no longer just textiles but goods from its heavy industry as well. Ships were exported from Japan during the war, and the industrial sector in particular could rely on unforeseen profits. With the financial surplus, the Japanese government could also use loans to China and Russia to gain more influence in the regions of her imperial ambitions.[74] However, the boom and subsequent recession after the war also politically challenged the existent order in Japan, when rice riots and strikes steadily shook the order and endangered the country's internal stability. Although the government in Tokyo could see itself in the camp of the victorious powers, it still was able to lose a lot in 1919. In Paris, the delegation therefore had to secure a success for Japan. Uchida had consequently prepared the Japanese diplomats to remember the following four points: "First, Japan approved the Wilsonian program in theory. Second, details of the program would create circumstances disadvantageous to Japan. Third, Japan should attempt to delay the program's actual implementation. Fourth, if its realization appeared inevitable, Japan should not press reservations to the point of nonparticipation or diplomatic isolation."[75] The Japanese prepared for the peace talks with a lot of care, as they feared a repetition of the diplomatic loss they had experienced during the negotiations leading to the Peace Treaty of Portsmouth in 1905. The ambassadors to London and Paris, Chinda Sutemi (1857–1929) and Matsui Keishirō (1868–1946), were chosen to represent Japan at the Versailles Peace Treaty Conference, but the former had informed the government in Tokyo that he might not be suitable for this task, as the other states were sending plenipotentiaries that were heads of state at the time.[76] Since Prime Minister Hara Takashi (1856–1921) was not willing to leave Japan and was also not willing to send his foreign minister, whose support he needed at home, the cabinet eventually appointed Marquis Saionji Kinmochi (1849–1940) to lead the Japanese delegation, because "[h]is qualifications included Imperial lineage, past service as premier and foreign minister, and stints as Japanese minister in Austria, Belgium, and Germany. During a decade–long stay in

---

73 Burkman, Japan and the League of Nations, p. 2.

74 Ibid., pp. 2–3.

75 Ibid., p. 45.

76 Ibid., p. 57.

Paris as a student, he had acquired fluency in the French language and the friend-
ship of Georges Clemenceau.[77] Moreover, the sixty–nine–year–old Saionji was a
recognized senior statesman of quasi–*genrō* status."[78] Regardless of Saionji's official leadership, Makino Nobuaki (1861–1949) "acted as the real strategist and
major spokesman for the delegation" and made sure that Japan's interests were
taken into full consideration by the other powers.[79]

On 21 April 1919 the delegation received a message from Foreign Minister
Uchida requesting them to deny Japan's participation in the League of Nations if
the other powers did not accept the takeover of German rights in Shandong Province by the Japanese government. It was therefore clear that Uchida wanted to
use the idealist plan for the internationalist postwar order as leverage to gain the
Germans' colonial rights in China for Japan.[80] In the end, US President Woodrow
Wilson sacrificed the Chinese territorial integrity for his vision of an international
order based on free trade and peaceful understanding. Japan ripped away Chinese rights and claimed to be a guarantor of this new order when it became a
founding member of the League of Nations.[81] Japan was unable, however, to secure racial equality as a foundation of the new order, which meant full acceptance by the Western powers. The negotiations in Paris were another blow for
Japan's ambition to be accepted as a full member of the imperial club, and its
policy would change in the years to come when Tokyo would eventually argue in
favor of freeing Asia from white supremacy while replacing it with Japanese hegemony. Due to the political impact of the First World War, what Frattolillo and
Best called "a search for a new cultural identity among intellectuals and radical
activists"[82] began as well. Eventually, the discourse of the Meiji period, when
leading figures argued in favor of leaving Asia,[83] was replaced by demands for a
return to Asia, especially since it was obvious that the West had never accepted

---

77 Georges Clemenceau (1841–1929) was French Prime Minister during the peace conference
in Versailles.
78 Burkman, Japan and the League of Nations, p. 58.
79 Wada Hanako, Dai–ichiji Sekai Taisengo ni okeru Nihon gaikō zaigai kōkan, in: Journal of
the Graduate School of Humanities and Sciences, Ochanomizu University 8 (2005) 6, pp. 1–13.
80 Haruno Saru/Shen Chun Ye, Pari kōwa kaigi to Nichi–Bei–Chū kankei. „Santō mondai" o
chūshin ni, in: Hokusai kōkyū seisaku kenkyū 9 (2005) 2, pp. 189–206; Qian Yang, Pari kōwa
kaigi to taika ni jū ichi–kajō. Santō mondai o chūshin ni, in: Hokudai shigaku 58 (2018),
pp. 80–95.
81 Gates, Out with the New, p. 74.
82 Frattolillo/Best, Introduction, p. 6.
83 For a detailed discussion of Fukuzawa Yukichi's (1835–1901) „Datsu–A–ron" see: Fukuzawa
Naomi, Fukuzawa Yukichis Datsu–a–ron (1885). Wegbereiter des japanischen Imperialismus
oder zornige Enttauschung eines asiatischen Aufklarers?, in: Tātonnemen 13 (2011), pp. 210–224.

Japan as an equal. Regardless of its anti–Western resentment, Japan had profited from the war, but was forced to face a dangerous recession after the war
ended, which is why her interest in the Asian markets must have been even
stronger then than before the First World War. However, the war's economic impact was quite intense, and not only demanded a new foreign policy once the
European battles had ended. It is therefore necessary to take a closer look at the
socio–economic watershed,[84] as it was caused by the war that marked the beginning of the "age of extremes," and that, of course, not only in Europe but in
Asia as well.

3.3 The Economic Impact of the War

That the First World War caused tremendous changes in Japan is not a surprise,
especially when one considers the huge economic impact the conflict had on the
country's trade balance and industrial production.[85] In 1914 Japan was still paying interest, namely ¥80 million per annum, on the loans it had been granted a
decade before when it defeated Russia with American and British credit.[86] While
under economic pressure, the government, as mentioned before, also received
steady demands from the army and navy, whose representatives wanted to increase their share of the budget, making sure to strengthen Japan's military position on the Asian continent and the Pacific alike. This "budget rivalry in a time of
financial distress"[87] was a heavy burden for the Japanese state before the First
World War began. Although the Japanese Navy had suffered from budget cuts
and the Siemens Scandal, as described before, the rivalry with the army did not
cease to exist and would continue, even after the war. When the First World War
began, there was consequently not only a "grievous depression"[88] but also an
internal political instability that had the potential to cause more than just a small
problem.

---

84 Frank Jacob, Der Erste Weltkrieg als ökonomisch–soziale Zäsur der japanischen Moderne,
in: Stephan Köhn/Chantal Weber/Volker Elis (Eds.), Tokyo in den zwanziger Jahren Experimentierfeld einer anderen Moderne? Wiesbaden 2017, pp. 17–32.
85 Tamura Kosaku, who worked in the Ministry of Foreign Affairs and later became a professor at Tokyo's Chūō University had written an early analysis of the impact of the war on foreign trade. Tamura Kosaku, Dai–ichiji Sekai Taisen to Nihon gaikō, in: Diplomatic Archives of
the Ministry of Foreign Affairs, B10070135800.
86 Frattolillo/Best, Introduction, p. 3.
87 Ibid.
88 Young, Japan under Taisho Tenno, p. 90.

In some way, one could argue that the First World War presented some kind of salvation, because "[f]or some years the tendency of imports to exceed exports had been a source of anxiety to Japanese economists, and it was noted with satisfaction that in the first half of 1915 exports exceeded imports, though the satisfaction was somewhat damped by the fact that the change was even more due to the decline in imports than to the increase in exports."[89] Initially, the prices of the main Japanese trade goods, namely rice and silk, fell tremendously, and Prime Minister Ōkuma therefore established companies that acted on behalf of the government and bought rice and silk to stabilize the economy. This was a dangerous move, but once the Japanese stock market boomed after one year of the war, his strategy paid off, as it held Japan in order until the advantages of increasing trade volume due to the European conflict kicked in. Due to the events since 1914, their Western competitors had left the Asian markets to Japanese trade, which is why a boom was the natural consequence of the now hegemonic and monopolistic position of the single supplier for the goods needed in the region. Due to the immense surplus created by the war, Japan went through a speedy second phase of industrialization and urbanization, and income tax eventually the main direct taxation. For the Allied powers, Japan became the main source to buy arms from, but also textiles, war supplies, and other industrial goods were ordered in Tokyo and other larger Japanese cities, which is why the value of exports soon outnumbered that of imports and Japan eventually became a creditor, handing out loans to Britain, France, and Russia so that these allied nation states were able to buy goods from Japanese companies.

During the war years, Japan, when it comes to war–related sales, had a very fortunate trade relation with Russia, having "sent over a million rifles, with ammunition for small arms and artillery and kept the Osaka factories working night and day in supplying these, besides boots, hats, blankets, clothing and various supplies for the Russian army."[90] Since the Allies, like Britain, also forced their own economies to respond to the war necessities, they no longer produced for the colonial markets in Asia but for the battlefields in Europe. It was Japan that could exploit this situation as it began, step by step, to take over these markets as the main supplier for textile goods, and due to the lack of competition the prices rose. Japan's exports in the textile sector, in the meantime, increased by over 60%, and this development was greeted with joy, especially by politicians like Finance Minister Taketomi Tokitoshi (1856–1938).[91] While

---

89 Ibid.
90 The North American Review, 1918, p. 727.
91 Young, Japan under Taisho Tenno, p. 91.

demands for stronger Japanese involvement in the European war effort could be ignored, the country gained from the absence of its rivals, who tried to destroy themselves in the years of bloodshed. The short struggle against the Germans in Shandong was sufficient involvement for the Japanese government, whose representatives now, albeit while struggling for more influence in China, rather tended to enjoy the economic surplus created by the far–away conflict.

The prices charged for the Japanese goods were "extortionate,"[92] and by 1916 the First World War was widely "regarded [. . .] as a heaven–sent opportunity to make money"[93] while the war, i.e. the battles and the casualties, at least from a Japanese perspective, was already over. Japan's position with regard to the First World War was consequently an ambivalent one. On the one hand, it had actively participated in defeating Germany, even if it only did so in the Asian and Pacific context; on the other hand, it profited like a neutral nation state from the lack of competitors for Asian trade during the war and could sell goods to the Allied powers, whose demands were constantly high, because the conflict in Europe was a total one, demanding all economic capacity to be thrown at the enemy in this global battle of material. Within this global context, Ōkuma could observe the rise of a new Japan:

> The old Marquis was at the helm at the important crisis of the outbreak of war; he had embarked on a policy of successful aggression in China which most of his countrymen frankly admired. He had made daring deals in rice and silk, and had proved them to be good business. Above all, he saw the country pass from a state of commercial depression to one of unprecedented prosperity. New industries were started on all sides, often with bountiful subsidies, a special and lasting effort being made in the manufacture of electrical apparatus. Ships were in such demand and the supply of shipbuilding materials was so scarce that the firm of Suzuki, ordering a new steamer in September 1916, had to pay the unprecedented price of 385 yen (then about £40) a ton. The scenes on the stock exchanges were described as fit only for a madhouse.[94]

Having been dependant on foreign loans in the past, Japan had eventually become a creditor to many other great powers, something that definitely created a feeling of pride for the Asian island nation. And Japan's prosperity in these few years seemed to be unmatched: "The war had not progressed very far when Japan found herself in the position of a monopolist supplier of a multitude of goods. In the Indian and Chinese markets she had hardly a competitor. The Dutch Indies and Australia depended increasingly on her factories for a number of their commodities; and before the war was ended South Africa and South

---

92 Ibid., p. 92.
93 Ibid., p. 93.
94 Ibid., p. 95.

America were offering almost any price for her manufactures."[95] At the same time, however, Japan also had trouble with getting possession of the goods necessary to keep up its production rate, which is why, to name just one example, "new import–substitution industries, in areas such as chemicals and optics, to make up for the loss of trade with Germany"[96] had to be built up from scratch. Nikon was one of these companies, initially providing war–related materials to the Japanese Navy. While Japan had enormous financial reserves in 1918 – up to ¥1.6 billion – the following tables (Tables 3.2 and 3.3) show that this was only possible due to the rise in exports since 1914.

Table 3.2: Japan's Foreign Trade 1910–1924.[97]

Years	Imports in millions of ¥	Exports in millions of ¥
1910–1914	662.3	593.1
1915–1919	14.137	15.999
1920–1924	24.257	18.104

In particular, the war years 1915, 1916, and 1917 showed an extreme increase with regard to the excess of exports (Table 3.3), as a US report from 1919 indicates.[98]

Table 3.3: Japan's Foreign Trade 1914–1917.[99]

Year	Imports in thousands of ¥	Exports in thousands of ¥	Excess of Exports in thousands of ¥
1914	595,736	591,101	−4,635
1915	532,450	708,307	175,857
1916	756,428	1,127,468	371,040
1917	1,035,811	1,603,005	567,194

With regard to Japan's share of world trade during the First World War, her position seemed almost totally uncontested, especially since she was the Allied Powers' favorite trade partner during the first years of the conflict.

---

95 Ibid., p. 110.
96 Frattolillo/Best, Introduction, p. 5.
97 Xu, Asia and the Great War, p. 50.
98 United States Tariff Commission, Japan. Trade During the War, Washington (Government Printing Office) 1919.
99 Ibid., p. 8.

An increase in factories could be observed due to the economic surplus, with the number of those with more than five workers rising from 31,000 in 1914 to 43,000 in 1919.[100] The economy as a whole grew extremely fast until the early 1920s, and Japan's exports became dominated by manufactured goods, which needed to be produced by an increasing urban labor force. The cities were consequently growing, e.g. Tokyo, where the population tripled to around 1 million in 1920. Osaka, the "industrial capital of Japan," had even reached 2 million inhabitants by 1925.[101] This urbanization, in combination with increasing prosperity, created a new urban middle class in Japan, which was no longer only male: 10% of Tokyo's workforce during the war years were women, and therefore a female consumer culture developed as well. There were consequently not only geopolitical changes due to the Japanese wealth created by the war, but also social changes within the country that would have a tremendous impact. Due to the economic boom, as Andrea Revelant highlighted, "the state's dependence on agriculture had dramatically decreased"[102] and changed existent structures as well as the relationship between urban centers and countryside peripheries as well. At the same time, inflation became a problem in the early 1920s, further weakening the economic position of small farmers and other producers in the agricultural sector. When one considers the impact of the First World War on Japan and the long-term reasons for the protests in its aftermath, one has to take the social transformation of Japanese daily life into further consideration.

3.4 The War and Social Change in Japan

The above-mentioned urbanization in the war years led to a migration of people from the countryside to find employment in the new factories, where the wages had increased due to the increase in prices and a more expensive life. The cities, however, not only promised well-paid work, but also the chance to participate in a modern lifestyle.[103] This chance was nevertheless very often an illusion, and what awaited the migrants in reality was totally different. Miki Kiyoshi (1897–1945), a Japanese philosopher who described his arrival in Tokyo

---

100 Xu, Asia and the Great War, p. 50.
101 Ibid., p. 51.
102 Revelant, Rethinking Japanese Taxation, p. 120.
103 Susan C. Townsend, The Great War and Urban Crisis. Conceptualizing the Industrial Metropolis in Japan and Britain in the 1910s, in: Tosh Minohara/Tze-ki Hon/Evan Dawley (Eds.), The Decade of the Great War. Japan and the Wider World in the 1910s, Leiden 2014, pp. 301–322, here 301.

in 1917, for example, was shocked when he realized his loneliness in the urban environment.[104] The urban poverty also influenced the Marxist Kawakami Hajime (1879–1946), whose "Bimbō monogatari" ("Tale of Poverty", 1916)[105] provides an insight into the rather dark side of the war for those living in the larger cities of Japan at that time. Due to the rising poverty rate and low wages compared to company profits and inflation, socialist ideas were also able to gain ground during the First World War. With the existence of more and more urban centers – there were only 39 in 1889, but this number had more than doubled to 83 by 1920[106] – a larger number of people started to wish for opportunities for consumption, e.g. journals, movies, food, cosmetics, etc. On the other hand, the city space needed to be shared with more and more people, which is why the density of Japanese cities during the First World War was much higher than in other countries. In Tokyo, to name just one example, more than 25,000 people shared a square kilometer.[107] The rapid influx of new labor created a surplus of inhabitants, and while Osaka became known as the "Manchester of the Orient," the city life of the lower classes was characterized by long working hours and general poverty. Osaka was no longer only known for its textile industry, but also for its slums.[108] Even before the war, the city had appeared crowded to Western visitors: "This flourishing industrial city, with its 5000 factories, its teeming population in crowded, narrow streets, its forest of smoking chimneys, its numerous great stone buildings in 'foreign' style, and, unfortunately, its paupers and its slums, represents the 'new industrialism' of Japan in its most extreme form."[109] Already facing the consequences of fast industrialization and urbanization, the problems in the urban space, as the British historian Susan C. Townsend correctly highlighted, were tremendously worsened due to the economic boom in the war years between 1914 and 1918:

> [N]early a thousand new factories opened. Floods of immigrant workers or 'new arrivals' (*gairaisha*) poured into the heavily polluted slum areas around the factories on [the] city's

---

104 For Miki's experiences in Tokyo see: Miki Kiyoshi, Miki Kiyoshi zenshū, Tokyo 1984, vol. 1, pp. 366–400. On the philosopher's life and work see: Susan C. Townsend, Miki Kiyoshi 1897–1945. Japan's Itinerant Philosopher, Leiden 2009.
105 Kawakami Hajime, Bimbō monogatari, Tokyo 1983. A German translation can be found in: Reiner Schrader, Die Erzählung von der Armut, in: Oriens Extremus 30 (1983–1986), pp. 154–245.
106 Townsend, The Great War and Urban Crisis, p. 308.
107 Ibid.
108 Ibid., p. 311.
109 Sidney and Beatrice Webb, The Webbs in Asia. The 1911–12 Travel Diary, edited by George Feaver, Basingstoke 1992, p. 70. cited in ibid.

fringes 'where living conditions were so poor that they posed a threat to public morals.' The worst areas were those adjacent to factories erected close to the harbor and along the rivers, especially the incorporated districts of Nishinari–gun and Higashinari–gun. Nishinari–gun reported a 47 per cent increase from 170,000 to 250,000 during the First World War and Higashinari–gun a 43 per cent increase from 140,000 to 200,000 turning these areas [. . .] from residential purgatory into something like Hell.[110]

The urban labor force, impoverished and exploited, eventually presented a high potential of social unrest, as was explicitly expressed in the Rice Riots of 1918, when the wartime boom and rice speculations on the one hand met with popular discontent and sorrow on the other.

The end of the war did not lead to a recession immediately, as it took a while until the European factories and producers began to reach their former capacities. Accordingly, "the change came with a little breathing–space,"[111] and the boom went on. The Japanese leadership and many businessmen seem to have ignored that the end of the war would bring back the former competition for the Asian markets and that prices would drop due to this as well. Due to this fact the recession hit Japan even harder, but for the time being, her people could still enjoy the economic surplus and the advantages it had created. There was also much enthusiasm shared by the government in its time about their own place in the country's history: "Japan after the Great War resembled the heady days of early Meiji, when the entire country rallied to conform to the new standards of modern civilization as originally introduced by Commodore Matthew Perry. In fact, Japanese statesmen after 1918 referred explicitly to the latter nineteenth–century transformation in their proclamation of a new future."[112] With the same enthusiasm, those who got rich during the war began to display their new wealth, and "the ostentation and extravagance of the newly rich attracted attention and condemnation"[113] at the same time. It was a spectacular time period, due to which those who had made a fortune due to their export business or shipbuilding – the latter of whom were called *fune narikin* – were very often wasting money, which is why they were very often caricatured for their almost shameless relationship with money.[114] With "extra money and

---

110 Ibid., p. 313. Townsend here refers to Jeffrey E. Hanes, The City as Subject: Seki Hajime and the Reinvention of Modern Osaka, Berkeley/Los Angeles, CA 2002, pp. 197–200.

111 Young, Japan under Taisho Tenno, p. 145.

112 Dickinson, The First World War, p. 169.

113 Young, Japan under Taisho Tenno, p. 112.

114 For an example see: Iizawa Ten'yō, Envelope for the series "The Nouveau Riche at New Year" (Narikin no shinnen), Part 1, Leonard A. Lauder Collection, Museum of Fine Arts, Boston.

time to spend on recreation"[115] that now could no longer only be afforded by the rich, but also by a growing middle class, more possibilities that offered exactly this were created.

Some people spent their money on a European wing of their house, built in stucco, where they tended to entertain their Europhile Japanese friends. However, the luxury on the one hand could hardly cover the hardships on the other, and Japanese society was divided. While many gained financially from the war and the export business, many lived in poverty, exploited by global capitalism and the trade monopoly existent for their own country. One consequently has to be careful when evaluating the developments in Japan during the war period. Of course, a lot of people gained from the economic rise of the island nation, but many were further impoverished while they had to witness the reckless spending of many of the *nouveaux riches* as well. Regardless of this conflict, which will be described later in more detail together with its impact, i.e. protest movements in Japan in the aftermath of the First World War, the influx of money into the country also resulted in better infrastructure and therefore established a relatively high national connectedness of the people, no matter if they lived in the cities or in the countryside. In the four years between 1918 and 1922 the railway network in Japan was extended by more than 30% and the number of kilometers traveled by passengers tripled.[116] In 1914 ca. 165 million passengers and 35 million tons of freight were transported by train, increasing to 245 million and 49 million respectively in 1917, before reaching 405 million passengers and 57 million tons of freight three years later.[117] At the same time, wages actually decreased – ¥ 30.9 in 1914, ¥ 33.7 in 1915, ¥ 31.2 in 1916, ¥ 27.6 in 1917, ¥ 22.9 in 1918, and ¥ 20.0 in 1919 – due to inflation and higher living costs.[118] In 1920 the railway authorities reacted and raised the real wage to ¥ 36.3.[119] Due to the economic developments during the war years, the medical service provided by the employers for the railway employees also changed, and better opportunities were created for railway workers and eventually their families. The demand for and expansion of the railway network, like in many other economic branches as well, increased the demand for experienced

115 Gennifer Weisenfeld, MAVO. Japanese Artists and the Avant–Garde, 1905–1931, Berkeley/ Los Angeles, CA 2002, p. 167.
116 Dickinson, The First World War, p. 171.
117 Chaisung Lim, Railroad Workers and World War I. Labor Hygiene and the Policies of Japanese National Railways, in: Tosh Minohara/Tze–ki Hon/Evan Dawley (Eds.), The Decade of the Great War. Japan and the Wider World in the 1910s, Leiden 2014, pp. 415–438, here p. 423.
118 Ibid.
119 Ibid., p. 433.

employees, who were consequently able to gain not only better wages but also better benefits from the enterprise they worked for.[120]

The railway had become the symbol of advancement, not only technological, but also social, as more and more people were able to travel, extend their individual horizon, and therefore reach modernity with regard to time and space.[121] Between 1912 and 1925 almost 1,300 power plants were built, since the increase in produced manufactured goods also demanded more electricity in the factories. This also led to increased private use of electricity, or better, its availability in private homes. The increase in productivity also affected Japanese factories abroad. To name just one example, the number of cotton spindles in China, which were owned by companies from Japan, increased from ca. 50,000 in 1910 to more than 800,000 in 1920.[122] These "explosions" in almost all economic sectors did not remain unnoticed, and on 1 January 1917 the *Asahi Shimbun* in Osaka announced that "during the span of the past two years Japan has secured a place in the sun, and she has become one of the happiest countries in the world [. . .]. Her national wealth has increased by leaps and bounds, and the volume of her foreign trade has witnessed an unprecedentedly [sic!] tremendous increase."[123] Social changes could nevertheless not only be observed in the cities, where the new financial capacities created a new consumer culture.

In general, the productive structures in the agricultural sector did not change a lot, although many people left for the cities to make more money and to secure a supposedly better life. However, the relationship between landowners and tenants changed a lot. American sociologist Theda Skocpol emphasized that especially peasants have some kind of generic potential for unrest that is related to change,[124] but the rapidness of the events overwhelmed even the Japanese peasantry. Due to their gains, many rich landowners moved to the cities, namely Tokyo or Osaka, to participate in the new and luxurious urban life and culture, as it was represented by the new department stores.[125] Custodians took over the

---

120 Ibid., p. 438.
121 On this issue: Woflgang Schivelbusch, Geschichte der Eisenbahnreise. Zur Industrialisierung von Raum und Zeit im 19. Jahrhundert, Seventh Edition, Frankfurt am Main 2000. The development of railways in Japan is well documented: Nihon Kokuyū Tetsudō – Sōsaishitsu – Shūshika, Nihon kokuyū tetsudō hyakunenshi, 17 vols., Tokyo 1969–1974.
122 Dickinson, The First World War, p. 171.
123 Ōsaka asahi shinbun, 1 January 1917, cited in ibid.
124 Theda Skocpol, States and Social Revolutions, Cambridge 1979, p. 115.
125 Fujioka Rika. The Development of Japanese Department Stores in the Early 20th Century. The Process of Western Adaptation, http://www.gla.ac.uk/media/media_167604_en.pdf (3. 7. 2016). Also see: Hatsuda Tōru, Hyakkaten no tanjō, Tokyo 1993; Jinno Yuki, Hyakkaten ga tsukutta teisuto, Tokyo, 1994.

administration of their properties in the countryside, and the relations between owners and tenants loosened. The custodians had no close relationship to the tenants due to which the relationship was often soured, especially when money could not be paid on time. The last remains of the feudal order in Japan consequently disappeared, and capitalism on its full scale finally reached the Japanese countryside. A relationship that had been based on reciprocal gains transformed into a harsh dependency, only evaluated according to capitalist demands. This transformation also stimulated the decision of smaller farmers to leave the countryside, as they hoped for a better future in the city. On the other hand, more and more tenants began to organize themselves to argue for lower rent, especially since the costs for necessary supplies had increased during the war years as well.[126] Tenant conflicts (*kosaku sōgi*) were the consequence, and their number increased by the end of the war. Tenant unions eventually took over the representation of the peasants who had rented their land from rich landowners, and the conflict was brought out into the open more and more. It showed that not all parts of Japanese society had gained from the First World War and that the new splendor of city life was paid for by the work and debts of those who were exploited in the countryside. While life in the city became more and more luxurious and speculations with rice at the stockmarket produced enormous profits, the agrarian population was not allowed to participate in this development and, at the same time, lost human capital when people decided to give up their poor life in the countryside to move to the cities in the hope of gaining a glimpse of the richness that was promised to them.

Peasants were not the only ones who started to organize themselves; they were also joined by industrial workers, teachers, female office workers, and others. They all demanded higher wages, as life in the city had got more expensive since 1914. More and more unions began to be established, as the workforce had realized that a potential strike movement needed a large number of people to get involved to really threaten company owners and to have the possibility of gaining something through a strike declaration.[127] As part of the Union of Wage and Salary Earners in Tokyo (Tōkyō hōkyū seikatsusha dōmei kyōgikai), the first all–female union of office workers was established in 1920. Its members demanded the equal and gender–neutral payment of wages.[128] However, this was not the first female

---

126 Andrew Gordon, A Modern History of Japan. From Tokugawa Times to the Present, New York 2003, pp. 146–147.
127 Ibid., p. 150.
128 Andrew Gordon, The Short Happy Life of the Japanese Middle Class, in: Olivier Zunz/ Leonard Schoppa/Nobuhiro Hiwatari (Eds.): Social Contracts Under Stress. New York 2002, pp. 108–129, here p. 115.

union activity. During the war, many women had already joined Suzuki Bunji's (1885–1946)[129] Workers' Union that counted 30,000 members in 1919 and demanded better wages and working conditions.[130] During the war years, many workers joined unions or other labor–related organizations, where they also got in contact with Marxist or socialist ideas, especially in the aftermath of the Russian Revolution. They all demanded not only higher wages but also better working conditions, and it can be stated that the war did not solely create an increase in trade and production. It also increased the self–awareness of the worker and the demands of the working class, especially in the urban and industrial centers of Japan. The solidarity among the exploited therefore intensified at the same speed as the exploiting upper classes gained money from Japan's special position within the First World War.

The economic prosperity in the city, regardless of the fact that not everyone was on the winning side, "laid the foundations for a mass–consumer society and invited an unprecedented transfer of power that nurtured representative politics in Tokyo."[131] The urban middle class was no longer just willing but in many cases also now able to spend money, be it for educational institutions, in the new department stores, or new media like journals or cinemas.[132] The already mentioned large and very often Western–looking department stores provided "a place and space that became central to modern Japanese life and a disseminator of modernist aesthetics to the general Japanese public during the early twentieth century"[133] and "Mitsukoshi and its rival Shirokiya had led the way in introducing advanced technology and Western architecture as well as innovative retailing methods since their beginnings as department stores during the first decade of the twentieth century."[134] The higher wages of the war years now allowed more and more people to enjoy the things such a place could offer, and the excitement related to the new Mitsukoshi building, whose three stories were opened in 1914, is easily understood. The two large lions flanking its entrance gave the customers the feeling of visiting Trafalgar Square

---

129 On Suzuki's life and work see: Stephen S. Large, The Japanese Labor Movement, 1912–1919. Suzuki Bunji and the Yūaikai, in: The Journal of Japanese Studies 29 (1970) 3, pp. 559–579.
130 For the development of unions in wartime Japan see: Chen Ta, Labor Conditions in Japan, in: Monthly Labor Review 21 (1925) 5, pp. 8–19.
131 Dickinson, The First World War, p. 175.
132 Dickinson, World War I, p. 7.
133 Elise K. Tipton, The Department Store. Producing Modernity in Interwar Japan, in: Roy Starrs (Ed.), Rethinking Japanese Modernism, Leiden 2011, pp. 428–451, here p. 428.
134 Ibid., p. 431.

in London.[135] At the same time, it was supposed that the store could provide a feeling of life in America, especially to female customers.[136]

A visit to a department store also opened different culinary experiences to the customers in the form of diverse restaurants. Furthermore, the shopping experience in the department stores in the big Japanese cities was no different from "Macy's in New York, Wanamaker in Philadelphia, and [. . .] Marshall Field in Chicago."[137] New journals were introduced that addressed the specific needs of the new urban middle class and thereby also opened up new possibilities for discussion, e.g. of gender roles, aesthetics, and many other things. The growing middle class wanted to spend money, and it did not seem hard to find opportunities for that in the consumer–oriented world of the big cities after the First World War. Consumption, however, was not only used to create leisure and excitement, it was also an expression of class, as the rise of the new gentry of the Taishō period was based on the unspoken agenda to spend money extravagantly. Referring to Ernest Gellner's (1925–1995) theories about nationalism, the new middle class that was established by the second industrialization wave during the war developed class consciousness and therefore demanded an expression of their own status, especially due to the spending of money, yet not only for the education of the next generation, as we will see later, but first and foremost to express their own belonging to the new middle class.[138] The members of the new Taishō middle class spent money to prove that they had achieved their social advancement, and in now amusement was available for everyone who could afford it. Even before the First World War, cinemas had shown films from Hollywood, which now reached even more spectators who looked for relaxation from their daily life, especially when watching movies. Japanese also danced to American Jazz, and like the Meiji oligarchs, defined their status especially by the consumption of foreign goods, including music. Money was also spent on Western clothes or food, and one market that gained tremendously from the prosperity of the new middle class was the print market. Books, magazines, and daily newspapers boomed because a larger audience could now be reached. This not only stimulated the establishment of what Benedict Anderson (1936–2015) called an "imagined community"[139] that

---

135 Ibid., p. 433.
136 Hatsuda, Hyakkaten, p. 124,.
137 Tipton, The Department Store, p. 434.
138 Ernest Gellner, Change and Thought, Chicago 1964.
139 Benedict Anderson, Imagined Communities. Reflections on the Origin and Spread of Nationalism, London 1983.

was based on print capitalism, but also allowed people who had been outside of the general mainstream before to participate in discourses about Japanese society.

Journals like *Friend of the Housewife* (*Shufu no tomo*, 1917–1935)[140] provided articles that were written for a female audience, including fashion tips, news about the modern female lifestyle, and other things. The journal therefore provided new role models for women as well as new social definitions of womanhood. It was the financial potential of the female readers that had stimulated the production of such journals, but other players, like the cosmetic company Shiseidō, also realized the potential of the female buyer. Beauty products became more popular, especially due to the discussions about their use in journals for women, and new images about beauty and the female gender were the consequence.[141] The role of women within society was discussed, and issues like education, political roles, workers' rights, the rights of mothers and daughters in the Japanese family, and sexual self–control became topics of popular interest.[142] In the early Taishō period social tensions were created by these discourses and conflict–laden energies were freed, especially indirectly by the economic impact of the First World War. In those days modern boys and girls, called *mobo* (modern boys) and *moga* (modern girls), appeared and were often staged as an expression of the new Taishō lifestyle in different mass media, though they were not representing a mass phenomenon. The style of these new representatives of Japanese modernity resembles that of the people in the so–called "Roaring Twenties" in Europe or the United States.[143] The self was eventually staged as representing the beginning of a new era, something that was only possible due to the increased financial capacities of the urban middle class who had gained from the developments during the war years.

Diversity was sought and expressed in many ways, including through entertainment and its consumption in any form. The more money was available, the more opportunities needed to be created because, as American philosopher Douglas Kellner highlighted correctly, "[d]ifference sells. Capitalism must constantly multiply markets, styles, fads, and artifacts to keep absorbing consumers into its

140 On this journal see: Christine Gross, Japanische Frauen. Ein Leitbild im Wandel. Die Zeitschrift Shufu no tomo 1917–1935, Dissertation, Universität Zürich, 2009.
141 Toya Riina, Ginza to Shiseidō. Nihon wo "modān" ni shita kaisha, Tokyo 2012.
142 Barbarba Molony, Women's Rights, Feminism, and Suffragism in Japan, 1870–1925, in: Pacific Historical Review 69 (2000) 4, pp. 639–661, here pp. 645–654.
143 James L. Huffman, Japan in World History, New York 2010, pp. 91–94.

practices and lifestyles."[144] Modern technologies also played an important role in creating these possibilities, which excited masses of people:

> [The] movie projector and against the mesmerizing images it cast on the big screen in the multiplex performance center of Entertainment Heaven (Rakutenchi); and carnies light-heartedly cajoled thrill-seekers into elevator rides up Tsûtenkaku Tower at the entrance to Luna Park in The New World (Shin Sekai) amusement park. The epoch-making technologies that embodied this new 'media culture' defined the spectacle of urban life; and the cultural processes of importation, adaptation, amplification, production, distribution, reproduction, and reinvention that helped assimilate these technologies into the everyday world had begun to work a powerful influence on the urban identity.[145]

Japan had not only turned into an "industrial dynamo"[146] during the First World War, but new technologies were very often also used to entertain the masses. This did not solely include the recently established urban middle class, but also the working class consumers, as "Japan witnessed a mass mania for conspicuous consumption fueled by status envy."[147] Japanese scholar Ishikawa Hiroyoshi has identified three periods of working class consumption. The first one (1916–1919) was marked by the wish for the consumption of food and drink, the second (1919–1922) by spending on clothes and housing, and the third (1922–1927) was dominated by the expectations of the working class as related to society and culture.[148] However, as Jeffrey E. Hanes emphasized, "[w]orkers and their families were not absorbed into the mass consumer market. With the help of able and willing (even enthusiastic) cultural producers, they carved out a distinct niche within it."[149] Those who offered pleasure and leisure related to new media in the Japanese metropolis at the same time, to quote Hanes once more, "offered to salve the workers' wounded spirits, interpret their unspoken dreams, and sell them an afternoon's excursion into a liminal world of sensory pleasure."[150] The entertainment industry in particular consequently

144 Douglas Kellner, Media Culture. Cultural Studies, Identity and Politics Between the Modern and the Postmodern, London 1995, p. 40.
145 Jeffrey E. Hanes, Media Culture in Taishō Osaka, in: Sharon Minichiello (Ed.), Japan's Competing Modernities. Issues in Culture and Democracy 1900–1930, Honolulu 1998, pp. 267–287, here p. 270.
146 Ibid.
147 Ibid., p. 271.
148 Ishikawa Hiroyoshi, Goraku no senzenshi, Tokyo 1981, pp. 100–102, cited in ibid.
149 Hanes, Media Culture, p. 271.
150 Ibid., p. 272.

provided the possibility of modern consumption for the masses as well, and cities like Osaka were able to offer any kind of entertainment to any kind of customer.

Greater income, however, was not only leading to consumption, but was also displayed through the education of the next generation, as recently wealthy people not only longed for leisure, but also the advancement to the next social level of their children, who would then naturally gain greater influence with regard to the political development of Japan.[151] Educational opportunities were plenty as a consequence of the described economic developments, because the larger financial capacities allowed the representatives of the new middle class to send their children to educational facilities. The number of male students in Japanese middle schools increased from 128,973 to 272,973 between 1912 and 1924. The number of female students that attended higher schools tripled, reaching 246,928. For the first time, parity between male and female students was achieved in Japan.[152] In addition to this trend, the famous private schools in Japan, i.e. Keiō, Waseda, Dōshisha, Chūō, and Meiji, were officially recognized as universities in the aftermath of the First World War, signaling the start of the further growth of Japan's university system that continued until 1930. In the Taishō period the number of academic professors increased from 792 to 8,946, and that of students from 4,567 to 52,186.[153] The indirect impact of the First World War, which means the direct impact of the increased financial capacities of the new urban middle class, could consequently also be felt with regard to the development of academia and higher education in Japan, a trend that reflected the necessities of those who had reached this new status and wanted the next generation to advance further.

This also caused gender–related changes, as the "attempt to strengthen the nation by educating its citizens was extended to females when girls' schools were built throughout the country [and] [b]y the time of the Great War (1914–1918), Japanese women's higher education had been developed into a gendered institution."[154] However, the girls and young women were no longer educated according to the Meiji agenda to create "good wives and wise mothers" (ryō-sai kenho) but rather to resemble a modernized society, in which the female right

---

151 A general discussion of the relation of income and political participation see: Jimmy Szewczyk, The Effects of Income Inequality on Political Participation. A Contextual Analysis. Honors Thessis, Sewanee 2015. https://www.sewanee.edu/media/academics/politics/The-Effects-of-Income-Inequality-on-Political-Participation.pdf (3. 7. 2016).

152 Dickinson, The First World War, p. 167.

153 Ibid.

154 Chika Shinohara, Gender and the Great War. Tsuda Umeko's Role in Institutionalizing Women's Education in Japan, in: Tosh Minohara/Tze–ki Hon/Evan Dawley (Eds.), The Decade of the Great War. Japan and the Wider World in the 1910s, Leiden 2014, pp. 323–348, here p. 323.

for a good education was addressed appropriately.[155] While the first Japanese female exchange students had already been sent to the United States in the 1870s, it was the First World War that "had minimized the enrollment disparity between girls and boys and thus established a good basis for developing higher education amongst all citizens, regardless of gender."[156] The years of the Great War had also witnessed a reconsideration of the role that women, especially well–educated ones, were supposed to play for the advancement of Japan's society. Educated mothers were supposed to raise the next generation of Japanese children and were therefore considered to be part of a national strategy, according to which their educational capacities would secure the country's prosperity in the future.[157] The education of girls and women was consequently turning into a necessary demand and was no longer perceived as something luxurious and probably inappropriate. With the import of Western ideas about education, new interpretations of gender roles also entered Japan and led to a discussion about Japanese society in general, often spearheaded by educators like Tsuda Umeko (1864–1929).[158] Initially, girls' schools were part of the work of Christian missionaries, especially during the early Meiji period when famous educational institutions like the United School for Girls (1871), the Aoyama Institute for Girls (1874), the Kobe Institute for Girls (1875), the Tokyo Academy for Girls (1876), the Doshisha School for Girls (1878) and others were established.[159] The internationalization of Japan during the First World War, with regard to both global trade and the further exchange of ideas, as Chika Shinohara highlighted, "fostered an awareness of women's important social roles, impacts, and their rights, particularly among highly educated women in Japan."[160] It was especially the latter ones who claimed more rights within society for themselves, and since the number of students who had studied abroad during the Great War increased the mass of people who shared similar ideas, there was not only an intellectual debate about gender roles but actual reforms were also initiated in these crucial years.

It was understood that a generally good education, not only the one provided to upper class girls and women, was essential to strengthen Japan's national

---

155 Ibid.

156 Ibid., pp. 330–331.

157 Ibid., p. 334.

158 On her life and works see: Yoshiko Furuki, The White Plum. A Biography of Ume Tsuda, Pioneer in the Higher Education of Japanese Women, New York 1991; Kameda Kinuko, Tsuda Umeko. Hitori no meikyōshi no kiseki, Tokyo 2005.

159 Shinohara, Gender and the Great War, p. 337.

160 Ibid., p. 342.

capacities that were deemed necessary to protect the wealth of the nation state. The percentage of girls who continued their study at institutes of secondary education doubled between 1905 and 1920, although it "only" reached 10%.[161] It was the indirect impact of the First World War that "shaped women's education and gender ideology or socially expected gender roles,"[162] although many women did not consider their education to contradict their position within the state as a supportive force. The discussion was consequently often not directed against the existent social norms, but rather pointed to the necessity of better education for female students, who would willingly fulfill this demand. The actual gender discourses in relation to education were consequently rather fueled by political ideas, not the sense of righteousness of female demands.

The dispute about gender roles was related to political discourse and led by the Japanese Left, whose members demanded more equality, and that not only for male workers. While the Left was dealing with other issues following the Russian Revolution, especially the ana–boru debate (anarchism vs. Bolshevism), due to which anarcho–syndicalists led a theoretical struggle against Marxist socialism, female anarchists and socialists argued about the shape of a post–revolutionary society from a woman's perspective.[163] Gender equality was one of the main aspects demanded by these women because this was one of the central expressions of revolutionary change, although the feminist perspectives of anarchists and socialists were quite different: "anarchist feminists generally espoused gynocentric or woman–centered feminism while socialist feminists adhered to a version of humanist feminism."[164] While the latter were represented by Yamakawa Kikue (1890–1980),[165] the anarchist position was argued

---

161 Ibid., p. 345.

162 Ibid., p. 346.

163 E. Patricia Tsurumi, Visions of Women and the New Society in Conflict. Yamakawa Kikue versus Takamure Itsue, in: Sharon Minichiello (Ed.), Japan's Competing Modernities. Issues in Culture and Democracy 1900–1930, Honolulu 1998, pp. 335–357, here p. 335.

164 Ibid.

165 Elyssa Faison, Women's Rights as Proletarian Rights. Yamakawa Kikue, Suffrage, and the "Dawn of Liberation", in: Julia C. Bullock/Ayako Kano/James Welker (Eds.), Rethinking Japanese Feminism, Honolulu 2018, pp. 15–33. On Yamakawa's role during the First World War also see Frank Jacob, The First World War, Women's Education, and Yamakawa Kikue's Socialist View of Gender Roles in Japan, in: Sebastian Engelmann/Bernhard Hemetsberger/Frank Jacob (Eds.), War and Education. The Pedagogical Preparation for Collective Mass Violence, Paderborn 2022, pp. 119–141.

for by Takamure Itsue (1894–1964).[166] While the theoretical struggle took place in the late 1920s, it was initiated by the changes taking place during the years of the First World War. Yamakawa Kikue published an article about "Women's Opinion that Stabs Women in the Back" ("Fujin o uragiru fujin ron") in the journal *Shin Nippon* (*New Japan*) in August 1918. This article expressed criticism against bourgeois–conservative feminism as it was expressed, e.g. by Yamada Waka (1879–1957),[167] in the tradition of the Meiji state's "good wife and wise mother" ideology. It was argued that the biological differences between the two sexes were overemphasized by conservative feminists and, according to the article, the conservatives used "biology as an excuse to defend male absolutism."[168] While "[a]ttacking Waka's arrogant proclamations about woman's nature, Kikue did not directly offer her own definition of woman's nature," and the socialist feminist "was content to express her hopes for the future in terms of the awakening of women, the building of a women's movement, a changed economic system, and equality of men and women."[169]

Kikue might have agreed with Yosano Akiko (1878–1942), another feminist of the Meiji and Taishō periods, that "more and better education was urgent," but she disagreed with regard to Yosano's "hopes for individual effort to achieve education, employment, financial independence, and political suffrage illusory within a society that systematically denied equal opportunity to the vast majority of its members."[170] For the socialist Kikue the problem was not an individual one but one that could only be saved by a transformation of the existent society. The individual path to emancipation was consequently only available for a few Japanese women who had access to sufficient monetary assets, i.e. the bourgeois women in Japan, especially since the majority of women were exploited, as "in the capitalist labor market women were paid very little, and their presence there was manipulated to lower remuneration for all laborers, while women's work within the family was entirely unremunerated."[171] Kikue pointed out that conservative feminists had neglected the social responsibility to reach gender equality and demanded that the problem be addressed on a broader scale, as the majority of women were not

---

166 For her autobiography see: Takamure Itsue, Hi no kuni no onna no nikki. Takamure Itsue jiden, Tokyo 1966. For a collection of her anarcho–feminist writings see: Takamure Itsue, Zoku anakizumu josei kaihō ronshū, Tokyo 1989.
167 On Yamada's life and impact see: Tomoko Yamazaki, The Story of Yamada Waka. From Prostitute to Feminist Pioneer, Tokyo 1985.
168 Cited in: Tsurumi, Visions of Women, p. 337.
169 Ibid., pp. 337–338.
170 Ibid., p. 339.
171 Ibid.

able to secure a better education because they were unable to afford it. The bourgeois conservative feminists had only made the argument for upper class women and not taken into consideration that most Japanese female workers or mothers had neither access to nor the capacities for a social advance on an individual level. According to Kikue, only a change of the existent economic system could eventually pave the way for the development of true equality. As long as women were exploited by a capitalist system, they would be unable to obtain a better education and therefore the precondition for true gender equality.[172] The female author was also influenced by the Russian Revolution, although she never demanded a combination of the socialist revolution with the liberation of women in Japan.

A different position was taken by the anarchist Itsue. Her works focused on two main aspects, namely 1) community care for Japanese mothers and 2) the abolition of marriage. Since women were responsible for the upbringing of the next generation, they should not take care of this task alone and in isolation, but should be supported by society: "Reproduction and child care were to be supported by a self–governing, nonhierarchical community in which men and women would be equal producers and womanhood highly esteemed. A corollary of this was [the] abolition of institutionalized marriage. The purpose of both was to allow [the] woman to enjoy passionate carnal and spiritual loving that, along with motherhood, was part of her basic nature."[173] She reflected upon the role of women, but in contrast to many others, did so not as a single reinterpretation of Western discourses but as it related to the development of the Japanese society in the recent years and decades. She consequently offers an original insight into the feminist discussions during the war and shows how it determined the necessity for such discourse. However, there were not only immediate consequences related to the First World War, but also a long–term impact on the perception of gender issues in Japan.

Usually the Taishō period is described as a dawn with regard to urban life in the metropolis, but such views neglect the other side of the coin, namely the Japanese countryside, where the "jump" into global capitalism and the consumer modernity it represented did not happen abruptly but took much longer to manifest itself. Nevertheless, it did not stay outside of the processes that took place, nor can it be considered traditional or premodern.[174] The "modern girls" eventually also reached the countryside, although they were not really

---

172 Ibid.
173 Ibid., p. 342.
174 Mariko Asano Tamanoi, The City and the Countryside. Competing Taishō "Modernities" on Gender, in: Sharon Minichiello (Ed.), Japan's Competing Modernities. Issues in Culture and Democracy 1900–1930, Honolulu 1998, pp. 91–113, here p. 92.

welcomed there and not considered modern, as a letter by a Japanese man, Suzuki Saburō, who lived somewhere in the countryside, to the journal *Ie no Hikari*
(*The Light of the Home*), shows: "I occasionally meet a woman who cuts her hair
very short and makes up her face with rouge, lipstick, and an eyebrow pencil.
But when I scrutinize her clothes, I find them not matching her hair style and
makeup. She seems to be satisfied with herself only because she can catch the
attention of others. I find her modern, but my feeling toward her is that of con-
tempt. She lacks something to be truly modern."[175] The modern urban girl of the
Taishō city was "a glittering, decadent, middle–class consumer who, through
her clothing, smoking, and drinking, flaunt[ed] tradition,"[176] but she was rather
an urban phenomenon of the war years and did not immediately show up in little villages, which remained rather peripheral. Regardless of this fact, however,
the migration of people to the cities, who then might have visited their hometowns or villages, would sooner or later spread new fashions even to far away
spots. The availability of train travel in particular made it easier for people to
cross the distances that separated the two spaces from each other.

When the boom created by the First World War ended in the early 1920s
and the prices for crops began to fall while taxes increased, many farmers in
the countryside began to detest modernity, resembled by the perverted city life,
globalized markets, and international stock markets. Even the silk farmers lost
due to the decrease in prices and suffered due to their steadily decreasing income. When the global depression then hit Japan in the late 1920s and early
1930s and the prices for rice and silk dropped even further, it caused "distress
[for] the roughly two million farm households engaging in agriculture throughout rural Japan."[177] When the now unemployed workers from the city then returned to their rural hometowns, it increased the economic and social pressure
there, where different ideas and experiences naturally clashed in such a time of
crisis. The above–mentioned tenant disputes tended to increase year by year
and socialist and communist ideas naturally spread because they offered an al-
ternative, especially for the impoverished farmers. The state, in the meantime,
tried to suppress dangerous ideas, i.e. anarchism, socialism, and communism,
to avoid the recruitment of "*Marukusu bo'oisu*" (Marx boys), as young Japanese

---

175 Ie no hikari, October 1928, p. 144 cited in ibid., p. 93.
176 Miriam Silverberg, The Modern Girl as Militant, in: Gail L. Bernstein (Ed.), Recreating Japanese Women, 1600–1945, Berkeley 1991, pp. 239–266, here p. 239 cited in ibid.
177 Tamanoi, The City and the Countryside, p. 95.

interested in politically left ideas were called, into the ranks of the labor movement and the related party structures.[178]

The growth of print capitalism was also responsible for a growing number of newspaper publications in the smaller villages, which thereby were more and more integrated into political discourses of the time, although the main topics of interest, e.g. the self–government of smaller villages, were quite different sometimes. Next to such discussions, the main information from the government and that which was related to state issues also reached this particular space of Japan. In some issues, the voices of women were also expressed, although this was still an exception and not the norm.[179] New media, i.e. the photograph or the radio, provided other forms of audio–visual communication that were used as platforms for the discussion of social issues, including gender roles. As a consequence of all these possibilities and the steady discourses about gender norms, as Mariko Asano Tamanoi's research confirms, "the clear division of labor by gender became blurred in the Taishō period; there emerged masculine women, independent and self–confident, as well as feminine men, dependent, fragile, and indecisive."[180] One of these local publications in 1925 summed up the demands for rural women, as they were requested to

(1) use time in the most effective way;
(2) curtail unnecessary costs in their everyday lives;
(3) save money for the education of their children;
(4) buy daily necessities with cash, not on credit;
(5) use public markets;
(6) use simple makeup;
(7) wear simple clothes;
(8) respect work, do side jobs, and utilize scraps;
(9) curtail unnecessary costs of weddings;
(10) respect the Shinto–style wedding ceremony; and, lastly,
(11) reserve one day a month as a day of women's volunteer work.[181]

At the same time, other articles criticized the modern girls in the cities, who should not have left their countryside home to begin with:

---

178 Ibid., pp. 96–97. The role of the countryside for revolution was later also debated by Marxist intellectuals. See: Germaine A. Hoston, Marxism and the Crisis of Development in Prewar Japan, Princeton, NJ 1986, pp. 223–250.
179 Tamanoi, The City and the Countryside, pp. 97–99.
180 Ibid., p. 100.
181 Motohara jihō, 15 June 1925, cited in ibid., p. 103.

> Why, Ms. N, do you have to transmogrify yourself with such heavy makeup every morn-
> ing? [. . .] When you walk carrying a big bag on the glittering city streets at night, you
> really look like a monkey. [. . .] Ms. N, I secretly adored you when you were here [in this
> village] working so diligently picking mulberry leaves, wearing a white cotton apron.
> Don't you know that the sweat on your forehead sparkled in the sun? A woman's beauty
> shines only when she works in the countryside.[182]

There obviously existed a conflict about different identities related to the city
and the countryside, respectively. For those in favor of the countryside, wom-
en's and girls' true beauty was destroyed by city life, as Japan's tradition might
be destroyed by the mix of influences in the urban space. Traditional Japan and
its beauty, represented by rural womanhood, could only be found far away
from the pulsing centers of modernity, i.e. the Japanese metropolises. The countryside was consequently part of the sphere that was impacted by the First
World War and discourses about modernity, here expressed through the discourse about gender roles and true beauty. The transformations eventually
reached all parts of Japan, although with a little delay, and demanded a discourse about modernity. It can consequently be stated that the war years were
the trigger for a national process of change that would lead into the second half
of the Taishō period, when its impact reached all regions of the country. That
the multiple socio–economic transformation processes would not be accepted
without hesitation or resistance, however, must be clearly understood, which is
why a much closer look must be taken at the protests that accompanied these
transformations.

3.5 The First World War and the Protests at Home

Although the Japanese economy had flourished during the war years, prices
rose at a faster pace than wages did. This increased the sorrows of those who
were not part of the new urban middle class or those who got tremendously rich
during the war. Many people suffered from low wages and the increasing living
costs, which is why socialist or communist ideas became more and more interesting for many people, especially in the cities. In the industries that boomed
during the war, e.g. shipbuilding, more and more unions were established to
represent the demands of the workers who, due to the actual demands of the
workforce, were in a position to better and more often successfully express their
demands. Although the war triggered the activities and establishment of unions

---

182 Kamishina jihō, 15 January 1925, cited in ibid., p. 104.

in all kinds of industries, the socialist activities during the war represented a continuation of the years before.

While socialist publications and anti-war activities had been suppressed during the Russo-Japanese War, the aftermath of the war was characterized by increased activity of the socialist movement in Japan. Socialists had been active in different mines since the early 1900s, and when in 1907 a riot at the famous Ashio copper mine occurred, the riots there spread to other mines across the country once the military had crushed the socialist-led riot after three days of protests.[183] The national impact of the riot at Ashio emphasized that the socialists had established a network of cooperation and solidarity and were actually no longer solely an intellectual phenomenon expressed in local study groups. The Left in Japan, however, was disunited about the future course it should take. The anarchists assembled around Kōtoku Shūsui (1871–1911)[184] demanded direct action, while the socialists led by Katayama Sen demanded reforms within the legal limits of the state.[185] Like the European Left, the Japanese anarchists and socialists discussed theory, often weakening their own movement due to internal divisions and struggles.[186] The government had already taken fierce action against the anarchist movement in 1911 due to the so-called High Treason Incident, when 26 anarchists were accused of having planned the assassination of the Meiji Emperor and were tried in secret. 11 of them, among them Kōtoku, were eventually executed, an act that showed that the government was not willing to accept the uncontested existence of dangerous ideas of the political Left. This caused further tension between anarchists and socialists on the one side and the state on the other.[187] The repression of the state was immediately felt when "[a]ll books on socialism were confiscated and all the public libraries were ordered to withdraw socialist books and papers. Even moderate papers like ours were severely censored and a few months after the said trial it was practically suppressed by the authorities."[188]

The First World War, however, also presented a chance for the socialist movement in Japan, whose members were now able to spread their ideas in unions and

---

183 Katayama Sen, The Labor Movement in Japan, Chicago 1918, p. 112. On the riot see: Kazuo Nimura, The Ashio Riot of 1907. A Social History of Mining in Japan, Durham, NC 1998.
184 On Kotoku's influence and the conflict with the state authorities see the important study Maik Hendrik Sprotte, Konfliktaustragung in autoritären Herrschaftssystemen. Eine historische Fallstudie zur frühsozialistischen Bewegung im Japan der Meiji-Zeit, Marburg 2001.
185 Katayama, The Labor Movement, p. 122.
186 Ibid., p. 124.
187 Ibid., p. 135.
188 Ibid., p. 140.

among workers, especially the recently increased working class of the cities, where the demand for manufactured goods had increased not only the number of workers representing the industrial proletariat of Japan but also the chances for them to use their potential for a fight for better wages. Katayama Sen therefore correctly argued that the members of the working class of Japan "have lately awakened."[189] This was also related to the impact of the Russian Revolution, which had shown that the dictatorship of the proletariat could be established, and many Japanese socialists admired the results of the protests in February 1917, although not all agreed with the Bolshevists' actions since October. As Katayama put it: "The living fact that the Russian revolution was accomplished by the joint action of the workers and the soldiers is the great revelation to the Japanese who are oppressed under militarism and conscription."[190] While the revolutionary events in Russia might have stimulated the discourse among the socialist intellectuals, it was the consequences of the growth of the war industry and global capitalism in Japan that were responsible for the workers' demands related to better wages and other benefits.[191] Katayama later described the rise of socialism during the First World War, but had remarked in an article in 1910 that the working class lacked "any form of lawful protection and [were] totally defenseless when [. . .] at the mercy of capitalist exploitation."[192] He added that there was "no law, no constitution, and no freedom"[193] for socialists and the Japanese police were, according to his own experiences, "worse than the Russian."[194] In 1911, he wrote that a small upper class that profited from the suffering of the working class ruled Japan, while emphasizing that this order was based on violence: "To perpetuate this regime of violence by a small minority over the large mass of the people, the government and the bourgeoisie have to betake themselves to police despotism and suppress every freer government."[195] According to Katayama, socialists suffered the most from this situation. The municipality of Tokyo was said to have spent ¥ 50,000 in 1910 to spy on 170 members of the Socialist Party, leaving no space for socialist activities at all.[196] The leadership was arrested within a year, and those who were still free were not only constantly monitored but also

---

[189] Ibid., p. 5.
[190] Ibid., p. 7.
[191] Ibid., pp. 5–6.
[192] Katayama Sen, Industrie und Sozialismus in Japan, in: Die neue Zeit. Wochenschrift der deutschen Sozialdemokratie 28 (1910) 25, pp. 874–880, here p. 878.
[193] Ibid., p. 880.
[194] Ibid.
[195] Katayama Sen, Die politischen Zustände Japans, in: Die neue Zeit. Wochenschrift der deutschen Sozialdemokratie 29 (1911) 4, pp. 107–111, here p. 109.
[196] Ibid.

struggled to earn a living.[197] In 1914, Katayama eventually left Japan and would never come back. He had surrendered and did not believe he was able to achieve anything in Japan, where police violence suffocated popular movements.[198] In exile, however, he remained in touch with leftist activists in Japan and was an active member of the global socialist network as well as a leading figure within the Communist International.

Due to the Russian Revolution of 1917, Katayama himself became more radical and wrote numerous works on behalf of Lenin's Bolshevism. He instructed members of the Socialist Party of America to join the Communist International in March 1919 and furthermore encouraged the founding of the Communist Party of the United States in September 1919. In addition, he led a group of Japanese communists who joined the American party.[199] In the same year, in a communication with the People's Russian Information Bureau in London, Katayama criticized Japan's position towards Soviet Russia, which is why his influence on the Japanese socialists was considered dangerous by the government in Tokyo. According to Katayama, the Japanese involvement in the Siberian Intervention was useless:

> Our soldiers in Siberia, since the beginning of the intervention, died 'a dog's death,' a useless death, and war expenses are simply wasted. We regret the loss on account of our mistaken policy, indeed! But by withdrawing our troops now we shall hereafter commit no more of such a senseless sacrifice and, moreover, the inimical attitude of the Russians can be eliminated. This is the opinion of the best people of Japan. [. . .] The Japanese Government's Siberian policy is upheld by the Allies, including America. It is a most outrageous policy. To them the Russian people are only the bourgeois class who are against the Bolshevik government and trying to sell Russia to the foreign capitalists![200]

Such criticism was considered dangerous in Japan, where the government intended to use the Siberian Intervention to push back the Russian zone of interest in East Asia and strengthen the country's position on the Asian continent.

---

197 Ibid., p. 111. Katayama declared the Japanese proletariat to be the most exploited in the world. Katayama Sen, Die Ausbeutung der Arbeiter in Japan, in: Die neue Zeit. Wochenschrift der deutschen Sozialdemokratie 29, 52 (1911), pp. 917–921, here 921.
198 Katayama Sen, Der Verfall des bureaukratischen Regimes in Japan, in: Die neue Zeit. Wochenschrift der deutschen Sozialdemokratie 32 (1914) 1, pp. 16–20, here p. 18.
199 Rudolf Hartmann, Japanischer Revolutionär und proletarischer Internationalist. Sen Katayama, in: Beiträge zur Geschichte der Arbeiterbewegung 26 (1984) 2, pp. 238–246, here p. 243.
200 Katayama Sen, Japan and Soviet Russia, London, 6 September 1919, Warwick Digital Collection, 36/R30/22, 2.

Critical anti–government voices such as that of Katayama were suppressed, especially during the later years and immediately after the First World War. Katayama therefore also emphasized that Soviet Russia was the victim of corrupt capitalist governments, like that of Japan:

> All lies, falsehoods and twisting the facts about the Russian Soviet Republic and its doings have been poured on the people of the world over for the past eighteen months to fool and mislead them. These lies, skillfully fabricated by the capitalists and their paid agents – journalists, editors and pressmen of big dailies, even those truth–loving Christians and god–fearing men, may mislead and cheat the people for a while, but they are like a house built on sand, or storm clouds before the sun: they will soon fall away before the truth.[201]

In his criticism, Katayama seems to have been blinded by his hope in the Communist International and his strong belief in Lenin and that the Bolshevik leader was working for a better world. The Japanese socialist did not realize that Lenin was rather the leader of a regime that would use yet another ideology to suppress the people while employing the same brute force the Japanese government had used in the years before. Emphatically, Katayama argued: "Capitalistic governments and their diplomats will not make a lasting peace in the world. We know that. There is only one true lasting peace of the world, that is the Russian Bolshevik peace proposed by Lenin and Trotsky when they formed the Soviet government. At least this is the consensus of opinion among the great masses of the world, and I am glad to say that the Japanese Socialists are of firm belief on this aspect."[202] Such pro–Bolshevik statements from a leader whom the Japanese government perceived as an agent of the Comintern further discredited the socialist movement and naturally incited further anti–leftist persecution at the end of the First World War. The rice riots that will be discussed in more detail below were at the same time the result of Japan's economic problems, and the post–war crisis made the government tighten its grip on the labor movement to prevent instability and suppress its revolutionary potential.[203] It feared a repetition of the Russian events on Japanese soil too much to let the activities of the socialist movement among Japanese workers be carried out uncontested.

---

201 Ibid.
202 Ibid.
203 On the rice riots, see: Inoue Kiyoshi/Watanabe Tōru, Kome sōdō no kenkyū, Tokyo 1997.

In 1920, when Katayama gave the lecture "Recent Tendencies in the Labor Movement in Japan"[204] at the Rand School of Social Science in New York,[205] he argued that the First World War and its aftermath had vitalized the labor movement in Japan (Tables 3.4 and 3.5). Socialists had been effective as union leaders during the war, and Katayama's statistics, dated 31 December 1919, show the increase in union membership and provide numbers for the increasingly numerous strikes since 1914, especially those related to or within the workers' movement.[206]

Table 3.4: The Status of Unionism in Japan, December 31, 1919.

Industry	Total number of workers	Number of union organizations	Total number of members	Percentage of unionized workers	Average number of workers per union
Textiles	713,620	90	61,643	6.6	685
Machinery	222,366	82	40,125	18.0	495
Chemicals	141,769	67	9,047	6.4	135
Mining	433,843	94	52,135	12.0	555
Total	1,511,598	333	162,950	10.8	489

Table 3.5: The Increase in Strikes in Japan between 1914 and 1919.

Year	Number of strikes	Number of strikers	Average number of strikers per strike
1914	50	7,904	158
1915	60	7,852	123
1916	108	8,413	78
1917	397	57,309	144
1918	417	66,457	159
1919	497	63,137	127
Total	1,534	211,072	

---

204 Katayama Sen, Recent Tendencies in the Labor Movement in Japan, Rand School of Social Science Papers (Dep't of Labor Research), The New York Public Library, Astor, Lenox and Tilden Foundations, Box 2, Katayama–Tractenberg, Folder 1, Katayama–Laidler. Following quotes will refer to Katayama Sen, Labor Union Movement, New York, October 21, 1920, a handwritten lecture manuscript within the named folder.
205 On the school, see Rachel Cutler Schwartz, The Rand School of Social Science, 1906–1924. A Study of Worker Education in the Socialist Era, PhD Thesis, State University of New York at Buffalo, 1984.
206 Katayama, Labor Union Movement, p. 2. The two charts are taken from these notes (pp. 2–3).

The government, frightened by possible further unrest in the country, suppressed the strikes by force: "In Aug[ust] 1919, there was a general [printers' union] strike of [. . .] the daily papers (17) in Tokyo for few days. The metropolis of 2,000,000 without a daily paper! But violent suppression of [the] strike and arrests of strikers executed during and after the strike and many other big strikes were suppressed by brutal police forces and some by calling out troops killing many strikers."[207] Katayama reported that the government's brutality was a consequence of "Japanese workers [showing] . . . a deep interest in the Russian revolution."[208] However, the interest in the revolution in Russia was not as important as the actual sorrows the workers in Japan had to face in their daily struggle against inflation and too low wages.

The rice riots of 1918 were a chance for the socialists to gain the attention and support of the masses who had suffered from the economic boom, while the upper class had simultaneously made a fortune out of it, especially due to the exploitation of cheap labor.[209] Katayama therefore considered the rice riots to be "direct revolutionary training,"[210] and the 7,831 rioters who were arrested and tried were the first representatives of the coming revolution. The Japanese government could consequently not tolerate such "revolutionary activities," especially not during the war itself. Thus, the fact that the "labor strikes [that] developed from the riots [. . .] [had] always [been] crushed by troops" was not a surprise at all, at least not for Katayama.[211] The strike of 26,000 laborers at the Yedamitsu Steel Works, to name just one example, was violently crushed, and many strikers were injured or killed.[212]

Katayama's account highlighted that the Japanese government, 14 years after the end of the Russo–Japanese War, continued its harsh anti–left course. The war had initially caused an economic boom, which was, however, followed by a recession after the war, and the danger of internal turmoil needed to be prevented again. Like in 1905, anti–left persecution and violence seem to have been the accurate means used to achieve these governmental aims. More than 50,000 workers had already participated in close to 400 strikes in 1917, which means that the potential for unrest was not suddenly expressed, but rather increased during the war. The financial gains of the nouveaux riches were criticized, not only by the workers but by publicists in Japan as well, but there was little one

---

207 Ibid., p. 4.
208 Ibid., p. 5.
209 James, The Rise and Fall, pp. 160–161.
210 Katayama, Labor Union Movement, p. 5.
211 Ibid., p. 6.
212 Ibid.

could do against the capitalist development that had created this super-rich class. Its representatives continued to gain from cheap labor and the political authorities did not seem interested in challenging them or their wrongdoings.[213] However, when the price of rice took off and due to ruthless speculation reached a level unknown before,[214] many people saw no other option but to openly challenge this development and the political order it stood for.

Between 1914 and 1920 the price of rice had increased by 174%, which is why it got more and more unattainable, especially in the non–urban parts of the country, where wages had not gained value during the war years.[215] This became even more problematic once the boom ended in 1920 and more and more people felt the beginning recession.[216] The end of war–related exports to the Allied powers hit the Japanese economy quite hard, and while the political leaders discussed the future world order at Versailles, Japanese producers had to face the end of the golden years created by the financial surplus due to the steady export of manufactured goods to the warring Europeans. Regardless of this initial shock, Japanese companies were able to recover and continued to record positive balances until the crash followed with its full impact in 1920. The economic bubble in Japan burst, and prices fell so fast that factory workers lost their job without any warning. The price of Japanese yarn dropped by 60%, and that of silk by 70%. The stock market in Tokyo crashed and lost 55%.[217] The unavailability of competitors in Asia had led to an overproduction of Japanese manufactured goods that now, after the return of the European trade companies, could no longer be sold. The consequence, in addition to dropping prices, was overproduction, and a financial crisis was inevitable. This crisis had been accompanied by rice riots since 1918, due to which the newly rich and other upper class representatives, as well as speculators, were accused of being responsible for the misery of the poor people in Japan.[218]

Producers and export companies had probably acted too jauntily during the war years, not considering that the economic boom could and would end with the conclusion of the First World War. They were probably intoxicated by

---

213 Young, Japan under Taisho Tenno, p. 114.

214 Ibid., p. 115.

215 Tobata Seiichi, Nihon nōgyō no ninaite, in: Nihon Nōgyō Hattatsushi Chōsakai et al. (Ed.), Nihon nōgyō hattatsushi, vol. 9, Tokyo 1956, pp. 561–604.

216 Andrew Gordon, A Modern History, pp. 139–140.

217 Ōno Ken'ichi, World War I and the 1920s. Export–led Boom and Bust, http://www.grips. ac.jp/teacher/oono/hp/lecture_J/lec07.htm (4. 7. 2016).

218 Michael Lewis, Rioters and Citizens. Mass Protest in Imperial Japan, Berkeley et al. 1990, pp. 100–110.

the extreme margins and profit and did not wish for this trend to end, eventually neglecting the simple possibility that time would change again. The overpriced products of the war years could no longer compete on the Asian markets and left many of the nouveaux riches impoverished again. Their luxurious lifestyle disappeared as quickly as it had occurred. Due to the crisis of the silk market and the crash of the Japanese stock market, the banks also faced a severe crisis, and the money owned by the common people lost a lot of its worth. On the one hand, the number of unemployed workers rose, while on the other, the rift between poor and rich got more intense, especially since most of the wages remained low while the rice prices exploded. This situation was intensified due to speculations with rice. In more than 350 cities, rice riots (*kome sōdō*) protested against the exploitation of ordinary consumers.[219] The latter attacked real and supposed speculators and many rice traders.

Considering the long–term perspective with regard to the postwar years, the developments were even worse. The Japanese economy entered a "chronic crisis."[220] This was also due to the international crises in the 1920s and 1930s, which further intensified the problems already faced at the end of the First World War. The gross national income rose by 6.2% between 1914 and 1919, but this trend declined to 0.7% in 1931.[221] The economist and political scientist Shizume Masato divided Japan's economic history from 1914 (when the First World War started) to the late 1930s (when the Second World War began in East Asia in 1937/39) into five time periods.[222] First, there was an economic boom between 1914 and 1919, with high rates of economic growth and inflation, then came a decade of deflationary measures between 1920 and 1929 before the Shōwa depression in 1930/31. Between 1932 and 1936 the economy partly recovered, before another upswing occurred in the first period of the Sino–Japanese War (1937–1945).[223]

Regardless of these long–term developments, we should return to the local riots between 1918 and 1920 once more, as they resembled the global unrest at the end of the Great War and therefore must be seen as a symptom for the

---

219 Reinhard Zöllner, Geschichte Japans: Von 1800 bis zur Gegenwart, Second edition, Paderborn 2008, p. 341.
220 Shizune Masato, The Japanese Economy during the Interwar Period. Instability in the Financial System and the Impact of the World Depression, in: Bank of Japan Review. Institute for Monetary and Economic Studies, 2009–E–2, Tōkyō 2009. https://www.boj.or.jp/en/research/wps_rev/rev_2009/data/rev09e02.pdf (10. 4. 2016).
221 Ibid.
222 Ibid.
223 Ibid. On the Shōwa depression see: Iwata Kikuo, Shōwa kyōkō no kenkyū, Toyko 2004.

shortcomings of a globalized capitalist world order that had been based on imperialism and the exploitation of the working class alike. In 1918 the Japanese authorities had to face a strong and, due to union and socialist party activities, well-organized working class. At the same time, the unrest of the farmers in the countryside was followed by protests by the fishermen, although the price for fish had increased as well, "but there was a complicated system of marketing under which commodities passed through several hands before reaching the consumer, so that the producers were the last to feel the benefit of a rise in market prices."[224] Even if more money for fish was available and the income of the fishermen increased, it could hardly match the prices of other consumer goods that needed to be bought in exchange. The food producers, i.e. farmers and fishermen, were consequently left out from the economic gains of the new middle and upper class, suffering even while making more money than in the past.

In Kobe, protests against the price of rice, which went up by 300% between 1915 and 1918, eventually culminated in a violent eruption when the nouveaux riches, the rice speculators, and other traders were attacked by an angry mob in early August 1918, and the deployment of troops was necessary to avoid a further spreading of the violent potential in the city.[225] However, Kobe can only be considered the peak of the protests that spanned the whole country; rice riots seem to have taken place almost everywhere in Japan, in which people demanded some kind of moral economy instead of capitalism-oriented exploitation.[226] Consequently, the protests could be understood as an expression of anti-globalization in Japan, where the producing and working classes demanded an end to a capitalist-driven and in some way immoral form of economy. In Kobe in August 1918, this was one of the sentiments that made the masses act and attack those they had identified as the ones responsible for their misery. It was there that the riots also reached their most violent potential:

> Crowds collected at Minato-gawa [. . .]. They were harangued by spokesmen whom the tide of excitement carried on its crest. The names of the principal profiteers were denounced. Presently the crowd began to move towards Suzuki's, a firm which had become very wealthy during the war and whose operations on the rice market particularly attracted the mob's hostile attention. Actually Suzuki's had been buying rice chiefly on the Government's behalf as commission agents, but it was believed that they were responsible for forcing up the price. Doors were battered in, kerosene poured over the furniture

---

224 Young, Japan under Taisho Tenno, p. 115.
225 James, The Rise and Fall, p. 161.
226 On the rice riots see the following recent article: Tomie Naoko, 1918-nen kome sōdō ni okeru „seizonken". Moraru ekonomī to shitizenshippu, in: Fukushi shakai gakken 14 (2017), pp. 95–119.

and the premises fired. The fire brigade – a branch of the police service – was driven away when it came up, and its hoses were cut. The firemen attempted to play on the flames from the windows of a Japanese newspaper office that stood opposite, whereupon the mob burnt the office as well. The same night the offices of a big house agency which had got the greater part of the dwellings in Kobe into its avaricious hands were burnt, besides the houses of a couple of unpopular money–lenders.[227]

Troops needed to intervene the following day to end the riots. Soldiers had to be brought in from Himeji, because they could not be sent from the nearer Osaka as this city was facing a similar situation, where angry crowds smashed shop windows as well as cars. The mob, naturally, like in Kobe as well, "expended its energies in minor mischief, but came into no extensive collisions with the troops."[228] It took the government a few days to reestablish order in the cities and bring life back to normal. In twenty places all over Japan, the military had to intervene and suppress the activities of angry mobs. At least a hundred protesters had been killed, although there is no exact number, because the government prohibited any news about the riots in their aftermath. The Japanese press, however, did not follow this order and even protested against it, which is why at least some reports provide a contemporary image of the events.

Regardless of their intensity, the riots could be suppressed, as they happened in a rather unorganized and very spontaneous manner. The fact, however, that protesters assembled all over Japan also highlights the dangerous situation the government in Tokyo had to face. The army remained loyal, however, and did not support the protests. Many people were arrested during and after the riots and were harshly sentenced in the aftermath, some protesters even facing the death sentence.[229] The Prime Minister, Terauchi Masatake (1852–1919), nevertheless, could not survive the discussions related to the events and had to resign on 17 September 1918. The new Prime Minister, Hara Takashi (1856–1921), was appointed a few days later and was "enthusiastically greeted" by labor leaders like Suzuki Bunji because he "was a common man, not a peer, and his cabinet was a party government."[230] Social change was supposed to be resembled by the new government, and although these hopes might have been a bit too high, there were, of course, also some long–term impacts from the events of 1918 on the Japanese labor movement.

---

227 Young, Japan under Taisho Tenno, p. 116.
228 Ibid., p. 117.
229 Ibid.
230 Takenaka, Failed Democratization, p. 92.

In May 1919 the first meeting of the Rōdō Dōmeikai (Labor League) met in Tokyo, and next to Suzuki Bunji, Ōsugi Sakae (1885–1923),[231] "a man of powerful mind, profoundly read in all revolutionary literature, and with a fanatical devotion to individual liberty,"[232] was a central figure. While a quarter of the participants of this meeting were supposedly policemen, the course of the meeting showed that confrontations between the labor movement and the state had become more severe since 1918: "[I]n spite of this ejectment the speeches continued to offend the police, who stopped them one after the other, until the assembly broke up in a storm of indignation. This became the type of Labour meeting henceforth, and though the most passionate outbursts greeted these prohibitions, disobedience and force were very rarely attempted."[233] Once the Treaty of Versailles had been signed, politicians thought they had established a return to a peaceful international order, but "the restlessness which pervaded the whole world manifested itself in industrial strikes, and Japan had rather more than her share."[234] With prices rising again, again faster than the real wages of the workers, it became quite common to request an adjustment through a strike. Considering the intensity of these developments, A. Morgan Young speaks of "an epidemic"[235] Japan had never faced before. It might have been this impression that led to the consideration that the Taishō period was a time of strong liberal demands and public unrest, i.e. a "Taishō democracy."[236] The struggle between the government and the labor movement continued in numerous ways during the period, but it is clear that the First World War had been a stronger trigger to mobilize the masses due to the created public interest than the war against Russia a decade before. In 1905, riots criticized the loss of Japan at the diplomatic table in the struggle for its future empire. In 1918 and afterward, people protested against capitalist exploitation instead. The impact of the Great War on unrest and protests in Japan, especially in the months after the war's end, can consequently not be neglected.

---

231 On his life and impact see: Thomas A. Stanley, Ōsugi Sakae, Anarchist in Taishō Japan. The Creativity of the Ego, Cambridge, MA 1982; Herbert Worm, Studien über den jungen Ōsugi Sakae und die Meiji-Sozialisten zwischen Sozialdemokratie und Anarchismus unter besonderer Berücksichtigung der Anarchismusrezeption, Hamburg 1981.
232 Young, Japan under Taisho Tenno, pp. 152–153.
233 Ibid., p. 153.
234 Ibid., p. 167.
235 Ibid.
236 Harald Meyer, Die „Taishō–Demokratie". Begriffsgeschichtliche Studien zur Demokratierezeption in Japan von 1900 bis 1920, Bern 2005.

3.6 Conclusion

The First World War had established Japan as the "only major non–Western colonial power in the twentieth century,"[237] and in 1919, Tokyo controlled parts of the neighboring mainland as well as some islands in the Pacific Rim. The Japanese government had used the war as a pretext for its imperialist expansion in China, which it needed to secure at Versailles at all cost, eroding the principles of the League of Nations before it even existed. At the same time, Japan had gained from its rather "light" involvement in the Great War, as it had economically profited from its trade with the Entente powers and the absence of European competitors for manufactured goods on the Asian markets. Japan's economy boomed, and the nouveaux riches enjoyed the urban city life in the metropolises. As has been shown above, however, the consequence was social transformations, and not only in the urban context, and new consumer markets led to discussions about Japanese society as a whole. New gender roles were as publicly discussed as the situations of those who were not able to participate in the advantageous boom of the economy.

Regardless of its growing publicity, which print capitalism had provided for broader audiences, the social question did not become really interesting before the end of the war when the boom abruptly ended and rice prices went through the roof. At the same time, low real wages were leading to massive impoverishment and, marking the start for more critical and confrontational mass eruptions in Japan, the rice riots of 1918 marked a new period of consciousness for the Japanese working class and the socialist movement. The latter's leading figures could use the steady suffering caused by capitalist exploitation, which had been globalized and therefore increased during the war years, to make themselves heard among the workers, whether in union or party meetings.

Once social unrest had erupted in Kobe and many other Japanese cities at the end of the war, the government also realized the danger and tried to contain dangerous ideas and punish protesters to avoid increasing revolutionary potential spreading. The anger of the protesters, however, was less stimulated by revolutionary dreams, as Katayama Sen might have had them, than by capitalist realities that caused sorrows for the majority of Japanese people, which could be felt in the cities and the countryside as well. The protests in Japan were consequently an expression of social unrest that must be seen in their global

---

237 Michele M. Mason/Helen J.S. Lee, Introduction, in: Michele M. Mason/Helen J.S. Lee (Eds.), Reading Colonial Japan. Text, Context, and Critique, Stanford, CA 2012, pp. 1–17, here p. 1.

context. Many people had reasons to rebel against the existent order around the globe, and it was a pity that the leaders in Versailles were unable to establish a better one but instead continued to believe in principles that had just turned the world to ashes. In Japan, the new order was greeted enthusiastically, but in reality and from a long–term perspective, it worsened the situation of the workers' movement and led the country into a war that was neither glorious like the Russo–Japanese War nor economically profitable, but would instead destroy much of the country and the region for the sake of capitalist exploitation and the imperialist ruling class.

4 Korea, the First World War, and the Hopes for a New World Order

4.1 Introduction

The impact of the First World War on Korea was similar to its impact on China, especially with regard to there being a nationalist eruption at its end, although the direct implications of the war were less distinct than in the national contexts of China or Japan. With regard to the Korean position during the war years, it can be emphasized that thoughts about the country's independence were often only shared or debated among Koreans, no matter if they lived within the national borders or somewhere abroad. The Japanese annexation in 1910 had been accepted relatively silently, but the end of the First World War and the debates about a new and peaceful world order sparked the nationalist ambitions of many Koreans, who demanded their sovereignty and independence be regained from Japan. It can therefore be argued that the "confrontation with Western imperialism" caused a stress test that the different dynasties in China, Japan, and Korea had to react to, and while "the painful disintegration of the Qing imperial state in China" would cause internal power struggles and factionalism that weakened the former center of East Asia, "the creation of the centralized Meiji state out of the ruins of the Tokugawa shogunate in Japan"[1] paved the way for Japanese expansion toward the Asian mainland, where Korea would soon be turned into a colonial space for Tokyo's imperialist ambitions. The intertwined course of the three countries, however, met yet another possible turning point at the end of the First World War, when Chinese nationalists demanded maintaining independence from Japan, while nationalists throughout Korea demanded their status as an independent nation again. Considering these preconditions for the course of events that will be recaptured in this chapter from a Korean perspective, one could argue that the three national contexts can be understood as a kind of East Asian microcosm of Immanuel Wallerstein's world system, where Japan is the expansionist core, China the semiperiphery, where Japanese ambitions for control were still held back by some kind of national interest, and Korea an almost completely suppressed and exploited colonial space. The three histories are consequently linked to each other not only by individual ties between people but

---

1 Anne Walthall, From Private to Public Patriarchy. Women, Labor and the State in East Asia, 1600–1919, in: Teresa A. Meade and Merry E. Wiesner-Hanks (Eds.), *A Companion to Gender History*, New York 2006, pp. 444–458, here p. 444.

also by international developments within East Asia, which, as a space, must be considered to be highly connected according to the economic, social, and political dynamics Wallerstein emphasized with regard to the functioning of larger world systems.[2]

Stressed by the arrival and the demands of the foreign powers, Japanese foreign policy turned into an aggressive and expansionist Asian form of colonialism that sought to expand the country's influence in Korea and China and thereby became, together with Italy and Germany, one of the imperialist latecomers, but it was also "the only non-Western colonizer in modern history."[3] In contrast to the Western colonial powers in many of their colonies, Japan considered its colonial territories not only as "markets for exports, but also as strategically integrated parts of the so-called 'Greater Japan.' Therefore, the Japanese colonial state put considerable effort into developing infrastructure in the colonies."[4] Due to this fact, those who seek to whitewash or at least somehow excuse Japanese colonialism tend to emphasize the many positive developments, e.g. economic growth, in the territories that had been controlled by Imperial Japan in the past.[5] Such arguments are similar to the narratives of the "White Man's Burden"[6] or a "Civilizing Mission"[7] in the name of the progress and modernization that was necessary to bring culture and civilization to underdeveloped parts of the world and which are repeated even today to glorify the empires of the past.[8]

---

2 Immanuel Wallerstein, Welt-System-Analyse. Eine Einführung, Wiesbaden 2019, pp. 17–22. Also see Daniel Chirot and Thomas D. Hall, World-System Theory, in: Annual Review of Sociology 8 (1982), pp. 81–106, here p. 84. On the value of Wallerstein's concept as a theoretical approach in different fields also see Frank Jacob (Ed.), Wallerstein 2.0. Thinking and Applying World-Systems Theory in the 21st Century, Bielefeld 2022.
3 Jitendra Uttam, Political Economy of Korea: Transition, Transformation and Turnaround, London 2014, p. 73.
4 Ibid.
5 Dong-No Kim, National Identity and Class Interest in the Peasant Movements of the Colonial Period, in: Hong Yung Lee, Yong-Chool Ha and Clark W. Sorensen (Eds.), *Colonial Rule and Social Change in Korea, 1910–1945*, Seattle, WA 2013, pp. 140–172, here p. 140.
6 Rudyard Kipling, The White Man's Burden (1899), in: *Modern History Sourcebook*, Fordham University. Accessed May 28, 2022. https://sourcebooks.fordham.edu/mod/kipling.asp.
7 Alice L. Conklin, A Mission to Civilize. The Republican Idea of Empire in France and West Africa, 1895–1930, Stanford, CA 1997.
8 One example for such an approach toward the history of the British Empire, which Kim Wagner correctly called a "whitewash for Britain's atrocities" would be Jeremy Black, Imperial Legacies. The British Empire Around the World, New York 2019. For Wagner's full review see Kim Wagner, Imperial Legacies by Jeremy Black. Review – Whitewash for Britain's Atrocities,

Japan's rise to hegemony in East Asia was related to its successful economic and military policy that demanded it match the Western powers to prevent the colonization of its own territory. At the same time, older expansionist traditions that reached back to the 16th century[9] were revived, and the idea of invading Korea had already been prominently discussed in the 1870s.[10] Following the Sino-Japanese War (1894–1895) and the Russo-Japanese War (1904–1905), not only was Japan eventually able to become accepted as a great international power, but its military victories also allowed it to push its geostrategic influence further toward the other Asian countries.[11] While the so-called Triple Intervention by France, Germany, and Russia in 1895 prevented the Japanese Empire from annexing the Liaodong Peninsula in China,[12] the Sino-Japanese War had decided the struggle for influence in Korea between China and Japan, and the war against Russia would eventually cement Japan's standing on the Korean Peninsula, a space the Japanese decision-makers considered to be exclusively Japanese. Operating there with a free hand, Korea was soon turned into a colony that was supposed to serve Japanese interests, and its governor-general was appointed by the Emperor. This important post was given to "a military man directly responsible to the Japanese prime minister"[13] and whose main task was to secure uncontested rule in the name of Japan. The colony was, as Jitendra Uttam emphasizes, hierarchically centralized to tighten the Japanese grip as much as possible:

> The governor-general appointed all the provincial governors and the county superintendents, who finally appointed heads of each district and village. The colonial administration took one step further to assume the nation's tradition of centralized governance. The total

---

in: The Guardian, August 10, 2019. Accessed May 28, 2022. https://www.theguardian.com/books/2019/aug/10/imperial-legacies-jeremy-black-review-empire-multiculturalism.

9 Toyotomi Hideyoshi (1537–1598) had already attempted to establish an Asian Empire under Japanese rule. For a detailed discussion of these attempts see Kitajima Manji, Hideyoshi no Chōsen shinryaku, Tokyo 2002; Kenneth Swope, A Dragon's Head and a Serpent's Tail. Ming China and the first great East Asian War, 1592–1598, Norman, OK 2016.

10 The so called "debate about the invasion of Korea" (seikanron) in 1873 caused trouble for the Japanese government, although it there was no disagreement about the idea of an invasion as such, but rather about the suitable timing of such an advance. Pŏm-sŏk Kang, Seikanron seihen. Meiji rokunen no kenryoku tōsō, Tokyo 1990.

11 Frank Jacob, The Russo-Japanese War and Its Shaping of the Twentieth Century, London 2018, pp. 46–73.

12 Urs Matthias Zachmann, Imperialism in a Nutshell: Conflict and the "Concert of Powers" in the Tripartite Intervention, 1895, in: Japanstudien 17 (2006) 1, pp. 57–82.

13 Uttam, Political Economy, 72.

number of officials in 1910 numbered 10,000; however, by 1937 that number grew to reach 87,552, comprising 52,270 Japanese and 35,282 Koreans.[14]

Ultimately, the Japanese not only intended to exploit their colony but also wanted to assimilate it to turn it into an integral part of their empire.

From 1905, and even more so after 1910, when the country was officially annexed, it was therefore the colonial experience that determined the experience of every Korean. This colonial experience, to cite Korean scholar Dong-No Kim, cannot be overemphasized with regard to understanding modern Korean history: Understanding Japanese colonialism in Korea is essential not only for reconstructing Korea's historical experience, but also for understanding the current functioning of contemporary Korean society, which has been considerably conditioned by its colonial legacy.[15] The First World War determined the second half of Korea's first decade as a Japanese colony and, at the same time, marked the first nationalist eruption against Japanese rule when the March First Movement in 1919 challenged the existent order. What has been called a "Korean Revolution"[16] was part of an international wave of protests at the end of the war,[17] especially since the peace treaty negotiations seemed to promise a better future based on enlightened ideas that were particularly linked to US President Woodrow Wilson.[18] As has been shown in the previous two chapters, there were riots and protests in all East Asian countries, but "[w]hereas in Japan men and women had rioted over the price of rice in 1918, in China they marched in support of national self-determination and democracy, and in Korea they demonstrated against Japanese imperialism."[19] The extent to which this "Wilsonian Moment"[20] influenced

---

14 Ibid.

15 Kim, National Identity, p. 140.

16 Korean Delegation, Petition. The Claim of the Korean People and Nation for Liberation from Japan and for the Reconstitution of Korea as an Independent State, Paris, April 1919, Columbia University Library, 97-84261-16, p. 4.

17 Marcel Bois and Frank Jacob (Eds.), Zeiten des Aufruhrs (1916–1921). Globale Proteste, Streiks und Revolutionen gegen den Ersten Weltkrieg und seine Auswirkungen, Berlin 2020. Also see Enrico Dal Lago, Róisín Healy and Gearóid Barry (Eds.), 1916 in Global Context. An Anti-Imperial Moment, London 2018.

18 Derek Heater, National Self-Determination. Woodrow Wilson and His Legacy, New York 1994; Massimo Mori, Friede und Föderalismus bei Kant, in: Zeitschrift für Politik 53 (2006) 4, pp. 379–392, here 379; Giuseppe Bottaro, Internazionalismo e democrazia nella politica estera Wilsoniana, in: Il Politico 72 (2007) 2, pp. 5–23.

19 Walthall, From Private to Public Patriarchy, p. 445.

20 James Chase, The Wilsonian Moment? in: The Wilson Quarterly 25 (2001) 4, pp. 34–41; Christopher Hobson, The Rise of Democracy. Revolution, War and Transformations in International Politics since 1776, Edinburgh 2015, pp. 140–170; Erez Manela, Imagining Woodrow

the events in Korea at the end of and after the First World War will therefore be taken into closer consideration in this chapter. Before that, however, an overview of the history of Japanese imperialism and the extent to which it changed Korean society from the 1870s, and in particular from 1905, will be provided to better contextualize the events of 1919.

4.2 Korea and Japanese Imperialism

In 1876, just about a quarter-century after its own forceful opening, Japan used international law to force Korea to open its borders and become part of the international economic and political system. The year consequently marked an important watershed in Korean history, as it "brought foreign economic and political penetration" and led to the growth of internal tensions because "the increased presence of foreign traders, missionaries, and even military troops provided a target for growing peasant discontent."[21] Although there were debates about reforms in the following years, the monarchy was initially not eager to allow more foreign contacts than necessary, especially since these contacts seemed to threaten not only the traditions within Korea but, first and foremost, the hierarchical order that had shaped the existent society. Young progressives, however, looked to Japan as an example of a successful modernization, i.e. Westernization, and therefore the young intellectuals who had founded the Enlightenment Party (*Kaehwadang*) demanded a similar course in Korean politics. One such intellectual was Park Yung-hyo (1861–1939),[22] who, as Anne Walthall remarks, while staying in Japan, "urged the king to modernize and strengthen Korea and insisted that elevating the status of women was essential to such efforts. He wanted to prohibit spousal abuse, child marriages, and concubinage. Women should be educated by the state, widows should be allowed to remarry, and marriage should be permitted between people of different statuses."[23] The treaty with Japan in 1876 – the so-called Ganghwa Treaty[24] – consequently "opened a Pandora's box of economic, intellectual,

---

Wilson in Asia: Dreams of East-West Harmony and the Revolt against Empire 1919, in: The American Historical Review 111 (2006) 5, pp. 1327–1351; Brad Simpson, The United States and the Curious History of Self-Determination, in: Diplomatic History 36 (2012) 4, pp. 675–694.

21 Michael Edson Robinson, Cultural Nationalism in Colonial Korea, 1920–1925, new edition, Seatlle, WA 2014 [1988], p. 14.

22 Sano-shi kyōdo hakubutsukan (Ed.), Kim Ok-kyun to Paku Yon-hyo wo meguru hitobito, Sano 2016.

23 Walthall, From Private to Public Patriarchy, p. 454.

24 Key-Hiuk Kim, The Last Phase of the East Asian World Order. Korea, Japan, and the Chinese Empire, 1860–1882, Berkeley, CA 1980, pp. 205–209.

political, and cultural forces that ultimately led to the fall of the Chosŏn dynasty"[25] that had ruled Korea since 1392. Although the Korean negotiators of the treaty were under the assumption that they had minimized future foreign influence as far as possible, the changes that followed, especially with regard to the capitalist transformation that would also have a tremendous impact on the country's social structure, would challenge more than just the economic order in Korea. Peasant unrest, also stimulated by anti-foreign sentiments, increased, and Christian missionaries were not only preaching a new religious belief but also acting as cultural mediators.[26] As Michael E. Robinson emphasized, they

> became the first Westerners to systematically study Korean history, culture, and language; their work formed a growing Orientalist literature on Korea, with its curious mixture of exotica, condescension, critique, and praise that subsequently shaped attitudes about Korea in the West for several generations. Mission schools were active in the 1890s and became models for the establishment of secular Korean schools devoted to a nontraditional, Western-studies curriculum, which also appeared in the 1890s. The missionary schools and hospitals attracted Koreans interested in new ideas and institutions.[27]

The rule of the monarchy that had been centralized over the previous centuries and forged a relatively homogenized mass of people now began to be eroded by pressure from without and by subsequent struggles within. The "monarch's authority was, in theory, absolute; his authority was augmented by Confucian ideology, a state orthodoxy that supported a stratified social structure,"[28] but the influx of new ideas that stimulated a debate about the future of Korea did not halt at the dynasty's role. Conflicts between the Korean monarchy and the social elites on the one hand and the masses of the people on the other were consequently intensified by the changes that occurred in the latter part of the 19th century as Japan gradually began to increase its influence and control over its neighbor.

The struggle with modernity within Korea, like in other national contexts, was also one regarding the elite's position and its legitimization. Confucianism, as well as education according to the Chinese classics and Chinese language, were essential for the self understanding of the Korean elites, as the "great houses of the . . . yangban [the gentry of dynastic Korea] followed meticulously formal Confucian family ritual, and relations between yangban families and

---

25 Michael E. Robinson, Korea's Twentieth-Century Odyssey. A Short History, Honolulu, HI 2007, p. 9.
26 Ibid., 9–10.
27 Ibid., 11. On the role of North American missionaries in Korea see Elizabeth Ann Underwood, Challenged Identities. North American Missionaries in Korea, 1884–1934, Seoul 2004.
28 Robinson, Cultural Nationalism, p. 15.

individuals were governed by strict adherence to rules of etiquette strongly influenced by Chinese norms."[29] The values of the elites, however, were, in the years after 1876, challenged by Christian ideas as well as by new religious movements, like the *Donghak* movement (Eastern Learning),[30] which challenged the existent order and led to internal struggles and turmoil in the late 19th century as well. King Kojong (1852–1919) was initially a relatively weak king, and his wife, Empress Myeongseong (1851–1895) – better known as Queen Min in the West –, an ambitious and powerful woman, could not make up for this weakness alone, especially since the king's father, Yi Ha-eung (1820–1898), who had ruled Korea under the title of *Heungseon Daewongun* (Grand Internal Prince Heungseon) between 1864 and 1873, tried to remain in power after his son had reached the age to take over rule from his father.[31] During his reign, however, "the Taewongun failed to redress the original balance of social and political forces that weakened the monarchy,"[32] a fact that weakened the Korean position toward the international menaces that were becoming more and more dangerous. Like Western colonialism in the Americas, the Japanese ambitions were consequently profiting from internal struggles that had been ongoing for several years before the country was eventually opened up to and connected with the existent world order. Furthermore, Korea had to sign a treaty in the tradition of the unequal treaties Japan itself had been trying to revoke since the 1860s as they weakened the international standing of all Asian countries. The fact that Japan used similar methods with regard to Korea already points to the fact that Japan's ambitions in that region were not really driven by Pan-Asianist ideas that considered Japan's Asian neighbors as equals.[33]

---

29 Ibid., 18. The yangban eventually were particularly criticized in nationalist writings, as they were considered to represent the major ills of Korean society. See Andre Schmid, Korea between Empires, 1895–1919, New York 2002, pp. 122–123.

30 Juljan Biontino and Sang-wook Yim, Der Deutsche Bauernkrieg und die "Tonghak Bauernrevolution". Rezeption in Südkorea und Perspektiven des Vergleichs, in: Zeitschrift für Geschichtswissenschaften 66 (2018) 2, pp. 147–166; George L. Kallander, Salvation through Dissent. Tonghak Heterodoxy and Early Modern Korea, Honolulu, HI 2016.

31 On this relationship and see Tatiana M. Simbirtseva, Queen Min of Korea. Coming to Power, in: Transactions of the Royal Asiatic Society, *Korea Branch* 71 (1996), pp. 41–54. On Empress Myeongseong and her role within Korean (foreign) politics see Frank Jacob, Queen Min, Foreign Policy and the Role of Female Leadership in Late Nineteenth-Century Korea, in: Elena Woodacre et al. (Eds.), The Routledge History of Monarchy, London 2019, pp. 700–717.

32 Robinson, Cultural Nationalism, p. 18.

33 Sven Saaler, Pan-Asianism in Modern Japanese History. Colonialism, Regionalism and Borders, London 2009. Pan-Asianist societies, like the Black Ocean Society (*Gen'yōsha*) or the Amur Society (*Kokuryūkai*) shared such an aggressive vision of pan-Asianism under Japanese leadership. On these societies see Frank Jacob, Die Thule-Gesellschaft und die Kokuryūkai.

From a Korean perspective, the danger was obviously downplayed, as its "leaders continued to view these arrangements as secondary to the primary relationship with China. Treaties simply recognized foreign demands, and multiple treaty arrangements balanced foreign powers against each other, thus preserving Korean autonomy."[34] The Korean political leadership simply underestimated the decline of China as the leading regional power and the new role of Japan as its replacement, a change in positions that would become even more obvious during and after the First World War. The opening of Korea intensified the problems the monarchy and the *yangban* had to face, and the foreign powers, first and foremost China and Japan, would use internal turmoil as a reason to intervene in their neighboring country. When a mutiny broke out in 1882 within the Korean Army due to poor pay and other issues within its organizational structure, both foreign powers sent troops to Korea. Due to the quick action of the Chinese, the rebels within the military were suppressed and Kojong was reinstalled in power, and the Treaty of Chemulpo, another unequal treaty with Japan, secured the latter's reimbursement for the destruction of Japanese property and allowed it to station Japanese soldiers in Seoul for the protection of the legation in Korea in the future.[35]

Korean progressives like the already-mentioned Park Yung-hyo and Kim Ok-gyun (1851–1894) were worried about these foreign interventions, and their *Kaehwadang* party tried to stimulate a more reform-oriented course within national politics. They had been influenced by their experiences in Japan, and intellectuals like Fukuzawa Yukichi (1835–1901), "a foremost popularizer of Western thought,"[36] as well as Pan-Asianists like Tōyama Mitsuru (1855–1944), influenced their pro-Japanese- and pro-modernization-oriented arguments.[37] The events of 1882 eventually "turned frustration into despair and desperation,"[38] such that Kim Ok-gyun and his followers began to think a coup was the only possible solution for Korea. The Gapsin Coup of 1884 was the consequence of these thoughts, and the progressives, who were supported by Japanese troops, seized control of

---

Geheimgesellschaften im global-historischen Vergleich, Würzburg 2013 and Frank Jacob, Japanism, Pan-Asianism and Terrorism. A Short History of the Amur Society (the Black Dragons), 1901–1945, Bethesda, CA 2014. There were, however, also Japanese intellectuals that interpreted pan-Asianist ideas from a more equal perspective. See, among others, Miyazaki Tōten, Sanjūsannen no yume, Tokyo 1902.

34 Robinson, Cultural Nationalism, p. 19.

35 Peter Duus, The Abacus and the Sword, paperback edition, Berkeley, CA 1998, p. 69.

36 Robinson, Cultural Nationalism, p. 21.

37 Ōshima Tōto, Tōyama-ō no doko ga erai ka, in: Fujimoto Hisanori (Ed.): Tōyama seishin Tokyo 1940, pp. 82–110.

38 Robinson, Cultural Nationalism, p. 21.

the government in Seoul. The king was kidnapped and some prominent conservatives murdered, but Kim and his men lacked popular support for their act, especially since their coup was publicly perceived as a Japanese plot against Korean independence. The Gapsin Coup failed, and not only did it fail to achieve a true change, but it also "besmirched the image of reform in the eyes of officials and the public alike."[39] Japanese right-wing forces had hoped that similar events would stimulate a crisis in Korea and a war with China, which is why they sent small sabotage units to the peninsula to stir up trouble,[40] but the war between the Middle Kingdom and Japan would not break out until 1894 when a Donghak rebellion shook Korea and forced the monarchy to ask for China's help, an act that allowed Japan to formulate a reason to go to war.[41] During the conflict, however, the Japanese military and other extremists used the opportunity to assassinate Empress Myeongseong, and Kojong had to escape to the Russian legation. While China was defeated in 1895, Russia had expressed its ambitions not only in the Triple Intervention against Japan but also in its support of Kojong, who tried to maneuver between the interests of the two great powers.

After the Sino-Japanese War, Kojong launched the Gwangmu Reform (1897–1904), and its agenda – "old foundation, new participation" (*kubon sinch'am*) – was supposed to bring about reforms without antagonizing the traditionalists too much.

However, it was not only the war between China and Japan that had further weakened Korea, which was already in turmoil before. The Donghak movement had also demanded more equality and was directed toward the strictly hierarchical and patriarchal family structures that existed in the country.[42] While the authorities had been able to repress the movement in the 1860s, in the 1890s, it reappeared stronger than before because economic changes had impoverished many peasants in the previous decades. This is why the Donghak movement, although it was based on religious considerations and motivations, also had a social component that made it attractive to many Koreans at the end of the 19th century. Its leaders had created it as a "syncretic religion combining Confucianism, Buddhism,

---

39 Ibid. On the history and consequences of the Kaspin Coup see Yŏng-ho Ch'oe, The Kapsin Coup of 1884. A Reassessment, in: Korean Studies 6 (1982) 1, pp. 105–124.

40 Jacob, Japanism, pp. 41–54; Miyagawa Gorīsaburō, Ten'yūkyō kyūen no keirinkō, in in: Fujimoto Hisanori (Ed.): Tōyama seishin Tokyo 1940, pp. 117–129; Ōsei Yoshikura, Ten'yūkyō, Tokyo 1981.

41 S.C.M Paine, The Sino-Japanese War of 1894–1895. Perceptions, Power, and Primacy, Cambridge 2003, pp. 109–164.

42 Walthall, From Private to Public Patriarchy, p. 458.

Taoism, and practices of lower-class popular religion,"[43] and they initially demanded reforms while backing the traditional role of the monarchy. When the Donghak movement reappeared in the 1890s, it was far more dangerous to Kojong, which is why he believed he had no other choice than to ask for help from abroad, especially since the demands of the movement were quite revolutionary with regard to the scale of the reforms requested. The issues that needed to be addressed, according to the followers of the movement, were "local governmental corruption, yangban privileges, rural poverty, and the growing foreign presence in Korea."[44] It was the impoverished peasants who flocked to the banners of the movement and made it powerful enough to threaten the political order, which, by asking for foreign help, could neither defend itself against the decline nor prevent Japanese expansionist ambitions from gaining ground on the Korean Peninsula.

There were, of course, also nationalist elements within the Donghak movement, as its name and the reference to the East emphasize. Strong anti-foreign sentiments moved the rural population as much as the increasing poverty they had been suffering from since the opening of Korea in 1876. Such sentiments would continue in the early 20th century, especially when the Righteous Army movements (*ŭibyŏng*, 1905, 1907–11) instrumentalized them against the Japanese. Japan had nevertheless taken advantage of the turmoil and used the Sino-Japanese War to claim special rights in Korea while the prestige of the monarchy further declined.

Regardless of these developments, young reform-oriented intellectuals and progressive officials took the initiative to stimulate further reforms in Korea. In 1896, they founded the Independence Club (*Tongnip hyŏphoe*),[45] which was led by Seo Jae-pil (1864–1951, a.k.a. Philip Jaisohn), a young medical student who had previously been exiled in the United States.[46] While the club was reform-oriented,[47] it was also nationalist in nature and initiated the demand to reform Korea as an empire and make the king its emperor so as to, in a way, gain independence from China and increase the country's status at the same time.[48]

---

43 Robinson, Cultural Nationalism, p. 23.
44 Ibid.
45 Vipan Chandra, Sentiment and Ideology in the Nationalism of the Independence Club (1896–1898), in: Korean Studies 10 (1986), pp. 13–34.
46 So Eung Oh, Dr. Philip Jaisohn's Reform Movement, 1896–1898. A Critical Appraisal of the Independence Club, Lanham, MD 1995; Robinson, Cultural Nationalism, p. 25; Robinson, Korea's Twentieth-Century Odyssey, p. 23.
47 Vipin Chandra, The Independence Club and Korea's First Proposal for a National Legislative Assembly, in: Occasional Papers on Korea 4 (1975), pp. 19–35.
48 Robinson, Cultural Nationalism, pp. 25–26.

Furthermore, the club published *The Independent* (*Tongnip sinmun*), which is "recognized as Korea's first vernacular (Han'gŭl script) newspaper and the first to include a section written in English."[49] The publication was therefore observed with suspicion by conservatives, especially since "classical Chinese had continued as the official court written language as well as the literary language of the yangban," and the use of *han'gŭl* was "controversial, opposed by conservative officials as vulgar and demeaning."[50] Furthermore, the Independence Club and the ideas expressed in *The Independent* were considered to be too radical, even if the members of the club presented themselves as Korean patriots. One could not support the monarchy and debate its policies at the same time. This was unheard of and caused a lot of criticism of and problems for the Independence Club.[51]

Regardless of these issues, the time was ripe for change, and more and more voices began to critically debate the future of Korea. The influx of Western knowledge had stimulated political debates, and study societies opened new spaces for debate about the ideas imported from the West. *The Independent*, regardless of the reactions the publication received from within official circles, paved the way for new journals that allowed young intellectuals to publicly debate their views and ideas while also enabling a growing number of readers to read about them and thereby become part of a wider and more diverse national print culture.

The Capital Daily (*Hwangsong sinmun*), published in a mix of Korean and Chinese, was one of the later successful publication projects between 1898 and the annexation in 1910, although it reached mainly upper- and middle-class intellectuals with its articles about reform ideas. The editorial board had prominent intellectuals as members, including the historian Chang Chi-yŏn (1864–1921) and the anarchist and historian Shin Chae-ho (1880–1936).[52] The "first truly mass publication in Korea,"[53] however, was the *Korea Daily News* (*Taehan maeil sinbo*), which was published in higher numbers, distributed all over the country, and thereby "shared a large role in enlightening the people and inspiring a patriotic fervor."[54] In addition to these daily newspapers, "[s]mall specialized magazines augmented

---

49 Mark E. Caprio, Marketing Assimilation. The Press and the Formation of the Japanese-Korean Colonial Relationship, The Journal of Korean Studies 16 (2011) 1, pp. 1–25, here p. 3.
50 Robinson, Cultural Nationalism, p. 26.
51 Ibid.
52 Yŏng-ho Ch'oe, An Outline History of Korean Historiography, in: Korean Studies 4 (1980), pp. 1–27.
53 Robinson, Cultural Nationalism, p. 29.
54 Chai-Shin Yu, A New History of Korean Civilization, Bloomington, IN 2012, p. 211.

the growth of the Korean press after 1900. These magazines focused on discussions of Western thought, translations of Western classical literature and political philosophy, and treatises on educational reform."[55] Journals were published by political societies, like the Korea Self-Strengthening Society (*Taehan cha'gan-ghoe*)[56] and other academic societies with a broad variety of topics. These publications helped to strengthen Korean nationalism as well, as they increased the existence of a sense of national belonging and created what Benedict Anderson named an "imagined community."[57] The new publications and the growing print capitalism helped to link intellectuals across the country, and the "growing nationalist intelligentsia"[58] would spread new ideas about the Korean nation in their spheres of influence. There were, of course, also debates about the right course for reforms. While the younger intellectuals often preferred a radical break with the past and traditions, more moderate voices argued on behalf of a symbiosis of Korean traditions and Western knowledge, something that was quite similar to the debates in China and Japan in the last decades of the 19th century.

A break with the past, however, could be observed in Korea with regard to education, since private schools boomed after 1900 and former students who returned from their study stays abroad, especially from Japan, opened such schools and taught according to radically different curricula. The intellectual Park Eun-sik (1859–1925), who would also write a history of the March First Movement,[59] "stressed the importance of instilling in students a new sense of cultural and social responsibility as a prerequisite to creating new citizens (*sinmin*). The new citizens would have an appreciation of science as well as a deep understanding of the Korean cultural and historical experience. It was important to galvanize identification with the nation or the fruits of the new education would be wasted."[60] Like in every other national context, the Koreans had to come to terms with regard to their own idea of a nation, and multiple positions and thoughts in the late 19th and early 20th centuries were struggling to define what was considered the ideal nation for Korea. It is almost tragic that this debate was being led while the Japanese continued to erode the existence of the Korean state, and thus the independent nation-state could not be created for another three and a half decades. The struggle between the nationalist

---

55 Robinson, Cultural Nationalism, p. 28. Robinson, Cultural Nationalism, p. 29.
56 The journal was called Taehan Chaganghoe wŏlbo.
57 Benedict Anderson, Imagined Communities. Reflections on the Origin and Spread of Nationalism, London 1983.
58 Robinson, Cultural Nationalism, p. 29.
59 Park Eun-sik, Han'guk tongnip undong chi hyŏlsa, Shanghai 1920.
60 Robinson, Cultural Nationalism, p. 30.

modernizers and reformers on the one hand and the traditionalist and conservative elites on the other eventually weakened the Korean position as it prevented unity. Some intellectuals cited Japan as a successful model of a combination of Western knowledge and Asian traditions, but although Western ideas were sometimes presented as being close to Confucian ideals, they were not convincing enough to create a powerful symbiosis that could attract the approval of the wider public. Ultimately, there was maybe just not enough time to find an answer, and Japan was the winner in this situation.

With its victory against Russia in 1905, and although the military victories on the battlefields and on the seas[61] were not turned into a diplomatic victory during the peace negotiations in Portsmouth, New Hampshire,[62] Japan was able to establish a kind of protectorate in Korea, and it used its influence to force Kojong to abdicate in 1907.[63] It was the Japanese victory that "ultimately determined the fate of the dynasty," and the Korean state "became a Japanese diplomatic dependency with no rights of self-representation in the world system."[64] With its international alliances and diplomatic agreements, such as the Anglo-Japanese Alliance (1902)[65] or the Taft-Katsura Agreement (1905),[66] Japan had secured its uncontested influence on the Korean Peninsula, and, after 1905, the Japanese resident-general would secure particular influence on the country's politics.[67] Kojong's protest against his forced abdication at the international court in The Hague did not result in any anti-Japanese protest or action from the international community, and when his son was installed as the new emperor in Seoul, it was the Japanese colonial authorities that used the

---

61 Frank Jacob, Tsushima 1905. Ostasiens Trafalgar, second edition, Paderborn 2021.

62 Jacob, Russo-Japanese War, pp. 90–113.

63 Todd A. Henry, Assimilating Seoul. Japanese Rule and the Politics of Public Space in Colonial Korea, 1910–1945, Los Angeles, CA 2014, p. 28.

64 Robinson, Korea's Twentieth-Century Odyssey, p. 12.

65 Ian Nish, The Anglo-Japanese Alliance. The Diplomacy of Two Island Empires, 1894–1907, London 1966.

66 Kirk W. Larsen and Joseph Seeley, Simple Conversation or Secret Treaty? The Taft-Katsura Memorandum in Korean Historical Memory, in: Journal of Korean Studies 19 (2014) 1, pp. 59–92. Also see Seung-young Kim, American Diplomacy and Strategy toward Korea and Northeast Asia 1882–1950 and After. Perception of Polarity and US Commitment to a Periphery, London 2009, pp. 13–66.

67 Mizuno Naoki, Shokuminchi Chōsen ni okeru Itō Hirobumi no kioku. Keijō no Hakubunji wo chūshin ni, in: Itō Yukio and I Sunhan (Eds.), Itō Hirobumi to Kankoku tōchi. Shodai Kankoku tōkan wo meguru hyakunenme no kenshō, Tokyo 2009, pp. 212–215. For Itō's vita see Kurokawa Hidenori, Nihon no dai-seijika. Itō Hirobumi mo, Chōsenjin ni totte ha gokuakunin datta! in: Kaku Kōzō (Ed.), Nihonshi jinbutsu "sono go no hanashi", fourth edition, Tokyo 1996, pp. 312–313; Takii Kazuhiro, Itō Hirobumi. Chi no seijika, Tokyo 2010, pp. 372–376.

boy to further intensify their control within Korea. In addition, Tokyo could also rely on pro-Japanese organizations like the *Iljinhoe* (Progress Party) that supported the idea of a "unification" with Japan.[68] Arguments were made on behalf of Japanese interventions with regard to the idea of necessary reforms in Korea, which is why the historical developments thereby further discredited the radical reform movement, as reforms in general came to be identified with Japanese aggression.

However, there was also resistance against the increasing Japanese influence and their tightened political grip on the monarchy and government in Seoul. Intellectuals would use the new print media to speak out against Japanese expansionism, and the above-mentioned Righteous Armies, i.e. small guerilla bands, were formed to fight against the Japanese police and military forces that had been stationed in the country. Between 1907 and 1911, the Japanese Army and the police exerted some amount of effort to deal with these nationalist elements in Korea, but the final annexation of the country could not be prevented.[69] This, however, does not mean that other forms of resistance against the developments in the aftermath of the Russo-Japanese War did not exist. The *Korea Daily News*, whose non-Korean editor Ernest Bethell (1872–1909)[70] could not be censored so easily by the Japanese authorities, could express criticism, at least for some years, before new publication laws prevented this critical voice against Japan from continuing its work.[71] However, with the steady intensification of Japanese rule in Korea, the nationalist reform movement went through a transformation, and in 1910, it turned into an independence movement directed against Japan. The latter's control over the peninsula was nevertheless made possible because there were also forces at work in Korea that collaborated with the Japanese authorities. The old elites, namely the royal and *yangban* families, were bought by stipends, and other collaborators received privileges or other forms of advantages within the new political order, which was increasingly centralized and occupied by representatives of the Japanese colonial government. When Resident-General Itō Hirobumi (1841–1909) was assassinated by a Korean nationalist, the Japanese finally had a suitable reason to formalize their colonial rule, and they annexed the country to become part of the Japanese Empire. On 22 August 1910, Japanese Resident-General Terauchi

---

68 William G. Beasley, Japanese Imperialism 1894–1945, Oxford 1987, p. 90; Jacob, Japanism, pp. 81–82.
69 Robinson, Cultural Nationalism, p. 38.
70 Joohyun Jade Park, Journalism behind Bars. Bethell's Anti-Japanese English-Korean Newspapers, in: Victorian Periodicals Review 51 (2018) 1, pp. 86–120.
71 Robinson, Cultural Nationalism, p. 38.

Masatake (1852–1919) and the Korean Prime Minister Yi Wan-yong (1858–1926) signed the official Treaty of Annexation,[72] which "further stipulated that the Japanese government assumed control of Korea's administration."[73]

At the same time, Koreans were turned into Japanese citizens, and although many left the country to escape Japanese rule, they would indirectly become agents of Japanese imperialism when the expansionists in Tokyo demanded that the borders be pushed into regions where Koreans – who, after 1910, were Japanese citizens – were living.[74] The American press at that time did not protest a lot but rather considered this step quite natural, especially since the Treaty of Portsmouth a couple of years earlier seemed to have prepared for precisely such a step. Considering the already-mentioned agreements with Western powers, Japan was assumably acting within the limits of its internationally accepted capacity.[75] The hope for foreign support was useless, as Kim Sik-hun, a Korean diplomat who was quite familiar with American politics due to his service in Washington, DC, remarked in an interview with the *New York Times*: "Everywhere, he says, there is a patriotic uprising burning fiercely despite frequent defeat of the Koreans by the better-equipped Japanese soldiers, and kept aflame by the hope that in the near future Japan will find herself with a more powerful enemy on her hands, when Korea can regain her 4,243-year-old independence and throw off the yoke of annexation."[76] Since nobody would interfere with Japanese imperialism in 1910, the outlook for Korea was rather hopeless. The country was also supposed to be Japanized according to an assimilation program, which was announced soon after the annexation was formalized. Korea, as mentioned earlier, was not only supposed to act as a colony for exploitation but was also to be transformed into an important part of the Japanese Empire.[77] Terauchi Masatake, who acted as the country's first governor-general after the annexation process had been formalized, therefore

---

72 The treaty's text can be found at https://international.ucla.edu/institute/article/18447. Accessed My 30, 2022.

73 Juergen Kleiner, Korea. A Century of Change, London et al. 2001, p. 29.

74 One of these regions was Manchuria. Frank Jacob, The Korean Diaspora in Manchuria. Korean Ambitions, Manchurian Dreams, Japanese Realities, in: Entremons UPF Journal of World History 6 (2014), pp. 1–11; Frank Jacob, Reflections on the Korean Diaspora in Manchuria, in: Florian Kläger and Klaus Stierstorfer (Eds.): Diasporic Constructions of Home and Belonging, Berlin 2015, pp. 111–122.

75 E. Taylor Atkins, Primitive Selves. Koreana in the Japanese Colonial Gaze, 1910–1945, Berkeley, CA 2010, p. 13.

76 Cited in ibid., p. 14.

77 Kleiner, Korea, p. 30.

"noted the close proximity, shared culture, and ethnic origins shared by Japan and Korea as proof of the possibility of eventual assimilation."[78]

The newly appointed governor-general was supposed to be assisted in his work, and for this purpose, "[s]ix central offices which functioned like ministries were established: for General, Home, Financial, Agricultural, Commercial and Industrial as well as Judicial Affairs."[79] With the annexation, the number of Japanese settlers and officials in Korea grew as well (Table 4.1).

Table 4.1: Number of Japanese living in Korea.[80]

Year	Number of Japanese
1910	171,500
1920	347,900
1939	650,100

At the same time, the number of policemen increased as well (Table 4.2), especially since the police force was turned into the "main instrument of Japanese control in Korea."[81]

Table 4.2: Number of policemen in colonial Korea.[82]

Year	Number of Policemen
1910	7,712
1918	14,358
1922	20,771
1937	20,647

Regardless of the strict and close control of life in colonial Korea, the resistance against Japanese rule on the peninsula did not totally vanish. However, it was at the end of the First World War when massive resistance erupted and thereby created a real stress test for the Japanese authorities in the colony. How the latter tried to assimilate the Korean population in the years between 1910 and the First World War will now be taken into closer consideration.

---

78 Robinson, Cultural Nationalism, p. 40.
79 Kleiner, Korea, p. 30.
80 Ibid., p. 31.
81 Ibid.
82 Ibid. and Chung-Shin Park, Protestantism and Politics in Korea, Seattle, WA 2003, p. 129.

4.3 Colonial Korea until the First World War

The first decade after the annexation by Japan is usually referred to as the "dark period,"[83] in which the Korean population, its traditions, its culture, and their national sense of being an independent people were suppressed by Japanese force. Yong-Chool Ha has emphasized that it is not easy to generalize the colonial experience of the Korean people, which is why he remarked that "in understanding colonial society it is essential to see the inherent contradictions created by the conflicting needs of colonial rule and the intersectoral imbalance or disequilibrium arbitrarily imposed by colonial control."[84] Ha further stressed that "essential elements of Japanese colonialism in Korea include foreign dominance, in which the domestic and numerical majority is controlled by a foreign and numerical minority with the intent of economic and strategic exploitation based on an overwhelming disparity in coercive force."[85] According to Ha's further elaboration, the Japanese tried to fully control the "Colonial Superstructural Space," which is to be understood as "the space in which the colonial authority attempts, within the inevitable constraints of material possibility, to establish its hegemony over the colonized and to inaugurate institutional, societal, and ideological arrangements to implement and maintain such hegemony."[86] A centralized and omnipotent bureaucracy was one aspect of this attempt, while the cultural assimilation of the Korean people, who had to speak Japanese, worship the emperor, and give up their own national identity, was a demanded consequence. In this regard, Japan was simply "aggressive, colonizing, and rapacious"[87] when satisfying its own cravings for expansion at the expense of its East Asian neighbors.[88]

In 1910, the power struggle for Korea was decided when Japan won against its competitors, i.e. China and Russia. Due to its military victories in 1895 and 1905, Japan had secured its power on the peninsula and could now exert it without any foreign intervention. The relationship between the two countries

---

83 Robinson, Cultural Nationalism, p. 42.
84 Yong-Chool Ha, Colonial Rule and Social Change in Korea. The Paradox of Colonial Control, in: Hong Yung Lee, Yong-Chool Ha and Clark W. Sorensen (Eds.), Colonial Rule and Social Change in Korea, 1910–1945, Seattle, WA 2013, pp. 39–75, here p. 39.
85 Ibid., p. 43.
86 Ibid., p. 47.
87 Sang-Kyung Kwak and Hun-Chang Lee, Conditions of Economic Devvelopment in Korea in the First Half of the Twentieth Century, in: Aiko Ikeo (Ed.), Economic Development in Twentieth-Century East Asia. The International Context, London/New York 1997, pp. 75–85, here p. 75.
88 Jinwung Kim, A History of Korea. From "Land of the Morning Calm" to States in Conflict, Bllomington, IN 2012, p. 321.

was consequently marked by a sense of Japanese entitlement regarding the inclusion of the Korean territory in its future Asian Empire. Although generalizing the economic developments in Korea is not recommended, in many ways, "Japan had a one-way economic relationship with Korea and the utilization of human and nonhuman resources was designed for the purpose of Japanese national strategy. Any economic relationships between Korea and Japan were focused on Japanese policy."[89] The colonial government and the authorities that represented it were therefore acting in Seoul on behalf of orders that were supposed to serve Tokyo more than the Korean population.[90] Regardless of these imperialist realities, the Japanese would argue that their actions were for the greater good of Korea. Considering these issues, it is tragic that the Korean attempts to modernize the country in the late 19th century failed, as this failure was also responsible for the internal weakness that made the aggressive moves of the Japanese possible. After 1910, however, the lives of the Korean people would be tremendously transformed, yet this transformation would no longer follow a genuine Korean interest.

The colonial government was probably the most intense and thorough form of foreign penetration in the long and brutal history of colonialism and imperialist expansion, as every angle of the Korean society was penetrated by the new ruling power. Michael E. Robinson highlighted in this regard that, "[n]ot content with simple compliance, the colonial state not only dominated Korea following the usual paternalistic logic of colonialists, but they also believed they could actually 'assimilate' Koreans culturally."[91] Using their experience from Taiwan,[92] the Japanese colonizers had a clear agenda to follow, and the authorities also "mobilized archeology, ethnography, and historical studies to justify their rule in Korea as a matter of lifting up a wayward sibling culture and returning it to its proper course as part of the destiny of the Yamato race."[93] As "the first steward of the state-building process as governor general,"[94] Terauchi was in a powerful position and willing to do everything necessary to fulfill the ambitions of Imperial Japan and the people that represented it. Appointed from

89 Kwak and Lee, Conditions, p. 76.
90 Kim, A History of Korea, p. 322.
91 Robinson, Korea's Twentieth-Century Odyssey, p. 36.
92 Leo T. S. Ching, Becoming "Japanese". Colonial Taiwan and the Politics of Identity Formation, Berkeley, CA 2001; Chih-Ming Ka, Japanese Colonialism in Taiwan. Land Tenure, Development, and Dependency, 1895–1945, London 2019; Ping-hui Liao and David Der-Wei Wang (Eds.), Taiwan Under Japanese Colonial Rule, 1895–1945. History, Culture, Memory, New York, NY 2010.
93 Robinson, Korea's Twentieth-Century Odyssey, p. 36.
94 Ibid., p. 37.

high army ranks – only Saitō Makoto (1858–1936), who served in this position between 1919 and 1927 as well as between 1929 and 1931, was an admiral in the Japanese navy before –, the governor-general was supposed to act under the supervision of the Diet, the Home Ministry, and the Ministry of Colonial Affairs, although the governor-general reported directly to the emperor and could thereby circumvent any form of political control.[95] The governor-general had a powerful position beyond his political might because he ruled over more than 20 million subjects, could collect and control taxes, was the commander of the Japanese Army and police in Korea, and directed the actions of the thousands of bureaucrats who kept the machinery of colonial control running.

After the annexation, the main task was to keep the peninsula pacified and to avoid the eruption of any nationalist or anti-Japanese protests. Once the guerilla bands of the Righteous Army were suppressed and the former elites sufficiently heavily bribed, the colonial government could rule relatively uncontested. Due to "a blatantly fabricated plot to assassinate the governor general in 1911,"[96] the Japanese arrested around 700 Koreans, though only around 100 were eventually prosecuted, and just five were sentenced to spend 5–10 years in prison. This was "the first major political show trial in the colony" and highlighted how easy it was to bring people to trial. The police in Korea also acted relatively brutally, and, together with a "rigid, highly intrusive administrative colonialism,"[97] they turned the life of the common people into one marked by agony and fear. The police and other representatives of the colonial government, as Robinson points out,

> counted everything and created a myriad of regulations governing daily life from slaughtering a worn-out draft animal to the placement of a family grave; they established new land and family registers, health regulations, detailed sanitation procedures in the reorganized city administrations, fishery regulations, rules governing water rights and irrigation ditches, standard operating procedures for periodic markets, and licenses and permission forms for just about everything else. The gendarmerie – swords dangling from the men's uniforms as symbols of their authority – was given summary powers to enforce the regulations.[98]

At the same time, the legal regulations and punishments for Koreans and Japanese who lived in Korea were different, e.g. with regard to whipping, which was only used as a punishment for the former group. Public resistance was no longer possible, and organizations like the New People's Association (*Sinminhoe*), which was organized by the intellectuals and social activists Shin Chae-

---

95 Ibid.
96 Ibid., p. 38.
97 Ibid.
98 Ibid.

ho, An Chang-ho (1878–1938), Park Eun-sik, and Lim Chi-jung (1880–1932), had to go into hiding and continue their activities in secret. It was through educational means in particular that the association members tried to forge new nationalist leaders for the future struggle against the Japanese, but their work was not easy in the colonial environment.[99] In the years after 1910, more and more Koreans were consequently imprisoned by the Japanese authorities because the latter feared a spread of Korean nationalism and anti-Japanese sentiments across the peninsula (Table 4.3).

Table 4.3: The number of imprisoned Koreans in the period 1911–1916.[100]

Year	Number of Imprisoned Koreans
1911	16,807
1912	19,494
1913	21,846
1914	24,434
1915	27,255
1916	32,836

Since, during the "dark period," Koreans were not allowed to join any political organization or spend time engaged in activities that could be interpreted politically, religious institutions and churches, e.g. the Protestant Church, whose missionaries would also link Korea to the outside world during the First World War,[101] became important spaces for political activism. Because the Japanese had divided the colony into 13 provinces and a large number of colonial bureaucrats and officers administered them locally, divided into cities and counties, there were not many alternatives left for the Korean population to organize or exchange anti-Japanese thoughts.[102] To avoid any threatening resistance, the Japanese decision-makers also sent additional troops to the colony over the years to tighten their grip there. It is therefore not surprising that Koreans abroad, in the United States but also in Japan, would play an important role in

---

99 For a discussion of Shin Chae-ho's nationalist interpretations see Michael Robinson, National Identity and the Thought of Sin Ch'aeho. Sadaejuŭi and Chuch'e in History and Politics, in: The Journal of Korean Studies 5 (1984), pp. 121–142.
100 Park, Protestantism, p. 130.
101 A. Hamish Ion, The Cross and the Rising Sun, vol. 2: The British Protestant Movement in Japan, Korea and Taiwan, 1865–1945, Waterloo, ON 2009, pp. 100–104.
102 Kim, A History of Korea, p. 322.

the spread of nationalist ideas and the organization of Korean resistance, which in a way culminated in March 1919.[103]

The economic structure of Korea was also adjusted to fit the Japanese demands.[104] To see how the Japanese changed the structures within the country, it is important to take a short look at the land allotment schemes that existed before the opening of Korea and its annexation by Japan. It has been assumed that, in the 17th and 18th centuries, "about 10% of the landholders owned 40% to 50% of the registered land, while middle or poor peasants comprising about 60% of the rural population controlled only about 10% to 20%."[105] The larger landowners were, of course, *yangban*, whose social status was closely linked to their possessions. While per capita landholding during the later years of the Chosŏn dynasty had declined, peasants avoided poverty through "crop specialization, technological innovation, and labor intensification."[106] The opening of Korea changed this situation, as export markets were now dictating domestic demands, and rice and beans became the dominant crops in Korean fields, as they "constituted more than 60% of total exports in the late nineteenth and early twentieth centuries."[107] Before 1905, Japanese economic interests had already influenced the Korean agricultural setting considerably,[108] but after 1900, and especially after 1910, the colonial interests of Japan would tremendously alter the existent land tenure structures and decrease the percentage of land that was actually owned by Koreans.

The Japanese authorities had already tried to take possession of Korean lands before the official annexation but met fierce resistance. With the official "integration" of Korea into the Japanese Empire, however, the governor-general simply confiscated large parts of public land and farmland (around 65,000 acres) as well as forests (around 45,000 acres).[109] Consequently, the colonial annexation was accompanied by a "real land grab"[110] since the Japanese also took control of the Royal Household's land possessions. Many of the new lands were handed over to "Korean investors and private land companies such as the

---

103 Kenneth M. Wells, Background to the March First Movement. Koreans in Japan, 1905–1919, in: Korean Studies 13 (1989), pp. 5–21.

104 Kim, A History of Korea, p. 324.

105 Gi-Wook Shin, Peasant Protest and Social Change in Colonial Korea, Seattle, WA 1996, p. 22.

106 Ibid., p. 25. Cotton, tobacco, silk, ginseng and other commercial crops were grown as a consequence.

107 Ibid., p. 28.

108 Karl Moskowitz, The Creation of the Oriental Development Company. Japanese Illusions Meet Korean Reality, in: Occasional Papers on Korea 2 (1974), pp. 73–121, here p. 77.

109 Kim, A History of Korea, p. 324.

110 Robinson, Korea's Twentieth-Century Odyssey, p. 40.

Fuji Land Company or the huge semigovernmental Oriental Development Company."[111] From its start, the Japanese colonial policy was consequently determined by the economic interests of Japanese investment companies as well. The loss of large parts of public land, the increased population, and volatile rice prices harshened the lives of many Korean peasants in the following years, such that, "[b]y the end of the colonial period, tenancy rates approached 80 percent in the densely populated and most productive rice-growing areas of the Cholla provinces in the southwest. And many peasants chose to leave the land altogether, ending up in the cities in search of jobs."[112] The new system of land possession and capitalist-oriented agriculture provided numerous advantages for landowners, which is why the *yangban* naturally supported, or at least did not resist, the Japanese measures. The farmers' voices were simply not heard, and the *yangban* maintained their position as the main landowning class in the new colonial order.[113]

With their control of the forests, mines, and fisheries established, the Japanese could also begin to effectively exploit Korea's resources, and they would soon also have tight control over the industrial sector and finances on the peninsula. The forests were of particular interest, which is why in May 1918, according to a new law, all forest owners had to register their possessions, and all former forest lands that had been owned by the Korean state were officially seized and became the property of the governer-general.[114] Eventually, the colonial authorities took over more than 50% of the forests and farmland and thereby physically controlled the country.[115] When Japanese companies lumbered large quantities of wood in the areas around the Yalu and Tumen rivers in the north of the country, the profits from the forests went to these companies as well.[116] Similar developments can be observed with regard to the exploitation of the vast Korean fishing grounds. In 1912, "the vast fishing grounds, held formerly by the Chosŏn royal household and private Koreans, were placed under the administration of the Government-General. The colonial government encouraged Japanese fishermen to immigrate to Korea."[117] With the more sophisticated Japanese fishing

---

111 Ibid.
112 Ibid.
113 Kim, A History of Korea, p. 325.
114 Ibid., p. 326.
115 For a detailed study of Japan's policies regarding the Korean forests see David Fedman, Seeds of Control. Japan's Empire of Forestry in Colonial Korea, Seattle, WA 2020.
116 The Japanese interest in the forests in the northern peninsula was not new. See United States Bureau of Manufactures (Ed.), Monthy Consular and Trade Reports 86, Washington, D.C. 1908, pp. 91–92.
117 Kim, A History of Korea, p. 326.

techniques, the number of fish that could be taken out of Korean waters increased tremendously, but the fishing grounds were systematically overfished, and the Japanese colonial policy thereby also harmed the ecosystem within the borders of the former Korean waters.

The mineral resources in the north of Korea were similarly exploited by Japanese mining companies, but these acts were legalized by a mining ordinance in December 1915. The profits went to Japanese *zaibatsu* like Mitsui, which had almost unlimited access to Korean ores.[118] Although attempts to relativize the economic gains colonialism created for Japan have been made, it can be said without any doubt that the Korean colony was exploited in numerous ways for the sake of Japanese prosperity in the first half of the 20th century.[119] The finance sector was also regulated by a new Company Law (1910), and a close surveillance of the banks – including the Bank of Chōsen, which was supposed to become the colony's central banking institution, and the Chōsen Industrial Bank – secured the financing of projects related to the colony's infrastructure, like building railways, as well as ventures that would stimulate further Japanese expansion toward the north, especially in Manchuria.[120]

As this short survey has already shown, "[v]irtually all industries were monopolized either by Japanese-based corporations or by Japanese corporations in Korea."[121] and access to natural resources and financial transactions was tightly controlled and increasingly limited for Koreans, whose enterprises were closely monitored by the Japanese colonial authorities as well. Without the approval of the latter, a new company could not be founded, and Korean economic activities were thereby systematically limited and even purposefully underdeveloped. Considering underdevelopment an essential aspect of colonial rule, Japan's hold over Korea was consequently similar to those of Western

---

118 Ibid.

119 Mitsuhiko Kimura, The Economics of Japanese Imperialism in Korea, 1910–1939, in: The Economic History Review 48 (1995) 3, pp. 555–574.

120 Robinson, Korea's Twentieth-Century Odyssey, p. 41. Also see Herbert P. Bix, Japanese Imperialism and the Manchurian Economy, 1900–31, in: The China Quarterly 51 (1972), pp. 425–443. Japan had actively applied a form of "railway imperialism." See Janet Hunter, Japanese Government Policy, Business Opinion and the Seoul–Pusan Railway, 1894–1906, in: Modern Asian Studies 11 (1977) 4, pp. 573–599; Jun Uchida, "A Scramble for Freight". The Politics of Collaboration along and across the Railway Tracks of Korea under Japanese Rule, in: Comparative Studies in Society and History 51 (2009) 1, pp. 117–150. More broadly on the "brokers of empire," see Jun Uchida, Brokers of Empire. Japanese Settler Colonialism in Korea, 1876–1945, Cambridge, MA 2011.

121 Kim, A History of Korea, p. 326.

imperialist powers in their respective colonies.[122] It is therefore hardly surprising that more than 90% of all invested capital in Korea was in Japanese hands, which is why arguments setting out the positive impact of Japanese colonialism on Korea's development – e.g. the increase of railroad lines from 677 miles in 1911 to 1,777 miles in 1930 – often seem to be quite absurd and only serve to relativize the abuse of power to exploit the peninsula for the sake of Japanese imperialism and the building of an East Asian empire.[123] The railways in particular served the interest of the colonial government, as they 1) linked the southern ports with the northern production and mining sites and 2) allowed troop transports that would be essential for further Japanese expansion toward the north.[124]

However, there was not only an economic side to Japanese colonialism in Korea. "After the annexation of Korea, the Japanese were ever sensitive to the education of the Koreans"[125] to assimilate the Korean population as well as possible. Robinson clearly emphasized the Japanese aims in this regard when he stated that "[f]rom the beginning of their colonial rule, the Japanese had intended that Korea would not be absorbed just politically by the empire but that it would also be culturally assimilated (dōka), to become one with Japan in all respects."[126] To secure "one voice" with regard to the intellectual and educational efforts aimed at the Korean population, the Japanese authorities limited the accessibility of information by issuing a Newspaper Law and a Publication Law in 1907 and 1909, respectively. Once the annexation was completed, access to any kind of unfiltered information became more and more restricted, and, as mentioned before, religious organizations and meetings remained the only space for Koreans' political activism. The colonial government also built large Shintō shrines in Korean cities to prepare for the locals' assimilation on this level as well, although this policy did not go uncontested. The cultural assimilation policy was also expressed by architectural changes when the former capital of the Korean dynasty was turned into a modern city space that was supposed to echo Japanese achievements.[127]

---

122 Christopher Chase-Dunn, Jackie Smith, Patrick Manning and Andrej Grubačić, Remembering Immanuel Wallerstein, in: Journal of World-Systems Research 26 (2020) 1, pp. 5–8, here p. 5. For theoretical considerations and reflections about colonial underdevelopment also see Walter Rodney, How Europe Underdeveloped Africa, Washington, D.C. 1982, pp. 1–30.
123 Kim, A History of Korea, p. 327.
124 Robinson, Korea's Twentieth-Century Odyssey, p. 43.
125 Kim, A History of Korea, p. 328.
126 Robinson, Korea's Twentieth-Century Odyssey, p. 43.
127 Henry, Assimilating Seoul, pp. 1 and 29.

Step by step, the intention was to reinterpret Korean national history such that it would fit better with the Japanese narratives of unity and pan-Asian solidarity, although the latter were exclusively understood according to their pro-Japanese interpretation. Between 1932 and 1937, a multi-volume *History of Korea* (*Chōsenshi*) was published, and, according to Robinson, it "rewrote the entire history of the peninsula into an elaborate justification of colonial rule."[128] Korean historians and intellectuals tried to counter such reinterpretations, but they often did not have the means or the access to the popular audiences to actively resist Japan's attempt to rewrite Korea's past in the name of its future assimilation. For the colonial administration, the task was to foster the acceptance of the idea that the Japanese policy in Korea was for the greater good of its people. According to their narrative, "[a]n incompetent Korean government had stifled Korean potential," but now, "[p]lacing the people under a benevolent government would allow them to realize their potential."[129] Regardless of such assumptions, there were also debates about the proper assimilation policies and the overall potential for such a task to be successful. The Japanese ethnohistorian Kita Sadakichi (1871–1939),[130] who was tied to the Ministry of Education, compared the Koreans to the Ainu[131] and argued that "assimilation was appropriate because it represented a return to the historical, and natural, relationship that the two peoples once shared."[132]

While those in favor of a fast assimilation process were particularly fond of their position and had high hopes after 1910, as this task could now be taken into full consideration by the colonial authorities, there were also those who cautioned against moving too fast, warning that "[d]espite the apparent ease that Japanese imagined in the people's assimilation, Koreans would first have to demonstrate their ability to rise to Japanese standards before they could be accepted into their inner circles."[133] After the Second World War, the historian Hatada Takashi (1908–1994) remarked in relation to Japan's assimilation attempts that

128 Robinson, Korea's Twentieth-Century Odyssey, p. 44.

129 Mark E. Caprio, Japanese Assimilation Policies in Colonial Korea, 1910–1945, Seattle, WA 2009, p. 81.

130 Etsuko H. Kang, Kita Sadakichi (1871–1939) on Korea. A Japanese Ethno-Historian and the Annexation of Korea in 1910, in: Asian Studies Review 21 (1997) 1, pp. 41–60.

131 The indigenous people of Japan that had been forcefully assimilated. Brett L. Walker, The Conquest of Ainu Lands. Ecology and Culture in Japanese Expansion, 1590–1800, Berkeley, CA 2009; Sasaki Toshikazu, Ainu shi no jidai he. Yoreki shō, Sapporo 2013.

132 Caprio, Japanese Assimilation Policies, p. 83.

133 Ibid., 85.

[d]espite the rhetoric of Korean-Japanese similarity provided by participants in the debate over assimilation policy, those painting images of Koreans portrayed the people in terms only slightly more encouraging than those that predated annexation. Koreans remained an underdeveloped people trapped in the distant past, a spiritless people in desperate need of enlightened government to awaken them to present reality. While some saw potential in the Korean people, the views of difference in others hardened as they observed one of the results of annexation: Japanese and Koreans residing in closer proximity.[134]

Some Japanese also had doubts about Koreans' rapid assimilation, since they were considered to be too different for immediate success in this regard. The politician Arakawa Gorō (1865–1944) had warned in 1906 that although Koreans "all look just like the Japanese," they would not match the intellectual level of their Japanese neighbors.[135]

The Japanese education policy in colonial Korea was consequently oriented toward achieving an assimilation in the future, and "Japanese reformers and educators thus sought to reorganize Korean education around a new pedagogy founded on moral instruction and disciplinary techniques"[136] that addressed the demands and regulations of Imperial Ordinance No. 229 of August 1911. Terauchi requested the schools in Korea to be classified according to three levels or categories, namely *futsū* (common), *jitsugyō* (industrial), and *senmon* (specialized).[137] Boys and girls would spend four years in primary education and four and three years, respectively, in a secondary educational institution after that. Koreans and Japanese were also separated within the schools, and only the latter could also send their children to Japan to get schooled there. In 1911, school textbooks were sanctioned and needed to be pre-approved by the colonial government to ensure the accuracy of the content that was being taught. The educational experiences of many Korean children and youths were consequently tremendously impacted by the colonial reality: "Japanese language study was compulsory in all accredited schools, and the Korean secondary system stressed vocational and technical education. The only higher liberal arts education available to Koreans was in private religious or secular colleges; in short, opportunities for Koreans in Korea to study law, medicine, engineering, and the humanities remained very limited."[138] Only a few Korean students

---

134 Cited in ibid., p. 89. Also see Takashi Hatada, Nihon to chōsen, Tokyo 1965.
135 Cited in ibid., p. 92.
136 Theodore Jun Yoo, The Politics of Gender in Colonial Korea. Education, Labor, and Health, 1910–1945, Berkeley, CA 2008, p. 61. On a discussion of the Japanese education policy in colonial Korea also see Caprio, Japanese Assimilation Policies, pp. 92–100.
137 Yoo, The Politics of Gender, p. 61.
138 Robinson, Korea's Twentieth-Century Odyssey, p. 45.

could afford to enroll in higher education institutions in Japan or other foreign countries, although the Korean independence movement would later especially rely on these students who had been part of the national diaspora abroad.

The reasons to leave Korea were numerous, but white-collar professions in particular were hardly accessible for Koreans because the financial sector, trading companies, public schools, railways, and the colonial bureaucracy were mostly dominated by Japanese or at least pro-Japanese personnel. In addition, a secondary degree of Japanese provenance was often necessary to have the possibility to work in one of these jobs. The small Korean elite was consequently kept that way through educational means.[139] One could consequently argue that the nationalist and anti-Japanese eruption of 1919 was related to increasing social tension, as especially a younger and probably more radical generation of Koreans realized that the colonial order would not grant them similar access to a secure and prosperous future. Similarly to in China, the hopes for change in the aftermath of the First World War would consequently generate what nationalist forces perceived as a window of opportunity to loosen the yoke of Japanese colonialism and the tight control of almost every aspect that had determined life in Korean society since 1910. In Korea itself, it was, as mentioned before, churches and religious organizations that allowed gatherings and discussions in a relatively secure space that the Japanese authorities could not control. The "Protestant church came to serve as a place for solace, a political forum, a communication network, and an organizational base for Korean nationalist activities,"[140] a fact that was also related to the Christian missionary history in Korea, where many schools for girls and women had been opened by foreign missionaries since the late 1880s.[141] In the colonial era, the Protestant Church's influence was quite important, as Chung-shin Park highlights:

> The Protestant church's organizational potential at the time was useful for Korean nationalists, but dangerous for the colonial government. The church contained thousands of pastors and church workers who led some 200,000 adherents and more than 2,000 churches in the peninsula. There were almost one thousand church-affiliated schools, and Protestants published their own newspapers and periodicals. These organizations were arranged in a hierarchy, and thus were connected closely in terms of organization and church administration. The Protestant church provided a nationwide communication

---

139 Ibid., p. 46.
140 Park, Protestantism and Politics, p. 117.
141 Walthall, From Private to Public Patriarchy, p. 455. On the relation between missionary work and geneder norms in colonial Korea also see Hyaeweol Choi, An American Concubine in Old Korea. Missionary Discourse on Gender, Race, and Modernity, in: Frontiers: A Journal of Women Studies 25 (2004) 3, pp. 134–161.

network. According to Ch'oe Myŏngsik, a political activist at the time, Korean patriotic activities indeed proceeded in and through churches, and the Protestant church was the best meeting place and political forum for nationalist activities. It is natural that a Korean nationalist leadership was formed in this religious community.[142]

Church leaders had also been active in the *Sinminhoe*, a connection that created close ties between church and nationalist activism even before the colonial period officially began in 1910. The *Sinminhoe*'s members secretly met at the Sandong Church in Seoul, and under Japanese colonial rule, church meetings turned out to become camouflaged resistance activities for those nationalists who had to act without being recognized by the Japanese colonial authorities as political radicals. In addition to such forms of church support, missionaries also intervened by making their own comments on the colonial order when they "interpreted the Scripture deliberately to reflect the current political situation. The church taught that the exodus of the people of Israel from Egypt could be likened to the need for Koreans to free themselves from Japan. This was an instance of political language in the guise of religious teaching."[143] Regardless of these numerous forms of resistance related to Korean church organizations, it was first and foremost the nationalists abroad who tried to draw attention to the situation within colonial Korea, especially at the end of the First World War.

There were many Korean nationalists who were either forced to leave the Korean peninsula or proactively chose to do so in the aftermath of the Russo-Japanese War and, in particular, from 1910. This decision was also influenced by the absence of organizational structures and activities that could be undertaken there. The Japanese had control of the press, prohibited political organizations, and anyone who acted suspiciously was probably soon to be surveilled by the police. Therefore, as Robinson worded it, "the situation within Korea appeared hopeless"[144] to many political activists, who instead chose to continue their activities in exile in Manchuria, Shanghai, or Vladivostok. In the Manchurian context, they could use their access to land in the region to support the cause of the resistance economically, and military bases could even be erected there. The most prominent example of such activities is probably the Military School of the New Rising (*Sinhŭng mugwan hakkyo*), where, in the late 1910s, Korean independence fighters would be trained. Similar training facilities were established on Russian soil during the First World War.[145]

---

142 Park, Protestantism and Politics, p. 120.
143 Ibid., p. 131.
144 Robinson, Cultural Nationalism, p. 41.
145 Kim, A History of Korea, p. 329.

Other Korean nationalists organized themselves in Shanghai, where a Mutual Assistance Society (*Tongjesa*) was founded in 1912. In 1919, the New Korea Youth Corps (*Sinhan ch'ŏngnyŏndan*) was established, and Kim Kyu-sik (1881–1950) chose to travel to Paris to attend the peace conference there and to make the voices of Korea heard.[146] Others like Syngman Rhee (1875–1965), who would become the first president of South Korea in 1948,[147] were active in the United States. Rhee founded the Korean National Association in 1909 in Hawai'i, and, a year later, he received a doctoral degree in political science from Princeton University after having studied at George Washington University and Harvard University. His close ties to the intellectual and politically influential circles of the United States helped him to publicize the situation of the Korean people, and he hoped that diplomatic means would eventually help to regain Korea's independence. Regardless of his being abroad, Rhee was elected as the first president of the Korean Provisional Government, which was announced in Shanghai in April 1919.[148] In August of the same year, he created the Korean Commission in Washington, DC, an organization that was supposed to lobby for Korea's independence. Although it was not successful with regard to this aim, Rhee became probably the most well-known Korean abroad, and his popularity would play an important role as South Korea's president after the end of the Second World War.

While Rhee had argued for a diplomatic solution, others like Park Yong-man (1881–1928) demanded a violent uprising against Japanese rule, and, like others in Manchuria or Russia, he established a military training school in Hawai'i. There, the Korean activists were split into two camps, one supporting Rhee, one supporting Park. However, these were not the only alternatives: An Chang-ho (1878–1938) founded the Society for the Fostering of Educational Activities (*Hŭngsadan*) in San Francisco in 1913 because he believed that the strengthening of a particularly Korean education would help spark national sentiments and activate the necessary powers for an anti-Japanese liberation. While Korean expatriates were united by their hope to end the colonial rule of Japan in their home country, they did not share the same ideas about the

---

146 Ibid., pp. 329–330. Timothy S. Lee called Kim one of the "most important figures in modem Korean history." Timothy S. Lee, A Political Factor in the Rise of Protestantism in Korea. Protestantism and the 1919 March First Movement, in: Church History 69 (2000) 1, pp. 116–142.

147 On his life and impact see Young Ick Lew, The Making of the First Korean President. Syngman Rhee's Quest for Independence, 1875–1948, Honolulu, HI 2013; David Fields, Foreign Friends. Syngman Rhee, American Exceptionalism, and the Division of Korea, Lexington, KY 2019.

148 Kim, A History of Korea, p. 330.

means and methods to achieve it.[149] That the influence of those political activists who worked outside of Korea between 1910 and 1919 should not be taken lightly is obvious when one considers that there were Korean immigrants to the United States who returned to their home country in 1919 to help to organize the March First Movement because they wanted to support the national struggle against Japan.[150] That even people who had lived abroad for years were willing and eager to return to Korea to participate in the demonstrations for Korean independence was also related to the fact that, almost ten years after the annexation by Japan, the First World War and the post-war quest for a new political order that was supposed to determine a better and more peaceful future had created an opportunity many Koreans considered suitable to reclaim what had been taken from them due to Japan's expansion since the end of the Russo-Japanese War: the right of self-determination.

4.4 The First World War and the Chances for a Wilsonian Moment

The First World War, although it was definitely not solely a European war, was not really a military concern for Korea. Japan's involvement was also relatively limited, both geographically and with regard to the time span for actual military activities by Japanese troops. Nevertheless, as recent studies have clearly emphasized, the war was well perceived in Japan and definitely had an impact on the country that should not be underestimated and goes way beyond economic developments.[151] In Korea, the "sudden outbreak of the Korean independence movement shook the Japanese empire to its core,"[152] especially since the colonial authorities were totally surprised at such massive protests throughout the whole peninsula.

---

149 Ibid.

150 Ji-Yeon Yuh, Moving within Empires: Korean Women and Trans-Pacific Migration, in: Catherine Ceniza Choy and Judy Tzu-Chun Wu (Eds.), Gendering the Trans-Pacific World, Leiden 2017, pp. 107–113, here p. 108.

151 The recently published and very important study about Japan and the First World War by Jan Schmidt shows clearly the transnational impact during and after the war. Jan Schmidt, Nach dem Krieg ist vor dem Krieg. Medialisierte Erfahrungen des Ersten Weltkriegs und Nachkriegsdiskurse in Japan (1914–1919), Frankfurt am Main 2021.

152 Jun Uchida, Brokers of Empire. Japanese and Korean Business Elites in Colonial Korea, in: Caroline Elkins and Susan Pedersen (Eds.), Settler Colonialism in the Twentieth Century. Projects, Practices, Legacies, London: Routledge, 2005), pp. 153–170, here p. 155.

These countrywide protests were stimulated or aroused by a "combination of catalytic factors"[153] that will be discussed later in some detail. One main element, however, was the perception of US President Woodrow Wilson's Fourteen Points that sparked the idea that Korean independence was in reach if sufficient people in the country expressed their wish to be freed from the Japanese yoke of imperialism. Korean nationalism had aimed for independence since 1910, but it was only in 1919 that the struggles of oppositional forces inside and outside Korea were able to link their own activities to an international idea that not only stimulated the hopes of the masses but also united them to actively demand independence for a sovereign Korean nation. The "heavy-handed control measures"[154] of the Japanese colonial authorities might have limited the possibilities for unified action from the different nationalist organizations and their respective representatives, but they had also alienated the masses of the Korean population. Therefore, as Robinson expertly formulated it, "Korea resembled an enormous pressure cooker,"[155] and in 1919, the steam had to get out. While some Koreans had tried to search for their own possibilities for reforms, change, and a future marked by common international ideas about modernity,[156] the search for identity, e.g. the discussions about the "new woman" (*Sin yŏja*), also stimulated reflections about the idea of the Korean nation and independence. Prominent women activists from Japan like Yosano Akiko (1878–1942) and Hiratsuka Raichō (1886–1971) became role models for some women in Korea, but at the same time, the critical thinking about gender roles also took place in a colonial context that naturally became an aspect of the intellectual struggle. Korean feminist Na Hyesŏk (1896–1948) criticized the Japanese ideal of the "good wife and wise mother" that had been prominent since the Meiji period and wrote about the "Ideal Woman" in 1914:

> I also believe that it is not wise to only pursue the customary ideal of "good wife, wise mother" (*yangch'ŏ hyŏnmo*). It seems that that ideal is one of the favorite marketing strategies used by teachers. The man is both husband and father; but I have never heard of any curriculum that emphasizes "good husband, wise father" (*yangbu hyŏnbu*). It is only women whose conduct as good spouse and wise parent is reinforced through our education, making women into mere appendages of men. Such an education does not develop the mind. Also, the idea of a warm and compliant womanhood, a necessary point of propaganda to turn women into slaves, cannot be an ideal for women.[157]

---

153 Ibid.
154 Robinson, Cultural Nationalism, p. 43.
155 Ibid.
156 Hyaeweol Choi, New Women in Colonial Korea. A Sourcebook, London 2012, p. 26; Yoo, Politics of Gender, p. 3.
157 Na Hyesŏk, "Isang chŏk puin," Hakchigwang 3 (December 1914), pp. 13–14, in: Choi, New Women, pp. 28–29, here p. 29.

She consequently demanded a drastic change with regard to the education of women, as Na demanded nothing less than enlightenment all Korean women:

> Until now, women have been raised in the ideology that instructs them to devote themselves entirely to the welfare of men. They are so accustomed to the domestic arena that they cannot tell right from wrong in matters that are outside of the private domain. Given this, how can a woman evolve into an ideal woman? Of course, she needs knowledge, skills, and artistic talent. She should be prepared to judge right from wrong in any matter, based on her common sense. She should be self-aware, with the desire to discover her unique abilities in realizing certain goals in life. She must understand contemporary thought, knowledge, and sensibility. Only then can she become a pioneer, equipped with all the power and qualifications that she needs in order to be an enlightened, ideal woman.[158]

The inaugural editorial of the journal *New Woman* (*Sin yŏja*) declared in 1920 that the experience of the First World War would demand a total reconfiguration of human society, not only in Korea, but in the world, where imperialism and exploitation had caused enormous destruction:

> Reform (*kaejo*)! This is the outcry of humankind after painfully grieving over the terrifying gunshots of the past five years [referring to World War I]. Liberation (*haebang*)! This is the call of women who have been confined to the deep, dark, inner chambers for thousands of years. Excessively greedy ambition and egoism caused the war, breaking the peace of springtime and bringing mountains of death and oceans of blood. This war opposed the will of heaven and the correct path of humankind. . . . Reform! Reform! This call for reform is echoed high and loud from every corner of the world. Truly the time has come for change. Ah, the new era has arrived. Time has come to break away from old things and bring in new things. The time has come to throw off the wrong-headed, evil practices of the past. The time has come to reform all things.[159]

The Japanese authorities were only interested in effective colonial bureaucracy and the strong assimilation of the Koreans; they did not pay attention to such thoughts about reforms. In 1915, the governor-general of Korea organized the Chosŏn Industrial Exposition, which "was clearly an embodiment of colonial hegemony"[160] and would prove, first and foremost to the Koreans themselves, what Japanese colonial rule had done for the people. The exposition was visited by more than one million people, who were supposed to witness the greatness of the Japanese Empire and come to appreciate the fact that, for half a decade, Koreans had been part of this empire. In an evaluation of this exhibition, Hong Kal argues that "the visually oriented spectacle of the 1915 exposition was far

---

158 Ibid.
159 "Ch'anggansa," Sin yŏja 1 (1920), pp. 2–3, in: Choi, New Women, pp. 29–30.
160 Hong Kal, Aesthetic Constructions of Korean Nationalism. Spectacle, Politics and History, London/New York 2011, p. 14.

more effective in reaching out to the masses and relate them to the idea of nation than any other medium available at that time."[161] The official report of the event further emphasized the Japanese narrative of a "civilizing mission" when it stated that

> [s]ince the decline of Korea from ancient times . . . the country's destiny was in danger. Koreans had been suffering, its industry had deteriorated, and its land had been ruined. In 1910, the empire set up the Government General of Korea, and . . . for the first time, the spirit of the country [Korea] was restored. However, it is not easy to awaken people from a hundred years of slumber. Under the blessing of the emperor, people have now realized the need to cultivate fields, plant trees, open ports, disseminate education, and improve morality. By the order of the emperor, the Government General has accomplished its colonial mission for the last five years. . . . It is worthwhile to compare the present achievement with the past. . . . Therefore, the Government General has organized the Korean Industrial Exposition.[162]

The exposition in particular tried to diminish the value of Korean precolonial production through a comparison with Japanese goods: "The comparison was also made between customary objects as they were invested with meanings of the old and the new: the old signified the Chosŏn era and the new signified colonial Korea or Japan by extension."[163] Japan, which had profited economically during the war years, displayed its full capacity as an industrialized role model whose impact on Korea was supposedly an important necessity for the country's own modernization, albeit within the realm and the realities of the Japanese Asian Empire. As Hong Kal, in her detailed analysis of the exhibition, further emphasizes,

> [t]his rhetoric was also evident in the Reference Hall (Ch'amgogwan) and the Machinery Hall (Kigyegwan) in which advanced industrial instruments, products and machines from Japan (and a few from Taiwan) were displayed as a visual witness of Japanese modernity and at the same time served as a visual reference for Koreans to follow in the course of progress under the guidance of Japanese colonialism.[164]

This "principle of hierarchical comparison located colonial Korea within a linear evolutionary trajectory of history in which Korea moved from its pre-industrial to an industrial phase under the tutelage of Japan."[165] The exhibition, in a way, proves that the Japanese colonial authorities considered their assimilation policy to have been successful, and this success was to be displayed to the visitors. At

---

161 Ibid., p. 15.
162 Cited in ibid., p. 16.
163 Ibid., p. 22.
164 Ibid.
165 Ibid.

the same time, they believed a silent agreement based on the admiration of Japan's achievements had been reached. It is probably because of this belief that the policy of assimilation's further course would remain uncontested that the eruption of nationalist demands for independence in 1919 initially shocked the Japanese.

It may be that the authorities had simply been unaware of this possibility, but with regard to the criticism directed at them, the colonial government was unable to understand that, regardless of the public absence of protests, disagreement with the Japanese rule was strong among many Koreans. The censors had tried during the First World War to keep any discussion about the idea of the self-determination of nations out of Korean newspapers, but Wilson's Fourteen Points[166] were popular and sparked hope for a new era in Korea's history with a return to independence.[167] Wilson's ideas also gained momentum because the aforementioned Korean expatriates were spreading the word about them and linking these ideals that had been formulated in a Kantian tradition with the ambition to regain the right to self-determination from Japan.[168] It was the Korean nationalists who looked at the European post-war developments and the American President and "adopted the Wilsonian vision of a new international order as an unprecedented opportunity for Korea to emerge – or to reemerge, as they saw it – as an independent, equal member in the expanding community of nations."[169] What has been described as a "dark period" was consequently ended by an *ex occidente lux*, personified by the academic and champion of democracy, Woodrow Wilson. That the Korean nationalists were inspired by his thoughts and demands was in a way also due to Japanese restrictions, because "Korean students, encouraged to attend Japanese universities as part of the assimilation policy, had access to literature promoting liberal ideas and criticizing Japanese rule that the military authorities had banned from Korea itself."[170]

---

166 Woodrow Wilson, Fourteen Points Speech, in: Arhurt S. Link et al. (Eds.), The Papers of Woodrow Wilson, Princeton, NJ 1984, vol. 45, p. 536. Also see Trygve Throntveit, The Fable of the Fourteen Points. Woodrow Wilson and National Self-Determination, in: Diplomatic History 35, no. 3 (2011), pp. 445–481.

167 Erez Manela, The Wilsonian Moment. Self-Determination and the International Origins of Anticolonial Nationalism, Oxford 2007, p. 119.

168 Robert Bernasconi, Ewiger Friede und totaler Krieg, in: Alfred Hirsch and Pascal Delhom (Eds.), Denkwege des Friedens Aporien und Perspektiven, München 2019, pp. 50–70, here p. 61. The connection between Kant and Wilson was already emphasized by contemporary authors. See, among others, Klaus Vorländer, Kant und der Gedanke des Völkerbundes, Leipzig 1919, pp. 67–85.

169 Manela, The Wilsonian Moment, p. 120.

170 Ibid., p. 125.

The Korean National Association in the United States was important in this regard, especially as its early leading members not only provided important information about the events related to the First World War but also because, since the early 1910s, they had tried to keep Korea and its fate as a topic in the public debates of the United States. In December 1918, an open letter by the association asked Koreans in North America to stay united and prepare for an independence struggle that would soon bring Korea back into the community of sovereign nation-states. It was furthermore argued at a meeting in San Francisco that "in light of Wilson's vision for the postwar settlement, Koreans should submit a petition to the peace conference after the war and make an appeal to the United States and to Wilson himself to recognize Korean independence."[171] Syngman Rhee, among others, was selected to be part of a delegation to the peace conference, where the representatives of the Korean cause were to make sure that the matter really got the attention it needed. The delegates also informed President Wilson early on of their trip to Paris and their intentions, and it is not surprising that they put all their hopes on the United States and its leading representative at that time. As Erez Manela explains, the perceptions of Wilson and US democracy were decisive for the Korean expatriates' assumption that their cause at the peace conference would best be served by the American delegation:

> As with other anticolonial activists, Korean perceptions of Wilson and their hopes for his support drew on long-standing views of the United States as an exemplar of modern civilization and the power most sympathetic toward colonial aspirations for independence. Among Korean nationalists, moreover, such perceptions of the United States were more common and more deeply entrenched than among other colonial peoples, given the impact of Protestant missions in Korea and the prominence among expatriate activists of men who studied and lived in the United States.[172]

Around the same time, there were also activities in Japan, where Korean students did not just passively observe the events but intended to use the opening window of opportunity at the end of the war to strengthen the chances of a successful attempt to regain independence.

Chang Tŏksu (1895–1947), a prominent Korean student and nationalist activist in Japan, met with Yŏ Unhyŏng (1886–1947), who ran a school for Koreans in Shanghai, where they established the New Korea Youth Association that was supposed to coordinate the work of Korean student exiles in China and Japan to use their power to demand independence. They also hoped to use their contact

---

171 Ibid.
172 Ibid., p. 127.

with the American businessman Charles R. Crane (1858–1939)[173] to get in touch
with Wilson, especially since Crane had outlined the idea of self-determination at
several events he spoke at in China.[174] Like the Korean National Association in the
US, the New Korea Youth Association elected a delegate to be sent to Paris. Kim
Kyu-sik, an orphan raised and trained by the US missionary Horace G. Underwood
(1859–1916) and who had studied in the United States – at Roanoke College, VA
and later Princeton University –, was elected, and although there were numerous
issues that made it almost impossible for him to get to Paris, he managed to travel
there with a Chinese passport and under a false name.[175] Another organization,
the Korean Youth Independence Association, which had been organized by Korean students in Japan, also became active during the peace talks that were held
in Paris. The students wanted to do something that would draw the international
community's attention to the Korean cause, which is why the writer Yi Kwang-su
(1892–1950) was requested to draft a declaration of Korean independence. On
8 February 1919, the declaration was read out loud in front of the YMCA building
in Tokyo.[176] The text was then sent by other Korean activists through their Chinese
channels to Korea, where it found a fruitful ground and much attention in the nationalist circles. The American consul general in Korea described the situation
there in January 1919 as follows:

> There can be no doubt that the present general movement throughout the world looking
> towards the self-determination of peoples, and particularly of the subject races, has pro-
> duced its effect on the thought of the people in this country. At the outset of the war there
> was a strong undercurrent among the Koreans of hostility to the Allies, a feeling that
> arose from a not unnatural antagonism to Japan, one of the Allies. As the war progressed,
> however, and the ultimate aims of the Allies were more carefully and fully stated, those
> Koreans who are accustomed to look beyond immediate conditions in their own country
> and to view affairs here in light of world conditions began to see that they might also be
> affected in no adverse manner by the victory of the Allies.[177]

The situation was then further intensified by the death of Kojong, the former
Korean emperor who had been forced to abdicate his throne in 1907 by the Japanese. William Massy Royds (1843–1919), the British consul-general in Seoul, reported in early March about the interrelationship of this event with the March

---

173 On Crane's life and activities see Norman E. Saul, The Life and Times of Charles R. Crane,
1858–1939. American Businessman, Philanthropist, and a Founder of Russian Studies in America, Lanham, MD 2013.
174 Manela, The Wilsonian Moment, p. 128.
175 Ibid., p. 129.
176 Kim, A History of Korea, p. 332.
177 Cited in Manela, The Wilsonian Moment, p. 131.

First Movement, stating that "His Highness' death . . . called forth remarkable manifestations of grief throughout the Peninsula"[178] and that

> Everywhere the ex-Emperor is spoken of as a martyr in his country's cause, the idea being that he took his own life to prevent his son's marriage, and a popularity, which had rather waned since his abdication, was revived tenfold in his death. For many days immediately following the event, crowds of people assembled daily outside his palace, and prostrated themselves on mats, weeping loudly, and the whole nation went into mourning.[179]

The preparations for the funeral coincided with the massive protests on 1 March 1919 that would find their place in the history books as the March First Movement. In his first report thereupon, William Massy Royds made this interrelationship between the immediate events in Korea and the and the prepared declaration of independence clear when he stated that

> [t]wo days before the funeral, a so called demonstration of independence took place in several parts of Seoul and in many large centres in the country simultaneously on a considerable scale. The city was then full of people from all parts of the country, who had been arriving for some time in large numbers, and the principal demonstration took place in front of the palace where the ex-Emperor's body was lying . . . several hundreds of students suddenly rushed the guards at the palace gate, and burst into the grounds wildly cheering their declaration of independence. No attempt was made by them to use force, and fortunately no weapons were used by the police or soldiers, with the result that the demonstrators withdrew without any damage being done and dispersed in smaller bands to different parts of the city, where similar outbreaks had occurred.[180]

After Kojong's sudden death, rumors spread that he had been poisoned by the Japanese. The funeral also caused many Koreans to travel to Seoul to pay their tribute to the former emperor of Korea. This large influx of people made nationalist leaders debate the possibilities of how to use the current situation for the sake of Korean independence. The March First Movement would eventually unite the Korean intellectuals and the masses in their struggle to regain national freedom from Japan, which supposedly had the support of the international community and, in particular, of the United States.[181]

---

178 William Massy Royds, British Consulate-General, Seoul to Sir W. Conyngham Greene, H.M. Ambassador, Tokio, March 4, 1919. FO-262-1406, p. 1.
179 Ibid.
180 Ibid., pp. 1–2.
181 For a short summary of the March First Movement see Kim, A History of Korea, pp. 331–334.

4.5 The March First Movement

Korean students in Japan had witnessed the local rice riots in the aftermath of the First World War and probably also realized that anti-Japanese sentiments in China had been on the rise since 1915. These observations, in addition to the wishes for an international order that had been expressed by US President Wilson and many others, might have encouraged them in early 1919 to move toward more concrete actions to regain Korean independence, especially a public declaration of it in the first place. On 1 March 1919, thousands of Koreans followed their example and marched through the streets of Korean towns, demanding freedom and national sovereignty. The outburst had, in addition, been stimulated by the harsh assimilation policy of the colonial government and the Japanese suppression of the Korean population.[182] In this light, it is correct to say that "[t]he disaster for the Japanese of the March First movement proved the failure of their initial colonial policy, and for Korea it signaled the maturity of the nationalist movement."[183] The mass protests were "a defining moment in modern Korean history," and they remain an important focal point within the Korean nationalist memory even today, as they presented "a shining moment of national unity during the long dark night of Japanese rule."[184] Japan was unable to contain the spread of information about the events within and outside of Korea, and, as part of a global protest wave against imperialism at the end of the First World War, the March First Movement countered the Japanese narrative of progress and unity within the Japanese Empire, especially in its colonial possessions. The Korean declaration of independence showed the unity of its people and their wish to get rid of the imperialist yoke of Japanese rule.

While radical students were part of the movement's preparation, the majority of its leadership had a religious background, as the churches and other religious organizations had been, as described before, the main organizational units for Korean resistance and nationalist activism since 1910. Information about the developments in international politics had made its way into the country through the Koreans living abroad, and the Wilsonian moment had sparked nationalist ambitions within the religious organizations that the time to claim independence had come. Originally, the protests were supposed to take place on the day of Kojong's funeral, 3 March 1919, but the fear that the

---

182 Caprio, Japanese Assimilation Policies, pp. 111–112.
183 Robinson, Cultural Nationalism, p. 43.
184 Robinson, Korea's Twentieth-Century Odyssey, p. 47.

Japanese police could prevent the plot caused the organizers to speed things up. The official declaration of independence itself had been signed by 33 leading Christian, Buddhist, and Ch'ŏndogyo religious leaders.[185] The proclamation document clearly stated as follows:

> We proclaim, herewith, Korea an independent state and her people free. We announce it to the nations of the world and so make known the great truth of the equality of all humanity. We also make it known to our posterity for ten thousand generations that they may hold this right as a free people for all time. With the authority and dignity of 5,000 years of history and the devotion and loyalty of 20,000,000 people behind us, we make this proclamation. Thus we take this responsibility on behalf of the eternal freedom of our people. In order that we may move in accord with the opportune fortunes of a new era, when the conscience of humanity has awakened, we so act. It is the evident command of God, the trend of the age in which we live, the natural step in accord with the right of all peoples to live and move together. There is nothing in the world that should prevent it or stand in its way.[186]

The declaration of independence also emphasized that, without such independence, there would be no future for Korea and the following generations of Koreans:

> If we would rid ourselves of resentment over the past; if we would be free from the agony of the present; if we would escape violence for the future; if we would awaken once again the conscience of our people, now oppressed, or rouse the fallen state to a true endeavor; if we would rightly develop character in every man; if we would not pass on to our unfortunate children an inheritance of shame and distress; if we would have future generations for all time enjoy the perfection of blessing, we must, first and foremost, secure complete independence for our people.[187]

Emphasizing the timing of the declaration, the text also argued that the future of East Asia would also depend on a peaceful path for the future, because Japanese expansionism, a "disturbance to the peace of the Far East," would eventually and "undoubtedly [only] result in calling down on the whole of East Asia the sad fate of universal destruction."[188] According to Wilson's Fourteen Points and the accompanying demands for a peaceful international order that would be formed by self-determination and equal coexistence, the proclamation also emphasized the beginning of a new era: "A new world opens before our eyes, the age of force departs and that of truth and righteousness comes on. The mind of humanity, refined, clarified, matured, trained by the ages of the past,

---

185 Ch'ŏndogyo was a successor movement of the Donghak.
186 Copy of the Proclamation of March 1, 1919. FO-262-1406, p. 1.
187 Ibid.
188 Ibid., p. 2.

now begins to cast the morning light of a new civilization on the history of the race. A new spring dawns upon the world and all life hastens to awaken."[189]

Of those who signed the proclamation, 29 met on 1 March at a restaurant near Pagoda Park, where the declaration of independence was also to be read out. That Saturday, flyers were handed out and posters were posted in the streets that public gatherings would be held that day. Naturally, masses of people attended the events, and when the declaration of independence was read out, people cheered and the nationalist outcry was heard almost everywhere in the country, where similar gatherings followed in the next days. Those who had signed the declaration later gathered at a hotel and called the authorities to be arrested.[190] The mass protests in the meantime remained peaceful and no acts of violence were committed by the Koreans, although "[a]t one point mounted gendarmes charged the crowd and inflicted some sabre cuts [and t]he police were arresting as many as they could."[191] Regardless of this immediate and aggressive response, around 1,500 demonstrations with around two million participants followed countrywide. Royds reported about these events on 13 March as follows:

> The unrest . . . brought about simultaneous disturbances of a violent nature in most of the large centres throughout Corea, showing the movement to be the outcome of a remarkable organization. In several places the troops and police used their weapons, with the result that a considerable number of people including gendarmes were killed or wounded. . . . A printed manifesto . . . was issued on the 1st instant, proclaiming the independence of Corea, and appealing to the Peace Conference to uphold their claims. Stress was laid on the fact that resistance should not be made to the Authorities, and that force should not be used, the protest to be made being solely of a peaceful nature. . . . Twenty-nine of the 33 signatories were at once placed under arrest.[192]

Due to the involvement of religious groups and organizations, the British diplomat was at the same time also worried for the foreign missionaries in Korea because, as he continued in his report, "the missionaries doubtless sympathize at heart with the natural desire of the Coreans to preserve their existence as a nation, though they all scrupulously refrain from any interference of a political nature and from any discussion of the subject with Coreans."[193] He furthermore emphasized that the Japanese assimilation policy was responsible for the nature

---

189 Ibid.

190 Martin Uden, Times Past in Korea: An Illustrated Collection of Encounters, Customs and Daily Life Recorded by Foreign Visitors, London/New York 2003, p. 67.

191 Ibid.

192 William Massy Royds, British Consulate-General, Seoul to Sir W. Conyngham Greene, H.M. Ambassador, Tokio, March 13, 1919. FO-262-1406, p. 1.

193 Ibid., p. 2.

of this massive protest movement, as the "Japanese policy at present openly aims at depriving the Coreans of even their own language and customs, and their total assimilation by Japan, and the deliberate attempt to enforce this policy by every available means is the cause of the universal hatred in which the Japanese are held throughout the land."[194]

While the demonstrations per se were peaceful, the Japanese reaction was rather harsh and, in some cases, particularly violent. The colonial authorities did not see this nationalist wave coming and were really surprised by the nationwide coordination of the protests. By mid-April, 7,500 demonstrators had been killed, 16,000 had been wounded, and more than 45,000 people had been arrested in relation to the events. In addition, more than 700 houses as well as two schools and 47 churches had been destroyed.[195] The March First Movement was so powerful because it united all Koreans in a national struggle for independence and, as the Korean Information Bureau stated in 1919, "farmers, mechanics and laborers are equally as eager as the educated class to contribute their mite [sic!] in the efforts to regain their political independence."[196] It was such organizations, as well as Western observers and concerned politicians or diplomats, that reported about the events in Korea and linked them to the current moment of modern history. Carlton Waldo Kendall, a delegate of the Paris Peace Conference, published *The Truth about Korea* in 1919, in which he linked the events with the diplomatic negotiations: "The time to strike had come. When the Peace Conference, with its ideals of 'self-determination,' met in Paris, it gave to the oppressed Koreans the longed-for chance to place their problem before the world."[197] Kendall further emphasized that the Korean protesters were not dangerous political radicals or violent revolutionaries, two things the world – and especially the US – feared in 1919, two years after the revolution in Russia.[198] He pointed out that the Korean organizers' "plan was to begin a 'Passive Revolution'. No one, not even the Japanese, was to be harmed. No property was to be destroyed or

---

194 Ibid.

195 Kim, A History of Korea, p. 333. Also see Kendall, The Truth about Korea, p. 10. These numbers are estimates by Korean historians. The Japanese authorities only confirmed 553 deaths, 1,409 injured people, and a number of 12,522 arrests. Robinson, Korea's Twentieth-Century Odyssey, p. 48. For the Japanese reports of the events see Chōsen sōjō keika gaiyō, Japan Center for Asian Historical Records (JACAR), A04017275800.

196 Korean Information Bureau, Little Martyrs of Korea, Philadelphia, PA 1919, p. 5.

197 Carlton Waldo Kendall, The Truth about Korea, second edition, San Francisco, CA 1919, p. 25.

198 Frank Jacob, The Russian Revolution, the American Red Scare, and the Forced Exile of Transnational Anarchists. Emma Goldman and Alexander Berkman and their Soviet Experience, in: Yearbook of Transnational History 4 (2021), pp. 113–134.

injured. No radicalism, no I.W.W.-ism, no Bolshevism was to be tolerated or associated in any way with the movement. But a persistent passive agitation was to be instituted and continued until success attended their object-freedom from Japanese Military Autocracy."[199] Kendall also argued that the organizers had focused on protests in Seoul as they wanted to use the proximity of the foreign legations to arouse international attention to the Korean cause.[200] The sheer mass of people who had answered the nationalist call across the whole country was simply too much for the Japanese to bear, and frustration might have played an important part in the violent measures taken by the colonial police in the aftermath of 1 March 1919.[201]

Six days after the initial protests, Governor-General Hasegawa Yoshimichi (1850–1924) urged the Koreans not to resist Japan's colonial rule due to false rumors when he published the following instructions: "Rumour was recently circulated that at the preliminary peace conference in Paris the independence of Chosen was recognized by foreign Powers, but the rumour is absolutely groundless. It need hardly be said that the sovereignty of the Japanese Empire is irrevocably established in the Peninsula and will never be broken in the future."[202] While the colonial authorities wanted to show strength in Korea, Tokyo tried to avoid attracting too much international attention to the recent events, but the reports by missionaries from Korea damaged the Japanese image abroad. The Korean Information Bureau published reports that emphasized that even children who wanted to support the nationalist cause of the people of Korea were severely punished by the Japanese police apparatus. One such report stated the following:

> After the leaders and adults had a demonstration in Seoul, the boys and girls of all the schools in that city, without the knowledge of their elders, gathered in Pagoda Park and declared themselves in sympathy with their elders. They read the Declaration of Independence, and then giving their national cry of "*Toknip Mansei*" (Independence Forever), they rushed down the principal streets of the city, holding up their hands and waving their caps, lustily shouting for their independence. These children were immediately met by the Japanese gendarmes and police, with drawn swords and fixed bayonets and were driven back with many casualties. About six o'clock, when the sun disappeared behind the western hills, these brave little patriots disappeared from the streets.[203]

---

199 The Truth about Korea, p. 25.
200 Ibid., p. 26.
201 Ibid., pp. 27–30.
202 Urgent Instructions by Governor-General, in: The Seoul Press, March 7, 1919, FO-262-1406.
203 Korean Information Bureau, Little Martyrs, p. 6.

Another report about a young Korean girl is quite heartbreaking:

> One of the girls in our school came to the principal, and said: "I must go home to see my mother on a very important matter." The principal immediately gave her permission to leave, so she packed her belongings and started for home. When she entered her home she greeted her mother, and then with a very determined look on her young face, said, "Mother, I have come to see you for a few minutes, as I have decided to give my life for my country, and wanted to see you once more and say good-bye." Her mother was ignorant of the demonstrations taking place all over the country, and asked her daughter for an explanation. The little girl then gave her some of the story she had heard of the independence movement, and then exclaimed, "Mother, I must do something for my country; I must go out and shout for our independence and give my life for our freedom."[204]

From the perspective of foreign observers, the "Japanese reaction bordered on hysteria,"[205] but when one considers the history of the industrial exposition in 1915 and the belief that the assimilation of the Koreans into the Japanese Empire had been fast and successful, the surprise of the mass protests must have aroused anger and desperation within Japanese colonial circles that caused them to respond extremely violently to the Korean wish for independence. Or, as a contemporary pamphlet argued, "shame and self-remorse quickly gave went to Prussianlike brutality."[206] Since the protests continued until the early summer, they could not easily be repressed, and therefore this added frustration further intensified the violent responses from the police and the Japanese authorities. As Michael Robinson has pointed out, it was Japanese helplessness that was leading to extreme forms of violence:

> By mid-April rioting was widespread, and police violence led to a number of well-documented atrocities: the burning of villages, shooting on crowds, mass searches, arrests, and the disappearance of demonstrators. The police also seized printing presses, closed schools, and declared a colony-wide curfew. Still the rioting continued sporadically into the summer of 1919 and was controlled only after additional troops arrived from Japan.[207]

The violent reactions were also causing problems for Japan's international reputation: "The horror and brutality of some of the deeds committed are beyond belief. In the name of crushing the Independence Movement, the military authorities have transgressed the laws of all civilization and proved beyond the shadow of a doubt that Japanese Military Autocracy is no longer fit to be

---

204 Ibid., p. 11.
205 Robinson, Cultural Nationalism, p. 44.
206 The Korean Independence Movement, Shanghai n.d. [1919?].
207 Robinson, Korea's Twentieth-Century Odyssey, p. 48.

respected by any civilized people."[208] The acts of the police were described in detail, and the fact that women and children were among the victims who "were knocked down with the butts of rifles"[209] gave rise to harsh criticism, and not only from the Korean communities abroad. The authenticity of reports about the atrocities and massacres conducted in Korea became a topic of international debate.[210]

A particularly cruel "incident" was reported in Cheam-ni, in the south of Seoul, on 15 April 1919, when the Japanese locked the doors of a church and set it on fire, and 29 people were burned alive. The "incident" became known as the "Cheam-ni Massacre,"[211] and although the Japanese officer responsible was charged and sentenced, the history of the massacre would further poison Japanese-Korean relations in the years to come. Considering the fact that the protests were answered so violently and yet did not cause any international intervention against Japanese rule, "a general tenor of disillusionment, frustration, and despondency set in."[212] The poet O Sang-sun remarked on these feelings in an editorial in his journal *P'yeho* (Ruins):

> Our land of Korea is in ruins. These are times of sorrow and agony. Saying this will wrench the heart of our youth. But I must, for it is a fact that I can neither deny nor even doubt. In ruins lie all our defects and shortcomings, inside and outside, physical as well as mental: emptiness, grievances, discontent and resentment, sighs and worries, pain and tears – all these evils will lead to extinction and death. As we stand before the ruins, darkness and death open their fearsome, cavernous mouths, threatening to gobble us up. Again, we are struck by the feeling that the old ruins spell extinction and death.[213]

The situation was particularly devastating for so many Koreans because the US President had not interfered on behalf of their right to self-determination; instead, he and the great international powers had simply accepted the realities Japan had created in Korea by the use of brute force. The Korean delegates who were sent to Paris had urged Wilson to understand the situation. They "simply wish[ed] to expose certain facts and truths and only solicite your impartial judgment for the sake of HUMANITY AND JUSTICE that are being trampled over under the iron heel of the Asiatic Kaiser who really surpasses his Prussian

---

208 Kendall, The Truth about Korea, p. 33.
209 Ibid., 31.
210 Japanese Atrocities in Korea. Reports Emphasized and Made Convincing by Japanese Propaganda, n.p. n.d. [1920].
211 Arita-chūi ni kakaru saiban senkoku no kudan hōkoku, JACAR, C03022465000.
212 Park, Protestantism and Politics, p. 139.
213 Cited in ibid.

pattern."[214] The petition that was handed to Wilson emphasized the injustice of Japanese colonial rule in Korea and warned the international community about the future, which would be dangerous for peace due to Japan's "continental policy" and its "policy in operation" in Korea.[215] There were, of course, Western voices that called for support for the Korean claim for independence, but they were unheard in the chambers of power where the new world order was eventually negotiated. Demands were, however, made, especially with regard to Wilson's ideas about self-determination:

> The principles which underlie the right of self-determination must be applied universally if they are to be applied at all. The doctrines which President Wilson has been preaching and for which America has so solidly stood throughout the war, and which are now being promulgated by the League of Nations, are mere words if they can not be applied concretely. No nation in the world has a better claim to independence than Korea. It is therefore timely to consider the plight of this people. . . . With the development of the doctrine of self-determination there has come a recrudescence of nationality in Korea, the Hermit Kingdom, the Land of the Morning Calm, that has manifested itself in rioting in Seoul and other large centers, the establishment of revolutionary headquarters in Siberia and in the sending of a delegate to the Peace Conference at Paris with a plea for recognition of the rights of the Korean people to govern themselves without the interference of Japan. . . . Self-determination is one of the accepted policies of the Peace Conference. It is just as important to the world that democracy should be safe in Korea as it is that, for the protection of the balance of power in Europe, the national aspirations of Poland, Czecho-Slovakia and Jugo-Slavia should be recognized. The Koreans, notwithstanding the assertions of certain eminent Japanese at present in this country, are capable of self-government and are entitled to it unless the Peace Conference is going to put the Far East and its subject nations upon a different basis from those of Eastern Europe. Such a result would be a stultification of all of the principles for which the war was fought and upon which the world expects peace to be established.[216]

Such interventions nevertheless could not change the fact that the Korean people and their fate were simply ignored. The international community was not willing to really live up to the ideals they had all claimed to long for, and the people of Korea were the victims of the fact that Japan was to be kept a member of the world's major powers, regardless of its colonial policies.

Eventually, Japan reacted by adopting a new course when the Hara Cabinet appointed a new governor-general, Saitō Makoto, and "replaced naked coercion

---

214 Letter by the Korean Delegation, Paris, May 14, 1919, in: Korean Delegation, Petition.
215 Korean Delegation, Petition, pp. 1–3.
216 Arthur MacLennan, Diplomacy and Force in Korea, San Francisco, CA 1919, pp. 1, 13 and 16.

with a softer but even more effective policy of manipulation and co-optation."[217] The "attitudinal changes"[218] in the aftermath of the March First Movement nevertheless did not change the fact that Korea was to be assimilated and remain an essential part of Japan's overseas empire. Korean political activists radicalized further, and those who had organized anti-Japanese resistance were now leaning more toward communist support from China than hoping for democratic lip service from Western powers.[219] Regardless of these trends, there were also numerous provisional governments that were formed in the aftermath of the March First Movement in which prominent figures of post-war Korean history, like Syngman Rhee, were active,[220] while the Koreans in exile continued to keep the fate of their home country in the global consciousness.

4.6 Conclusion

The March First Movement was tragic but also, at the same time, "a historic event that helped define a nation in a time of need."[221] It showed that the Korean nation was still alive and that Japanese assimilation policies had failed, regardless of the fact that the Japanese authorities claimed to have modernized Korea according to their own standards. The tragedy of Korea in 1919 was Japan's strength and importance after the First World War. The Western powers did not want to sacrifice their good relations with their war-time ally for an ideal like self-determination, even if President Wilson had argued on behalf of this ideal in the latter phase of the First World War. The war years had instead intensified Japanese rule, and Korea's attempt at its end to regain independence was not able to gain international support. For all nationalist activists,

---

217 Robinson, Korea's Twentieth-Century Odyssey, p. 49. Also see Uchida, Brokers of Empire. Japanese and Korean Business Elites, pp. 155–156. Regardless of Saitō's supposedly milder course, his aims were the same: "The kernel of Saitō's strategy for dealing with Korean nationalism, however, was to mobilize local men of influence, Korean as well as Japanese. From the outset, the Saitō administration labored hard to crystallize whatever tenuous ties the colonial state had forged with the Korean upper class." Ibid., p. 156.
218 Caprio, Japanese Assimilation Policies, p. 112.
219 Hongkoo Han, Colonial Origins of Juche. The Minsaengdan Incident of the 1930s and the Birth of the North Korea-China Relationship, in: Jae-Jung Suh (Ed.), Origins of North Korea's Juche. Colonialism, War, and Development, Lanham, MD 2012, pp. 33–62, here p. 34; Dongyoun Hwang, Anarchism in Korea. Independence, Transnationalism, and the Question of National Development, 1919–1984, Albany, NY 2016, p. 1.
220 Lew, The Making of the First Korean President, pp. 333–334.
221 Ibid., p. 89.

this marked the weakness of the post-war order and the failure to achieve a true Wilsonian moment that could have initiated a new, peaceful world order. Nationalisms and imperialist ambitions were still too powerful, and the Korean protesters seemed to have suffered without any tangible result. What they nevertheless proved was the fact that Korea had a strong national identity and that its people would not give in to the Japanese narrative of their benevolent empire.

The nationalist struggle therefore continued, but the hope for a democratic intervention was replaced with anger about international imperialism in general and Western indifference in particular. It is therefore also important to understand the shortcomings of the post-war order from a more global perspective, as the results of the peace treaties that were established in the aftermath of the First World War not only determined European history for the years to come but also poisoned the existent political relations in East Asia, especially between Japan and Korea.

Bibliography

Unpublished Sources

Dimplomatic Archives of the Foreign Ministry of Japan
Kokuryūkai, 8 Tai–Shi mondaikaiketsu iken, 9 October 1914, B–1–1–2–156.
Tamura Kosaku, Dai–ichiji sekaitaisen to Nihon gaikō, B10070135800.
Uchida Ryōhei, 15 Tai–Shi mondaikaiketsu iken, 29 October 1914, B–1–1–2–151.

Museum of Fine Arts Boston
Iizawa Ten'yō, Envelope for the series "The Nouveau Riche at New Year" (Narikin no shinnen),
Part 1, Leonard A. Lauder Collection.

National Archives, UK
FO–262–1406
FO 676/140

New York Public Library
Katayama Sen, Recent Tendencies in the Labor Movement in Japan, Rand School of Social
Science Papers (Dep't of Labor Research), The New York Public Library, Astor, Lenox and
Tilden Foundations, Box 2, Katayama–Tractenberg, Folder 1, Katayama–Laidler

Published Sources and Secondary Works

Ahlund, Claes (Ed.). Scandinavia in the First World War. Studies in the War Experience of the
Northern Neutrals, Lund 2013.
Anderson, Benedict. Imagined Communities. Reflections on the Origin and Spread of
Nationalism, London 1983.
Atkins, E. Taylor. Primitive Selves. Koreana in the Japanese Colonial Gaze, 1910–1945,
Berkeley, CA 2010.
Asada, Masafumi. The China–Russia–Japan Military Balance in Manchuria, 1906–1918,
in: Modern Asian Studies 44 (2010) 6, pp. 1283–1311.
Ban'no Junji– Meiji kenpō taisei no kakuritsu. Fukoku kyōhei to minryoku kyūyō, Tokyo 1992.
Beasley, William G. Japanese Imperialism 1894–1945, Oxford 1987.
Bergère, Marie–Claire. Sun Yat–Sen, trans. Janet Lloyd, Stanford 1998.
Bernasconi, Robert. Ewiger Friede und totaler Krieg, in: Alfred Hirsch and Pascal Delhom
(Eds.), Denkwege des Friedens. Aporien und Perspektiven, München 2019, pp. 50–70.
Billingsley, Phil. Bandits in Republican China, Stanford 1988.
Biontino, Juljan and Yim, Sang–wook. Der Deutsche Bauernkrieg und die "Tonghak
Bauernrevolution". Rezeption in Südkorea und Perspektiven des Vergleichs, in: Zeitschrift
für Geschichtswissenschaften 66 (2018) 2, pp. 147–166.
Bix, Herbert P. Japanese Imperialism and the Manchurian Economy, 1900–31, in: The China
Quarterly 51 (1972), pp. 425–443.
Black, Jeremy. Imperial Legacies. The British Empire Around the World, New York 2019.

Bois, Marcel and Jacob, Frank (Eds.). Zeiten des Aufruhrs (1916–1921). Globale Proteste, Streiks und Revolutionen gegen den Ersten Weltkrieg und seine Auswirkungen, Berlin 2020.

Bonavia, David. China's Warlords, New York 1995.

Bottaro, Giuseppe. Internazionalismo e democrazia nella politica estera Wilsoniana, in: Il Politico 72 (2007) 2, pp. 5–23.

Burkman, Thomas W. Japan and the League of Nations. Empire and World Order, 1914–1938, Honolulu, HI 2007.

Cai, Jianguo and Cai, Yuanpei. Gelehrter und Mittler zwischen Ost und West, Münster 1998.

Cai Shaoqing (Ed.), Minguo shiqi de tufei, Beijing 1993.

Calvo, Alex and Qiaoni, Bao. Forgotten Voices from the Great War. The Chinese Labour Corps, in: The Asia–Pacific Journal 13 (2015) 1. Accessed September 30, 2019. http://apjjf.org/-Bao-Qiaoni-Alex-Calvo/4411/article.pdf.

Caprio, Mark E. Japanese Assimilation Policies in Colonial Korea, 1910–1945, Seattle, WA 2009.

Caprio, Mark E. Marketing Assimilation. The Press and the Formation of the Japanese–Korean Colonial Relationship, The Journal of Korean Studies 16 (2011) 1, pp. 1–25.

Chandra, Vipan. Sentiment and Ideology in the Nationalism of the Independence Club (1896–1898), in: Korean Studies 10 (1986), pp. 13–34.

Chandra, Vipin. The Independence Club and Korea's First Proposal for a National Legislative Assembly, in: Occasional Papers on Korea 4 (1975), pp. 19–35.

Chase, James. The Wilsonian Moment? in: The Wilson Quarterly 25 (2001) 4, pp. 34–41.

Chase–Dunn, Christopher; Smith, Jackie; Manning, Patrick and Grubačić, Andrej. Remembering Immanuel Wallerstein, in: Journal of World–Systems Research 26 (2020) 1, pp. 5–8.

Chen, Joseph T. The May Fourth Movement in Shanghai. The Making of a Social Movement in Modern China, Leiden 1971.

Ch'i, Hsi–sheng. Warlord Politics in China 1916–1928, Stanford, CA 1976.

China Also Balks, in: The Sun (New York, NY), May 7, 1919, p. 1.

China Calls Decision of Big 3 "Unfair", in: New York Tribune, May 4, 1919, p. 4.

China's Grievances over Shantung, in: The Chinese Students' Monthly 15 (1919) 1, pp. 3–6.

Ching, Leo T. S. Becoming "Japanese". Colonial Taiwan and the Politics of Identity Formation, Berkeley, CA 2001.

Chirot, Daniel and Hall, Thomas D. World–System Theory, in: Annual Review of Sociology 8 (1982), pp. 81–106.

Ch'oe, Yŏng–ho. An Outline History of Korean Historiography, in: Korean Studies 4 (1980), pp. 1–27.

Ch'oe, Yŏng–ho. The Kapsin Coup of 1884. A Reassessment, in: Korean Studies 6 (1982) 1, pp. 105–124.

Choi, Hyaeweol. An American Concubine in Old Korea. Missionary Discourse on Gender, Race, and Modernity, in: Frontiers: A Journal of Women Studies 25 (2004) 3, pp. 134–161.

Choi, Hyaeweol. New Women in Colonial Korea. A Sourcebook, London 2012.

Clarke, Joseph I. C. Japan at First Hand. New York 1918.

Cohen, Paul A. and Schreckner, John E. (Eds.). Reform in Nineteenth–Century China, Cambridge, MA 1976.

Conklin, Alice L. A Mission to Civilize. The Republican Idea of Empire in France and West Africa, 1895–1930, Stanford, CA 1997.

Conrad, Sebastian. What is Global History? Princeton, NJ 2016.

Conze, Eckart. Die große Illusion. Versailles 1919 und die Neuordnung der Welt, Munich 2018.

Coudert, Frederik R. et al. Why Europe Is At War? The Question Considered from the Points of View of France, England, Germany, Japan and the United States, New York/London 1915.

Craft, Stephen G. Angling for an Invitation to Paris: China's Entry into the First World War, in: The International History Review 16 (1994) 1, pp. 1–24.

Craft, Stephen G. V.K. Wellington Koo and the Emergence of Modern China, Lexington, KY 2003.

Craft, Stephen G. John Bassett Moore, Robert Lansing, and the Shandong Question, in: Pacific Historical Review 66 (1997) 2, pp. 231–249.

Dal Lago, Enrico; Healy, Róisín and Barry, Gearóid (Eds.). 1916 in Global Context. An Anti–Imperial Moment, London 2018.

David, Mirela. Bertrand Russell and Ellen Key in China. Idividualism, Free Love, and Eugenics in the May Fourth Era, in: Chiang, Howard (Ed.), Sexuality in China. Histories of Power and Pleasure, Seattle, WA 2018, pp. 76–98.

Davis, Clarence B. Limits of Effacement. Britain and the Problem of American Cooperation and Competitionin China, 1915–1917, in: Pacific Historical Review 48 (1979) 1, pp. 47–63.

Da Yang. Leng yan jia wu. Kan Riben jun shi di guo de gou jian he bao fa (1868–1905), Beijing 2015.

Deutsch, Karl W. Nationalism and Social Communication. An Inquiry into the Foundations of Nationality, Cambridge, MA 1953.

Dickinson, Frederick R. The First World War, Japan, and a Global Century, in: Frattolillo, Oliviero and Best, Antony (Eds.), Japan and the Great War, New York 2015, pp. 162–182.

Dickinson, Frederick R. World War I and the Triumph of a New Japan, 1919–1930, Cambridge, MA 2013.

Ding Xianjun. Yangwu yundong shihua, Beijing 2000.

Dirlik, Arif. Ideology and Organization in the May Fourth Movement. Some Proplems in the Intellectual Historiography of the May Fourth Period, in: Republican China 12 (1987) 1, pp. 3–19.

Duiker, William J. Ts'ai Yuan–p'ei. Educator of Modern China, University Park, PA 1977.

Dunscomb, Paul E. Japan's Siberian Intervention, 1918–1922, Lanham, MD 2011.

Edmunds, Charles K. Modern Education in China, Department of the Interior, Bureau of Education, Bulletin 1919, No. 44, Washington, D.C. 1919.

Etō, Shinkichi. China's International Relations, 1911–1931, in: Fairbank, John K. and Feuerwerker, Albert (Eds.), The Cambridge History of China, Vol. 13: Republican China 1912–1949, Part 2, Cambridge 1983, pp. 74–115.

Fairbank, John King and Goldman, Merle. China. A New History, second edition, Cambridge, MA 2006.

Faison, Elyssa Women's Rights as Proletarian Rights. Yamakawa Kikue, Suffrage, and the "Dawn of Liberation, in: Bullock, Julia C.; Kano, Ayako and Welker, James (Eds.), Rethinking Japanese Feminism, Honolulu 2018, pp. 15–33.

Fay, Peter Ward. The Opium War, 1840–1842, paperback edition, Chapel Hill, NC, 1997 [1975].

Fedman, David. Seeds of Control. Japan's Empire of Forestry in Colonial Korea, Seattle, WA 2020.

Feuerwerker, Albert. Economic Trends, 1912–49, in: Twitchett, Denis and Fairbank, John K. (Eds.), The Cambridge History of China, vol. 12: Republican China 1912–1949, Part 1, Cambridge 1983, pp. 28–127.

Fields, David. Foreign Friends. Syngman Rhee, American Exceptionalism, and the Division of Korea, Lexington, KY 2019.

Fishel, Wesley R. The Far East and United States Policy: A Re-Examination, in: The Western Political Quarterly 3 (1950) 1, pp. 1–13.

Fitzgerald, Matthew P. and Monteath, Peter (Eds.). Colonialism, China and the Chinese, New York/London 2019.

Forster, Elisabeth. 1919 – The Year That Changed China. A New History of the New Culture Movement, Berlin/Boston 2018.

Frattolillo, Oliviero and Best, Antony. Introduction: Japan and the Great War, in: idem. (Eds.), Japan and the Great War, New York 2015, pp. 1–10.

Fukuzawa, Naomi. Fukuzawa Yukichis Datsu-a-ron (1885). Wegbereiter des japanischen Imperialismus oder zornige Enttauschung eines asiatischen Aufklarers?, in: Tātonnemen 13 (2011), pp. 210–224.

Furth, Charlotte. Intellectual Change. From the Reform Movement to the May Fourth Movement, 1895–1920, in: Twitchett, Denis and Fairbank, John K. (Eds.), The Cambridge History of China, vol. 12: Republican China 1912–1949, Part 1, Cambridge 1983, pp. 322–405.

Furuki, Yoshiko. The White Plum. A Biography of Ume Tsuda, Pioneer in the Higher Education of Japanese Women, New York 1991.

Gates, Rustin B. Out with the New and in with the Old. Uchida Yasuya and the Great War as a Turning Point in Japanese Foreign Affairs, in: Minohara, Tosh; Hon, Tze-ki and Dawley, Evan (Eds.), The Decade of the Great War. Japan and the Wider World in the 1910s, Leiden 2014, pp. 64–82.

Gellner, Ernest. Change and Thought, Chicago, IL 1964.

Gellner, Ernest. Nations and Nationalism, Ithaca, NY 1983.

Geng, Yunzhi. An Introductory Study on China's Cultural Transformation in Recent Times, Berlin 2014.

Goetzmann, William N.; Ukhov, Andrey D. and Zhu, Ning. China and the World Financial Markets 1870–1939. Modern Lessons from Historical Globalization, in: The Economic History Review 60 (2007) 2, pp. 267–312.

Gordon, Andrew. A Modern History of Japan. From Tokugawa Times to the Present, New York 2003.

Gordon, Andrew. The Short Happy Life of the Japanese Middle Class, in: Zunz, Olivier; Schoppa, Leonard and Hiwatari Nobuhiro (Eds.), Social Contracts Under Stress. New York 2002, pp. 108–129.

Griffis, William Elliot. Japan in the World War, in: The North American Review 208 (1918) 756, pp. 722–728.

Gross, Christine. Japanische Frauen. Ein Leitbild im Wandel. Die Zeitschrift Shufu no tomo 1917–1935, Dissertation, Universität Zürich, 2009.

Gu, Edward X. Populistic Themes in May Fourth Radical Thinking. A Reappraisal of the Intellectual Origins of Chinese Marxism (1917–1922), in: East Asian History 10 (1995), pp. 99–126.

Ha, Yong-Chool. Colonial Rule and Social Change in Korea The Paradox of Colonial Control, in: Lee, Hong Yung; Ha, Yong-Chool and Sorensen, Clark W. (Eds.), Colonial Rule and Social Change in Korea, 1910–1945, Seattle, WA 2013, pp. 39–75.

Han, Hongkoo. Colonial Origins of *Juche*: The Minsaengdan Incident of the 1930s and the Birth of the North Korea–China Relationship, in: Suh, Jae Jung (Ed.), Origins of North Korea's Juche. Colonialism, War, and Development, Lanham, MD 2012, pp. 33–62.

Han, Suyin. Eldest Son. Zhou Enlai and the Making of Modern China, 1898–1976, New York 1995.

Handō Kazutoshi. Nichiro Sensōshl, 3 vols., Tokyo 2016.

Hanes, Jeffrey E. Media Culture in Taishō Osaka, in: Minichiello, Sharon (Ed.), Japan's Competing Modernities. Issues in Culture and Democracy 1900–1930, Honolulu 1998, pp. 267–287.

Hanes, Jeffrey E. The City as Subject. Seki Hajime and the Reinvention of Modern Osaka, Berkeley/Los Angeles, CA 2002.

Harnisch, Thomas. Chinesische Studenten in Deutschland. Geschichte und Wirkung ihrer Studienaufenthalte in den Jahren 1860 bis 1945, Hamburg 1999.

Hartmann, Rudolf. Japanischer Revolutionär und proletarischer Internationalist. Sen Katayama, in: Beiträge zur Geschichte der Arbeiterbewegung 26 (1984) 2, pp. 238–246.

Haruno Saru and Shen Chun Ye, Pari kōwa kaigi to Nichi–Bei–Chū kankei. "Santō mondai" o chūshin ni, in: Hokusai kōkyū seisaku kenkyū 9 (2005) 2, pp. 189–206.

Hatano Yoshihiro. Chūgoku kindai gunbatsu no kenkyū, Tokyo 1973.

Hatsuda Tōru. Hyakkaten no tanjō, Tokyo 1993.

Hatsuse Ryūhei. Dentōteki uyoku. Uchida Ryōhei no kenkyū, Fukuoka 1980.

Hayot, Eric. Bertrand Russell's Chinese Eyes, in: Modern Chinese Literature and Culture 18 (2006) 1, pp. 120–154.

Heater, Derek. National Self-Determination. Woodrow Wilson and His Legacy, New York 1994.

Henry, Todd A. Assimilating Seoul. Japanese Rule and the Politics of Public Space in Colonial Korea, 1910–1945, Los Angeles, CA 2014.

Hirakawa Sukehiro. Wakon yōsai no keifu. Uchi to soto kara no Meiji Nihon, Tokyo 1992.

Hobson, Christopher. The Rise of Democracy. Revolution, War and Transformations in International Politics since 1776, Edinburgh 2015.

Hosoya Chihiro. Roshia kakumei to Nihon, Tokyo 1972.

Hosoya Chihiro. Ryō taisenkan no Nihon no gaikō, 1914–1945, Tokyo 1988.

Hosoya Chihiro. Shiberia shuppei no shiteki kenkyū, Tokyo 2005.

Hoston, Germaine A. Marxism and the Crisis of Development in Prewar Japan, Princeton, NJ 1986.

Huffman, James L. Japan in World History, New York 2010.

Hunter, Janet. Japanese Government Policy, Business Opinion and the Seoul–Pusan Railway, 1894–1906, in: Modern Asian Studies 11 (1977) 4, pp. 573–599.

Hwang, Dongyoun. Anarchlsm In Korea. Independence, Transnatlonallsm, and the Questlon of National Development, 1919–1984, Albany, NY 2016.

Inoue Kiyoshi and Watanabe Tōru. Kome sōdō no kenkyū, Tokyo 1997.

Inoue Kiyoshi. Meiji ishin, Tokyo 2003.

Ion, A. Hamish. The Cross and the Rising Sun, vol. 2: The British Protestant Movement in Japan, Korea and Taiwan, 1865–1945, Waterloo, ON 2009.

Ishikawa Hiroyoshi. Goraku no senzenshi, Tokyo 1981.

Itaya Toshihiko. Nihonjin no tame no Dai–ichiji Sekai Taisenshi. Sekai wa naze sensō ni totsunyū shita noka, Tokyo 2017.

Izao Tomio. Shoki shiberia shuppei no kenkyū. Atarashiki kyūseigun kōsō no tōjō to tenkai, Fukuoka 2003.

Jacob, Frank. 1917. Die korrumpierte Revolution, Marburg 2020.

Jacob, Frank. Der Erste Weltkrieg als ökonomisch–soziale Zäsur der japanischen Moderne, in: Köhn, Stephan; Weber, Chantal and Elis, Volker (Eds.), Tokyo in den zwanziger Jahren Experimentierfeld einer anderen Moderne? Wiesbaden 2017, pp. 17–32.

Jacob, Frank. Die Thule–Gesellschaft und die Kokuryūkai. Geheimgesellschaften im global–historischen Vergleich, Würzburg 2013.

Jacob, Frank. Japanism, Pan–Asianism and Terrorism. A Short History of the Amur Society (the Black Dragons), 1901–1945, Bethesda, CA 2014.

Jacob, Frank. Queen Min, Foreign Policy and the Role of Female Leadership in Late Nineteenth–Century Korea, in: Elena Woodacre et al. (Eds.), The Routledge History of Monarchy, London 2019, pp. 700–717.

Jacob, Frank. Reflections on the Korean Diaspora in Manchuria, in: Florian Kläger and Klaus Stierstorfer (Eds.): Diasporic Constructions of Home and Belonging, Berlin 2015, pp. 111–122.

Jacob, Frank. The First World War, Women's Education, and Yamakawa Kikue's Socialist View of Gender Roles in Japan, in: Sebastian Engelmann/Bernhard Hemetsberger/Frank Jacob (Eds.), War and Education. The Pedagogical Preparation for Collective Mass Violence, Paderborn 2022, pp. 119–141.

Jacob, Frank. The Korean Diaspora in Manchuria. Korean Ambitions, Manchurian Dreams, Japanese Realities, in: Entremons UPF. Journal of World History 6 (2014), pp. 1–11.

Jacob, Frank. The Russian Revolution, the American Red Scare, and the Forced Exile of Transnational Anarchists. Emma Goldman and Alexander Berkman and their Soviet Experience, in: Yearbook of Transnational History 4 (2021), pp. 113–134.

Jacob, Frank. The Russo–Japanese War and Its Shaping of the Twentieth Century, London 2018.

Jacob, Frank. Tsushima 1905. Ostasiens Trafalgar, second edition, Paderborn 2021.

Jacob, Frank (Ed.). Wallerstein 2.0. Thinking and Applying World–Systems Theory in the 21st Century, Bielefeld 2022.

Jacob, Frank; Shaw, Jeffrey and Demy, Timothy (Eds.). War and the Humanities. The Cultural Impact of the First World War, Paderborn 2019.

James, David H. The Rise and Fall of the Japanese Empire, London/New York 2010 [1951].

Jansen, Marius B. The Japanese and Sun Yat–sen, Stanford 1970 [1954].

Japanese Atrocities in Korea. Reports Emphasized and Made Convincing by Japanese Propaganda, n.d. [1920].

Jessen, Olaf. Verdun 1916. Urschlacht des Jahrhunderts, second edition, Munich 2017.

Jinno Yuki. Hyakkaten ga tsukutta teisuto, Tokyo, 1994.

Jonas, Michael. Scandinavia and the Great Powers in the First World War, London 2019.

Ka, Chih–Ming. Japanese Colonialism in Taiwan. Land Tenure, Development, and Dependency, 1895–1945, London 2019.

Kal, Hong. Aesthetic Constructions of Korean Nationalism. Spectacle, Politics and History, London/New York 2011.

Kallander, George L. Salvation through Dissent. Tonghak Heterodoxy and Early Modern Korea, Honolulu, HI 2016.

Kameda Kinuko. Tsuda Umeko. Hitori no meikyōshi no kiseki, Tokyo 2005.

Kang, Chao. The Development of Cotton Textile Production in China, Cambridge, MA 1977.

Kang, Etsuko H. Kita Sadakichi (1871–1939) on Korea. A Japanese Ethno-Historian and the Annexation of Korea in 1910, in: Asian Studies Review 21 (1997) 1, pp. 41–60.

Kang, Pŏm–sŏk. Seikanron seihen. Meiji rokunen no kenryoku tōsō, Tokyo 1990.

Katayama Sen. Der Verfall des bureaukratischen Regimes in Japan, in: Die neue Zeit. Wochenschrift der deutschen Sozialdemokratie 32 (1914) 1, pp. 16–20.

Katayama Sen. Die Ausbeutung der Arbeiter in Japan, in: Die neue Zeit. Wochenschrift der deutschen Sozialdemokratie 29 (1911) 52, pp. 917–921.

Katayama Sen. Die politischen Zustände Japans, in: Die neue Zeit. Wochenschrift der deutschen Sozialdemokratie 29 (1911) 4, pp. 107–111.

Katayama Sen. Industrie und Sozialismus in Japan, in: Die neue Zeit. Wochenschrift der deutschen Sozialdemokratie 28 (1910) 25, pp. 874–880.

Katayama Sen. Japan and Soviet Russia, London, 6 September 1919, Warwick Digital Collection, 36/R30/22, 2.

Katayama Sen. The Labor Movement in Japan, Chicago 1918.

Kaufman, Alison A. In Pursuit of Equality and Respect. China's Diplomacy and the League of Nations, in: Modern China 40 (2014) 6, pp. 605–638.

Kawakami Hajime. Bimbō monogatari, Tokyo 1983.

Kendall, Carlton Waldo. The Truth about Korea, second edition, San Francisco, CA 1919.

Kennan, George F. The Decline of Bismarck's European Order. Franco–Russian Relations, 1875–1890, Princeton, NJ 1979.

Kim, Dong–No. "National Identity and Class Interest in the Peasant Movements of the Colonial Period, in: Lee, Hong Yung; Ha, Yong–Chool and Sorensen, Clark W. (Eds.), Colonial Rule and Social Change in Korea, 1910–1945, Seattle, WA 2013, pp. 140–172.

Kim, Jinwung. A History of Korea. From "Land of the Morning Calm" to States in Conflict, Bloomington, IN 2012.

Kim, Key–Hiuk. The Last Phase of the East Asian World Order. Korea, Japan, and the Chinese Empire, 1860–1882, Berkeley, CA 1980.

Kim, Seung–young. American Diplomacy and Strategy toward Korea and Northeast Asia 1882–1950 and After. Perception of Polarity and US Commitment to a Periphery, London 2009.

Kimura, Mitsuhiko. The Economics of Japanese Imperialism in Korea, 1910–1939, in: The Economic History Review 48 (1995) 3, pp. 555–574.

Kimura Seiji. Dai–ichiji Sekai Taisen, Tokyo 2014.

Kimura Tokio. Kita Ikki to Ni–niroku jiken no inbō Tokyo 2007.

Kipling, Rudyard. The White Man's Burden (1899), in: Modern History Sourcebook, Fordham University. Accessed May 28, 2022. https://sourcebooks.fordham.edu/mod/kipling.asp.

Kitajima Manji. Hideyoshi no Chōsen shinryaku, Tokyo 2002.

Kitaoka Shin'ichi. Nihon rikugun to tairiku seisaku, 1906–1918, Tokyo 1978.

Kleiner, Juergen. Korea. A Century of Change, London et al. 2001.

Kobayashi Tatsuo (Hrsg.). Suiusō Nikki, Tokyo 1965.

Korean Delegation. Petition. The Claim of the Korean People and Nation for Liberation from Japan and for the Reconstitution of Korea as an Independent State, Paris, April 1919, Columbia University Library, 97–84261–16.

Korean Information Bureau. Little Martyrs of Korea, Philadelphia, PA 1919.

Kuhn, Dieter. Die Republik China von 1912 bis 1937. Entwurf für eine politische Ereignisgeschichte, thrid revised and extended edition, Heidelberg 2007.

Kurokawa Hidenori, Nihon no dai–seijika. Itō Hirobumi mo, Chōsenjin ni totte ha gokuakunin datta! in: Kaku Kōzō (Ed.), Nihonshi jinbutsu "sono go no hanashi", fourth edition, Tokyo 1996, pp. 312–313.

Kuß, Susanne and Martin, Bernd (Eds.). Das Deutsche Reich und der Boxeraufstand, Munich 2002.

Kuß, Susanne. Deutsches Militär auf kolonialen Kriegsschauplätzen. Eskalation von Gewalt zu Beginn des 20. Jahrhunderts, Berlin 2005.

Kwak, Sang–Kyung and Lee, Hun–Chang. Conditions of Economic Devvelopment in Korea in the First Half of the Twentieth Century, in: Ikeo, Aiko (Ed.), Economic Development in Twentieth–Century East Asia. The International Context, London/New York 1997, pp. 75–85.

Lanza, Fabio. Behind the Gate. Inventing Students in Beijing, New York 2010.

Large, Stephen S. The Japanese Labor Movement, 1912–1919. Suzuki Bunji and the Yūaikai, in: The Journal of Japanese Studies 29 (1970) 3, pp. 559–579.

Larsen, Kirk W. and Seeley, Joseph. Simple Conversation or Secret Treaty? The Taft–Katsura Memorandum in Korean Historical Memory, in: Journal of Korean Studies 19 (2014) 1, pp. 59–92.

Laurinat, Marion. Kita Ikki (1883–1937) und der Februarputsch 1936. Eine historische Untersuchung japanischer Quellen des Militärgerichtsverfahrens, Berlin 2006.

Lee, Chae–jin. Zhou Enlai. The Early Years, Stanford 1994.

Lee, Timothy S. A Political Factor in the Rise of Protestantism in Korea. Protestantism and the 1919 March First Movement, in: Church History 69 (2000) 1, pp. 116–142.

Leonhard, Jörn. Der überforderte Frieden. Versailles und die Welt 1918–1923, Munich 2018.

Leutner Mechthild and Mühlhahn, Klaus (Eds.). Kolonialkrieg in China. Die Niederschlagung der Boxerbewegung 1900–1901, Berlin 2007.

Lew, Young Ick. The Making of the First Korean President. Syngman Rhee's Quest for Independence, 1875–1948, Honolulu, HI 2013.

Liao, Ping–hui and Wang, David Der–Wei (Eds.). Taiwan Under Japanese Colonial Rule, 1895–1945. History, Culture, Memory, New York, NY 2010.

Lim, Chaisung. Railroad Workers and World War I. Labor Hygiene and the Policies of Japanese National Railways, in: Minohara, Tosh et al. (Eds.), The Decade of the Great War. Japan and the Wider World in the 1910s, Leiden 2014, pp. 415–438.

Linkhoeva, Tatiana. Revolution Goes East. Imperial Japan and Soviet Communism, Ithaca, NY 2020.

Linkhoeva, Tatiana. The Russian Revolution and the Emergence of Japanese Anticommunism, in: Revolutionary Russia 31 (2018) 2, pp. 261–278.

Lutum, Peter. Das Denken von Minakata Kumagusu und Yanagita Kunio. Zwei Pioniere der japanischen Volkskunde im Spiegel der Leitmotive wakon–yōsai und wayō–setchū, Münster 2005.

Lowe, Peter. Great Britain and Japan, 1911–1915. A Study of British Far Eastern Policy, New York 1969.

Lutum, Peter. Das Denken von Minakata Kumagusu und Yanagita Kunio. Zwei Pioniere der japanischen Volkskunde im Spiegel der Leitmotive wakon–yōsai und wayō–setchū, Münster 2005.

MacLennan, Arthur. Diplomacy and Force in Korea, San Francisco, CA 1919.

Manela, Erez. Imagining Woodrow Wilson in Asia: Dreams of East–West Harmony and the Revolt against Empire 1919, in: The American Historical Review 111 (2006) 5, pp. 1327–1351.

Manela, Erez. The Wilsonian Moment. Self–Determination and the International Origins of Anticolonial Nationalism, Oxford 2007.

Mao, Haijian. The Qing Empire and the Opium War. The Collapse of the Heavenly Dynasty, Cambridge 2016.

Mao Haijian. Wuxu bianfa shi shikao, Beijing 2005.

Mao Tse-tung. The Chinese Revolution and the Chinese Communist Party, in: Selected Works of Mao Tse-tung, vol. 2. Accessed September 17, 2019. https://www.marxists.org/refer ence/archive/mao/selected-works/volume-2/mswv2_23.htm#p4.

Mao Tse-tung. The May 4th Movement, in: Selected Works of Mao Tse-tung, vol. 2. Accessed September 17, 2019. https://www.marxists.org/reference/archive/mao/selected-works/ volume-2/mswv2_13.htm.

Mason, Michele M. and Lee, Helen J.S. Introduction, in: idem. (Eds.), Reading Colonial Japan. Text, Context, and Critique, Stanford, CA 2012, pp. 1–17.

Matsumoto Ken'ichi. Kita Ikki ron, Toyko 1996.

Matsusaka, Y. Tak. Japan's South Manchuria Railway Company in Northeast China, 1906–34, in: Elleman, Bruce A. and Kotkin, Stephen (Eds.), Manchurian Railways and the Opening of China. An International History, New York/London 2009, pp. 37–58.

May, Ernest R. American Policy and Japan's Entrance into World War I, in: The Mississippi Valley Historical Review 40 (1953) 2, pp. 279–290.

McCord, Edward A. Warlordism in Early Republican China, in: Graff, David A. and Highman, Robin (Eds.), A Military History of China, Lexington KY, 2012, pp. 175–192.

McCormack, Gavan. Chang Tso-lin in Northeast China, 1911–1928. China, Japan, and the Manchurian Idea, Stanford, CA 1977.

McGuire Mohr, Joan. The Czech and Slovak Legion in Siberia from 1917 to 1922, Jefferson, NC 2012.

Meisner, Maurice. Li Ta-Chao and the Origins of Chinese Marxism, Cambridge, MA 1967.

Melzer, Jürgen. Warfare 1914–1918 (Japan), in: 1914–1918-online. International Encyclopedia of the First World War, ed. by Ute Daniel, Peter Gatrell, Oliver Janz, Heather Jones, Jennifer Keene, Alan Kramer, and Bill Nasson, issued by Freie Universität Berlin, Berlin, October 19, 2017. Accessed May 30, 2022. https://encyclopedia.1914-1918-online.net/arti cle/warfare_1914-1918_japan.

Meyer, Harald. Die "Taishō-Demokratie". Begriffsgeschichtliche Studien zur Demokratierezeption in Japan von 1900 bis 1920, Bern 2005.

Mi Rucheng. Di guo zhu yi yu Zhongguo tie lu, 1847–1949, Beijing 2007.

Miki Kiyoshi, Miki Kiyoshi zenshū, Tokyo 1984, 20 vols.

Minohara, Tosh; Hon, Tze-ki and Dawley, Evan. Introduction, in:idem. (Eds.), The Decade of the Great War. Japan and the Wider World in the 1910s, Leiden 2014, pp. 1–17.

Mitter, Rana. 1911. The Unanchored Chinese Revolution, in: The China Quarterly 208 (2011), pp. 1009–1020.

Miyagawa Gorīsaburō. Ten'yūkyō kyūen no keirinkō, in in: Fujimoto Hisanori (Ed.): Tōyama seishin Tokyo 1940, pp. 117–129.

Miyazaki Tōten. Sanjūsannen no yume, Tokyo 1902.

Miyazaki, Tōten. My Thirty-Three Year's Dream. The Autobiography of Miyazaki Toten, transl. and ed. by Marius B. Jansen and Etō Shinkichi, Princeton 2014.

Mizuno Naoki. Shokuminchi Chōsen ni okeru Itō Hirobumi no kioku. Keijo no Hakubunji wo chūshin ni, in: Itō Yukio and I Sunhan (Eds.), Itō Hirobumi to Kankoku tōchi. Shodai Kankoku tōkan wo meguru hyakunenme no kenshō, Tokyo 2009, pp. 212–215.

Molony, Barbarba. Women's Rights, Feminism, and Suffragism in Japan, 1870–1925, in: Pacific Historical Review 69 (2000) 4, pp. 639–661.

Mori, Massimo. Friede und Föderalismus bei Kant, in: Zeitschrift für Politik 53 (2006) 4, pp. 379–392.

Moskowitz, Karl. The Creation of the Oriental Development Company. Japanese Illusions Meet Korean Reality, in: Occasional Papers on Korea 2 (1974), pp. 73–121.

Murao, Hideo. The Ideas and Philosophy of Nishihara Kamezō. In the Context of His Role in the Nishihara Loans, in: Nagasaki kenritsu daigaku ronshū 30 (1997) 3, pp. 433–473.

Nakano Takeshi. Fukoku to kyōhei. Chisei keizaigaku josetsu, Tokyo 2016.

Naraoka, Sōchi. A New Look at Japan's Twenty–One Demands. Reconsidering Katō Takaaki's Motives in 1915, in: Minohara, Tosh; Hon, Tze–ki and Dawley, Evan (Eds.), The Decade of the Great War. Japan and the Wider World in the 1910s, Leiden 2014, pp. 189–210.

Nathan, Andrew J. A Constitutional Republic. The Peking Government, 1916–28, in: Twitchett, Denis and Fairbank, John K. (Eds.), The Cambridge History of China, vol. 12: Republican China 1912–1949, Part 1, Cambridge 1983, pp. 256–283.

Nathan, Andrew J. Peking Politics, 1918–1923. Factionalism and the Failure of Constitutionalism, Berkeley/Los Angeles 1976.

Nihon Kokuyū Tetsudō – Sōsaishitsu – Shūshika, Nihon kokuyū tetsudō hyakunenshi, 17 vols., Tokyo 1969–1974.

Nimura, Kazuo. The Ashio Riot of 1907. A Social History of Mining in Japan, Durham, NC 1998.

Nish, Ian. Alliance in Decline. A Study in Anglo–Japanese Relations, 1908–1923, London 1972.

Nish, Ian. Japan and China, 1914–1916, in: Hinsley, F. Harry (Ed.), British Foreign Policy Under Sir Edward Grey, Cambridge 1977, pp. 452–465.

Nish, Ian. Japan and the Outbreak of War in 1914, in: The Collected Writings of Ian Nish, Vol. 1, Tokyo 2001, pp. 173–187.

Nish, Ian. The Anglo–Japanese Alliance. The Diplomacy of Two Island Empires, 1894–1907, London 1966.

Ogden, Suzanne P. The Sage in the Inkpot. Bertrand Russell and China's Social Reconstruction in the 1920s, in: Modern Asian Studies 16 (1982) 4, pp. 529–600.

Oh, Se–Eung. Dr. Philip Jaisohn's Reform Movement, 1896–1898. A Critical Appraisal of the Independence Club, Lanham, MD 1995.

Okabe Makio (Ed.). Minami Manshū tetsudō gaisha no kenkyū, Tokyo 2008.

Ōno Ken'ichi, World War I and the 1920s. Export–led Boom and Bust. Accessed July 4, 2016. http://www.grips.ac.jp/teacher/oono/hp/lecture_J/lec07.htm.

Osatake Takeki. Meiji ishin, Tokyo 1978.

Osei Yoshikura. Ten'yūkyō, Tokyo 1981.

Ōshima Tōto. Tōyama–ō no doko ga erai ka, in: Fujimoto Hisanori (Ed.): Tōyama seishin Tokyo 1940, pp. 82–110.

Otsubo, Sumiko. Fighting on Two Fronts. Japan's Involvement in the Siberian Intervention and the Spanish Influenza Pandemic of 1918, in: Minohara, Tosh; Hon, Tze–ki and Dawley, Evan (Eds.), The Decade of the Great War. Japan and the Wider World in the 1910s, Leiden 2014, pp. 461–480.

Paine, S.C.M. The Chinese Eastern Railway from the First Sino–Japanese War until the Russo–Japanese War, in: Elleman, Bruce A. and Kotkin, Stephen (Eds.), Manchurian Railways and the Opening of China. An International History, New York/London 2009, pp. 13–36.

Paine, S.C.M. The Sino–Japanese War of 1894–1895. Perceptions, Power, and Primacy, Cambridge 2003.

Park, Chung-Shin. *Protestantism and Politics in Korea*, Seattle, WA 2003.

Park Eun-sik, Han'guk tongnip undong chi hyŏlsa, Shanghai 1920.

Park, Joohyun Jade. Journalism behind Bars. Bethell's Anti-Japanese English-Korean Newspapers, in: Victorian Periodicals Review 51 (2018) 1, pp. 86–120.

Peckham, Robert. Epidemics in Modern Asia, Cambridge 2016.

Petersson, Niels P. Imperialismus und Modernisierung. Siam, China und die europäischen Mächte 1895–1914, Munich 2000.

Pires, Ana Paula; Schmidt, Jan and Tato, María Inés (Eds.), The Global First World War. African, East Asian, Latin American and Iberian Mediators, London/New York 2021.

Platt, Stephen R. Imperial Twilight. The Opium War and the End of China's Last Golden Age, New York 2019.

Radtke, Kurt W. Nationalism and Internationalism in Japan's Economic Liberalism. The Case of Ishibashi Tanzan, in: Stegewerns, Dick (Ed.), Nationalism and Internationalism in Imperial Japan. Autonomy, Asian Brotherhood, or World Citizenship? London/New York 2003, pp. 169–195.

Revelant, Andrea. Rethinking Japanese Taxation in the Wake of the Great War, in: Frattolillo, Oliviero and Best, Antony (Eds.), Japan and the Great War, New York 2015, pp. 116–141.

Rhoads, Edward. Stepping Forth into the World. The Chinese Educational Mission to the United States 1872–1881, Hong Kong 2011.

Rinke, Stefan. Latin America and the First World War, New York, NY 2017.

Robinson, Michael Edson. *Cultural Nationalism in Colonial* Korea, *1920–1925*, new edition, Seatlle, WA 2014 [1988].

Robinson, Michael E. Korea's Twentieth-Century Odyssey. A Short History, Honolulu, HI 2007.

Robinson, Michael. National Identity and the Thought of Sin Ch'aeho. *Sadaejuŭi* and *Chuch'e* in History and Politics, in: The Journal of Korean Studies 5 (1984), pp. 121–142.

Rodney, Walter. How Europe Underdeveloped Africa, Washington, D.C. 1982.

Russell, Bertrand. The Problem of China, London 1922.

Saaler, Sven and Koschmann, J. Victor (Eds.) Pan-Asianism in Modern Japanese History. Colonialism, Regionalism and Borders, London 2007.

Sasaki Toshikazu. Ainu shi no jidai he. Yoreki shō, Sapporo 2013.

Saul, Norman E. The Life and Times of Charles R. Crane, 1858–1939. American Businessman, Philanthropist, and a Founder of Russian Studies in America, Lanham, MD 2013.

Schencking, J. Charles. Making Waves. Politics, Propaganda, and the Emergence of the Imperial Japanese Navy, 1868–1922, Stanford, CA 2005.

Schiffrin, Harold Z. Military and Politics in China. Is the Warlord Model Pertinent? in: Asia Quarterly 3 (1975), p. 195.

Schiltz, Michael. "Separating the Roots of the Chrysanthemum". Nishihara Kamezō and the Abortive China Loans, 1917–18, (2007), MPRA Paper No. 7100. Accessed October 3, 2019. https://mpra.ub.uni-muenchen.de/7100/1/MPRA_paper_7100.pdf.

Schivelbusch, Woflgang. Geschichte der Eisenbahnreise: Zur Industrialisierung von Raum und Zeit im 19. Jahrhundert, Seventh Edition, Frankfurt am Main 2000.

Schmid, Andre. Korea between Empires, 1895–1919, New York 2002.

Schmidt, Jan. Nach dem Krieg ist vor dem Krieg. Medialisierte Erfahrungen des Ersten Weltkriegs und Nachkriegsdiskurse in Japan (1914–1919), Frankfurt am Main 2021.

Schmidt, Jan and Schmidtpott, Katja (Eds.). The East Asian Dimension of the First World War. Global Entanglements and Japan, China and Korea, 1914–1919, Frankfurt am Main 2020.

Reiner Schrader, Die Erzählung von der Armut, in: Oriens Extremus 30 (1983–1986), pp. 154–245.

Schwartz, Benjamin I. Themes in Intellectual History. May Fourth and After, in: Twitchett, Denis and Fairbank, John K. (Eds.), The Cambridge History of China, vol. 12: Republican China 1912–1949, Part 1, Cambridge 1983, pp. 406–450.

Schwartz, Rachel C. The Rand School of Social Science, 1906–1924. A Study of Worker Education in the Socialist Era, PhD Thesis, State University of New York at Buffalo, 1984.

Sheridan, James E. The Warlord Era. Politics and Militarism under the Peking Government, 1916–28, in: Twitchett, Denis and Fairbank, John K. (Eds.), The Cambridge History of China, vol. 12: Republican China 1912–1949, Part 1, Cambridge 1983, pp. 284–321.

Shin, Gi–Wook. *Peasant Protest and Social Change in Colonial Korea*, Seattle, WA 1996.

Shinohara, Chika. Gender and the Great War. Tsuda Umeko's Role in Institutionalizing Women's Education in Japan, in: Minohara, Tosh; Hon, Tze–ki and Dawley, Evan (Eds.), The Decade of the Great War. Japan and the Wider World in the 1910s, Leiden 2014, pp. 323–348.

Shizume Masato, The Japanese Economy during the Interwar Period. Instability in the Financial System and the Impact of the World Depression, in: Bank of Japan Review. Institute for Monetary and Economic Studies, 2009–E–2, Tōkyō 2009. Accessed April 10, 2016. https://www.boj.or.jp/en/research/wps_rev/rev_2009/data/rev09e02.pdf.

Silverberg, Miriam. The Modern Girl as Militant, in: Bernstein, Gail L. (Ed.), Recreating Japanese Women, 1600–1945, Berkeley 1991, pp. 239–266.

Simbirtseva, Tatiana M. Queen Min of Korea. Coming to Power, in: Transactions of the Royal Asiatic Society, *Korea Branch* 71 (1996), pp. 41–54.

Simpson, Brad. The United States and the Curious History of Self–Determination, in: Diplomatic History 36 (2012) 4, pp. 675–694.

Sizer, Nancy F. John Dewey's Ideas in China 1919 to 1921, in: Comparative Education Review 10, (1966) 3, pp. 390–403.

Skocpol, Theda. States and Social Revolutions, Cambridge 1979.

Sprotte, Maik Hendrik. Konfliktaustragung in autoritären Herrschaftssystemen. Eine historische Fallstudie zur frühsozialistischen Bewegung im Japan der Meiji–Zeit, Marburg 2001.

Stanley, Thomas A. Ōsugi Sakae, Anarchist in Taishō Japan. The Creativity of the Ego, Cambridge, MA 1982.

Stegewerns, Dick. The End of World War One as a Turning Point in Modern Japanese History, in: Edström, Bert (Ed.), Turning Points in Japanese History, London/New York 2002, pp. 138–162.

Sturfelt, Lina. Introduction. Scandinavia and the First World War, in: Scandia 80 (2014) 2, online at: https://project2.sol.lu.se/tidskriftenscandia/index-q=node-1096.html. Accessed May 30, 2022.

Summerskill, Michael. China on the Western Front. Britain's Chinese Work Force in the First World War, London 1982.

Suzuki Takeo (Ed.). Nishihara shakkan shiryō kenkyū, Tokyo 1972.

Swope, Kenneth. A Dragon's Head and a Serpent's Tail. Ming China and the first great East Asian War, 1592–1598, Norman, OK 2016.

Szewczyk, Jimmy. The Effects of Income Inequality on Political Participation. A Contextual Analysis. Honors Thessis, Sewanee 2015. Accessed July 3, 2016. https://www.sewanee.edu/media/academics/politics/The-Effects-of-Income-Inequality-on-Political-Participation.pdf.

Ta, Chen. Labor Conditions in Japan, in: Monthly Labor Review 21 (1925) 5, pp. 8–19.

Takamure Itsue. Hi no kuni no onna no nikki. Takamure Itsue jiden, Tokyo 1966.

Takamure Itsue. Zoku anakizumu josei kaihō ronshū, Tokyo 1989.

Takashi Hatada. Nihon to chōsen, Tokyo 1965.

Takenaka, Harukata. Failed Democratization in Prewar Japan. Breakdown of a Hybrid Regime, Stanford, CA 2014.

Takenaka, Toru. Siemens in Japan. Von der Landesöffnung bis zum Ersten Weltkrieg, Stuttgart 1996.

Takii Kazuhiro. Itō Hirobumi. Chi no seijika, Tokyo 2010.

Tamanoi, Mariko Asano. The City and the Countryside. Competing Taishō "Modernities" on Gender, in: Minichiello, Sharon (Ed.), Japan's Competing Modernities. Issues in Culture and Democracy 1900–1930, Honolulu 1998, pp. 91–113.

Tanaka Sōgorō. Kita Ikki. Nihonteki fashisuto no shōchō, second edition, Tokyo 1971.

The Korean Independence Movement, Shanghai [1919?].

The Shantung Controversy, in: The Revolutionary Age 2 (July 26, 1919) 4, p. 2.

Throntveit, Trygve. The Fable of the Fourteen Points. Woodrow Wilson and National Self-Determination, in: Diplomatic History 35, no. 3 (2011), pp. 445–481.

Thunig-Nittner, Gerburg. Die Tschechoslowakische Legion in Russland. Ihre Geschichte und Bedeutung bei der Entstehung der 1. Tschechoslowakischen Republik, Wiesbaden 1970.

Tipton, Elise K. The Department Store. Producing Modernity in Interwar Japan, in: Roy Starrs (Ed.), Rethinking Japanese Modernism, Leiden 2011, pp. 428–451.

Tobata Seiichi. Nihon nōgyō no ninaite, in: Nihon Nōgyō Hattatsushi Chōsakai et al. (Ed.), Nihon nōgyō hattatsushi, vol. 9, Tokyo 1956, pp. 561–604.

Toya Riina. Ginza to Shiseidō. Nihon wo "modān" ni shita kaisha, Tokyo 2012.

Tsao, Y. S. A Challenge to Western Learning. The Chinese Student Trained Abroad – What He Has Accomplished – His Problems, in: News Bulletin (Institute of Pacific Relations), December 1927, pp. 13–16.

Tsurumi, E. Patricia. Visions of Women and the New Society in Conflict. Yamakawa Kikue versus Takamure Itsue, in: Minichiello, Sharon (Ed.), Japan's Competing Modernities. Issues in Culture and Democracy 1900–1930, Honolulu, HI 1998, pp. 335–357.

Townsend, Susan C. Miki Kiyoshi 1897–1945. Japan's Itinerant Philosopher, Leiden 2009.

Townsend, Susan C. The Great War and Urban Crisis. Conceptualizing the Industrial Metropolis in Japan and Britain in the 1910s, in: Minohara, Tosh; Hon, Tze-ki and Dawley, Evan (Eds.), The Decade of the Great War. Japan and the Wider World in the 1910s, Leiden 2014, pp. 301–322.

Tōyama Shigeki. Meiji ishin, Tokyo 2018.

Uchida, Jun. Brokers of Empire: Japanese and Korean Business Elites in Colonial Korea, in: Elkins, Caroline and Pedersen, Sudan (Eds.), Settler Colonialism in the Twentieth Century. Projects, Practices, Legacies, London 2005, 153–170.

Uchida, Jun. Brokers of Empire. Japanese Settler Colonialism in Korea, 1876–1945, Cambridge, MA 2011.

Uchida, Jun. "A Scramble for Freight". The Politics of Collaboration along and across the Railway Tracks of Korea under Japanese Rule, in: Comparative Studies in Society and History 51 (2009) 1, pp. 117–150.

Uden, Martin. Times Past in Korea. An Illustrated Collection of Encounters, Customs and Daily Life Recorded by Foreign Visitors, London/New York 2003.

Underwood, Elizabeth Ann. Challenged Identities. North American Missionaries in Korea, 1884–1934, Seoul 2004.

United States Bureau of Manufactures (Ed.), Monthy Consular and Trade Reports 86, Washington, D.C. 1908.

United States Tariff Commission, Japan. Trade During the War, Washington, D.C. 1919.

Uttam, Jitendra. *Political Economy of Korea. Transition, Transformation and Turnaround*, London 2014.

Vorländer, Klaus. Kant und der Gedanke des Völkerbundes, Leipzig 1919.

Wada Hanako. Dai-ichiji Sekai Taisengo ni okeru Nihon gaikō zaigai kōkan, in: Journal of the Graduate School of Humanities and Sciences, Ochanomizu University 8 (2005) 6, pp. 1–13.

Wagner, Kim. Imperial Legacies by Jeremy Black review – whitewash for Britain's atrocities, in: The Guardian, August 10, 2019. Accessed May 28, 2022. https://www.theguardian.com/books/2019/aug/10/imperial-legacies-jeremy-black-review-empire-multiculturalism.

Wallerstein, Immanuel. Welt–System–Analyse. Eine Einführung, Wiesbaden 2019.

Walker, Brett L. The Conquest of Ainu Lands. Ecology and Culture in Japanese Expansion, 1590–1800, Berkeley, CA 2009.

Walthall, Anne. From Private to Public Patriarchy. Women, Labor and the State in East Asia, 1600–1919, in: Teresa A. Meade and Merry E. Wiesner–Hanks (Eds.), *A Companion to Gender History*, New York 2006, pp. 444–458.

Wang, Fan-sen and Fu, Ssu-nien. A Life in Chinese History and Politics, Cambridge/New York 2006.

Wang, Peili; von Humboldt, Wilhelm and Cai. Yuanpei. Eine vergleichende Analyse zweier klassischer Bildungskonzepte in der deutschen Aufklärung und in der ersten chinesischen Republik, Münster/New York 1996.

Wang, Peter Chen-main. Caring beyond National Borders: The YMCA and Chinese Laborers in World War I Europe, in: Church History 78 (2009) 2, pp. 327–349.

Wang, Yuru. Economic Development in China between the Two World Wars (1920–1936), in: Wright, Tim (Ed.), The Chinese Economy in the Early Twentieth Century. Recent Chinese Studies, London 1992, pp. 58–77.

Webb, Sidney and Beatrice. The Webbs in Asia. The 1911–12 Travel Diary, edited by George Feaver, Basingstoke 1992.

Weisenfeld, Gennifer. MAVO. Japanese Artists and the Avant–Garde, 1905–1931, Berkeley/Los Angeles, CA 2002.

Wells, Kenneth M. Background to the March First Movement. Koreans in Japan, 1905–1919, in: Korean Studies 13 (1989), pp. 5–21.

Wendorff, Jean Jaques. Der Boxeraufstand in China 1900/1901 als deutscher und französischer Erinnerungsort. Ein Vergleich anhand ausgewählter Quellengruppen, Frankfurt am Main 2016.

Werner, Edward T.C. China of the Chinese, London 1920.

Whiting, Allen S. The Soviet Offer to China of 1919, in: The Far Eastern Quarterly 10 (1951) 4, pp. 355–364.

Wilson, Woodrow. Fourteen Points Speech, in: Arhurt S. Link et al. (Eds.), The Papers of Woodrow Wilson, Princeton, NJ 1984, vol. 45, p. 536.

Winter, Jay (Ed.). The Cambridge History of the First World War, vol. 1: Global War, Cambridge 2014.

Womack, Brantly. China between Region and World, The China Journal 61 (2009), pp. 1–20.

Wood, Ge-Zay. China Versus Japan, New York 1919.

Worm, Herbert. Studien über den jungen Ōsugi Sakae und die Meiji–Sozialisten zwischen Sozialdemokratie und Anarchismus unter besonderer Berücksichtigung der Anarchismusrezeption, Hamburg 1981.

Wu, Chengming. A Brief Account of the Development of Capitalism in China, in: Wright, Tim (Ed.), The Chinese Economy in the Early Twentieth Century. Recent Chinese Studies, London 1992, pp. 29–43.

Xu, Guoqi. Asia, in: Winter, Jay (Ed.), The Cambridge History of the First World War, vol. 1, Cambridge 2014, pp. 479–510.

Xu, Guoqi. Asia and the Great War. A Shared History, New York 2017.

Xu, Guoqi. Strangers on the Western Front. Chinese Workers in the Great War, Cambridge, MA 2011.

Xu, Jilin. Historical Memories of May Fourth. Patriotism, but of What Kind?, in: China Heritage Quarterly 17 (2009). Accessed September 30, 2019. http://www.chinaheritagequarterly. org/features.php?searchterm=017_mayfourthmemories.inc&issue=017.

Yamamuro Shin'ichi et al. Gendai no kiten Dai–ichiji Sekai Taisen, 4 vols., Tokyo 2014.

Yamanoue Shōtarō. Dai–ichiji Sekai Taisen. Wasurerareta sensō, Tokyo 2010.

Yamazaki, Tomoko. The Story of Yamada Waka. From Prostitute to Feminist Pioneer, Tokyo 1985.

Yang, Qian. Pari kōwa kaigi to taika ni jū ichi–kajō. Santō mondai o chūshin ni, in: Hokudai shigaku 58 (2018), pp. 80–95.

Ye, Weili. Searching Modernity in China's Name. Chinese Students in the United States, 1900–1927, Stanford 2001.

Yoo, Theodore Jun. The Politics of Gender in Colonial Korea. Education, Labor, and Health, 1910–1945, Berkeley, CA 2008.

Young, A. Morgan. Japan under Taisho Tenno 1912–1926, London/New York 2010.

Yu, Chai–Shin. A New History of Korean Civilization, Bloomington, IN 2012.

Yuh, Ji–Yeon. Moving within Empires. Korean Women and Trans–Pacific Migration, in: Choy, Catherine Ceniza and Wu, Judy Tzu–Chun (Eds.), Gendering the Trans–Pacific World, Leiden 2017, pp. 107–113.

Zachmann, Urs Matthias. Imperialism in a Nutshell. Conflict and the "Concert of Powers" in the Tripartite Intervention, 1895, in: Japanstudien 17 (2006) 1, pp. 57–82.

Zachmann, Urs Matthias (Ed.). Asia After Versailles. Asian Perspectives on the Paris Peace Conference and the Interwar Order, 1919–33, Edinburgh 2018.

Index

www.ingramcontent.com/pod-product-compliance
Lightning Source LLC
Chambersburg PA
CBHW030313100426
42812CB00002B/690